EXPLORATIONS
at the Edge of Time

Written under the auspices of the Center of International Studies, Princeton, University

The United Nations University's Programme on Peace and Global Transformation was a major world-wide project whose purpose was to develop new insights about the interlinkages between questions of peace, conflict resolution, and the process of transformation. The research in this project, under six major themes, was co-ordinated by a 12-member core group in different regions of the world: East Asia, South-East Asia (including the Pacific), South Asia, the Arab region, Africa, Western Europe, Eastern Europe, North America, and Latin America. The themes covered were: Conflicts over Natural Resources; Security, Vulnerability, and Violence; Human Rights and Cultural Survival in a Changing Pluralistic World; The Role of Science and Technology in Peace and Transformation; The Role of the State in Peace and Global Transformation; and Global Economic Crisis. The project also included a special project on Peace and Regional Security.

EXPLORATIONS
at the Edge
of Time

The Prospects for World Order

RICHARD FALK

*Produced in association with
the United Nations University*

Temple University Press

PHILADELPHIA

Temple University Press, Philadelphia 19122
(UN) United Nations University Press, The United Nations University,
Toho Seimei Building, 15-1 Shibuya 2-chome,
Shibuya-ku, Tokyo 150, Japan

The paper used in this publication meets the minimum
requirements of American National Standard for Information
Sciences—Permanence of Paper for Printed Library Materials,
ANSI Z39.48-1984 ∞

Library of Congress Cataloging-in-Publication Data

Falk, Richard A.
    Explorations at the edge of time : the prospects for world order /
Richard Falk.
        p.   cm.
    Includes bibliographical references and index.
    ISBN 0-87722-860-4 (alk. paper)
    1. International organization—Philosophy.   2. International
relations and culture—Philosophy.   3. Civilization, Modern—1950–
4. Social evolution.   5. Politics and culture.   I. Title.
JX1954.F248   1991
327'.01—dc20   91-6823

The poetry excerpts on page 32 are from Gary Snyder, *Regarding Wave* (New York: New Directions, 1970), p. 39. Copyright © 1970 by Gary Snyder. Reprinted by permission of New Directions Pub. Corp. The following articles and essays by Richard Falk have been reprinted in revised form and are used with permission: *Chapter I*: "In Pursuit of the Postmodern," *The American Theosophist* 75, no. 5 (May 1987): 121–32; "In Pursuit of the Postmodern," reprinted from *Spirituality and Society: Postmodern Visions*, edited by David Ray Griffin (Albany: State University of New York Press, 1988), pp. 81–98, by permission of the State University of New York Press, © 1988 State University of New York. *Chapter II*: "Religion and Politics: Verging on the Postmodern," *Alternatives* 13, no. 3 (July 1988): 379–94; "Religion and Politics: Verging on the Postmodern," Center on Violence and Human Survival, John Jay College, City University of New York, Occasional Paper No. 4 (1988), 20 pp.; "Religion and Politics: Verging on the Postmodern," reprinted from *Sacred Interconnections: Postmodern Spirituality, Political Economy, and Art*, edited by David Ray Griffin (Albany: State University of New York, 1990), pp. 83–102, by permission of the State University of New York Press, © 1990 State University of New York. *Chapter III*: "Culture, Modernism, Postmodernism: A Challenge to International Relations," in *Culture and International Relations*, edited by Jongsuk Chay (New York: Praeger, 1990), pp. 267–79. *Chapter IV*: "Solving the Puzzles of Global Reform," *Alternatives* 11, no. 1 (January 1986): 45–81. *Chapter VI*: "The Global Promise of Social Movements: Explorations at the Edge of Time," *Alternatives* 7, no. 2 (April 1987): 173–96. *Chapter VII*: "The Extension of Law to Foreign Policy: The Next Constitutional Challenge," in *Constitutionalism: The Philosophical Dimension*, edited by Alan S. Rosenbaum (Westport, Conn.: Greenwood Press, 1988), pp. 205–21. *Chapter VIII*: "The Special Challenge of Our Time: Cultural Norms Relating to Nuclearism," reprinted from *Cultural Norms, War and the Environment*, edited by Arthur H. Westing (Oxford: Oxford University Press, 1988), pp. 53–63, by permission of Oxford University Press. *Chapter IX*: "Evasions of Sovereignty," from *Contending Sovereignties: Redefining Political Community*, edited by R.B.J. Walker and Saul H. Mendlovitz. Copyright © 1990 by Lynne Rienner Publishers, Inc. Reprinted by permission of the publisher. *Chapter X*: "The Realist School and Its Critics," from *Centerstage: American Diplomacy since World War II*, edited by L. Carl Brown (New York: Holmes & Meier, 1990), pp. 365–81. Copyright © 1990 by Holmes & Meier Publishers, Inc. Reprinted by permission of the publisher.

For June

CONTENTS

ACKNOWLEDGMENTS

THIS BOOK emerged out of my work on the Peace and Global Transformation Project, carried out under the auspices of the United Nations University. It was a stimulating intellectual process that was collaborative in the best sense, inspired by the overall project director, Rajni Kothari. At Princeton, this process was sustained by a multidisciplinary group of faculty and graduate students that met regularly over the course of four years under the rubric of "Normative International Relations" and shared many of the concerns addressed in this volume.

Like earlier work, this research and writing was done with the benefit of the facilities and encouragement of the Center of International Studies of Princeton University, especially its director, Henry Bienen. I was also helped by a dedicated research associate, Philomena Fischer.

My perspective has been shaped through years of close connection with the World Order Models Project and its principal associates. The Core Group of the Global Civilization Project has exerted a particular influence in recent years.

I was particularly encouraged and stimulated by Jane Cullen's invariably affirming approach on behalf of Temple University Press, and by her colleagues who assisted me with the final preparation of the manuscript.

Finally, I am deeply grateful to June Garson, to whom this volume is dedicated, for her many contributions to my well-being as an author and her warm friendship and loyalty.

EXPLORATIONS
at the Edge of Time

INTRODUCTION

Why Postmodern? Why Explorations at the Edge of Time? Why Rooted Utopianism?

AS WE GET closer to a new millennium, there is an almost irresistible tendency to dwell on endings and beginnings. This book has succumbed to this mood but places its emphasis on cultural and structural endings rather than on the end of the Cold War and the end of the postwar world. It devotes attention to the end of modernism as a framework for politics, both underpinning the territoriality of the state and the reliance upon the collective benefit of each state pursuing its own particular interests. The postmodern alternative involves a sequel to this territorial or spatial allocation of authority and capability. A positive sequel is by no means assured, but the possibility is definitely enhanced by its anticipation in thought and action. It is in this spirit that I treat explorations moving in postmodern directions as serious political attempts to go beyond the obsolescent constraints of modernist conceptions of the feasible.

Such an outlook also explains my adoption of the label "rooted utopianism." The idea is to affirm visions of the desirable that go beyond the horizon of realistic expectation but to retain the process of envisaging the "political" by insisting that it be rooted in some series of speculations about making a transition from here to there. The "courage" to be utopian involves the willingness to commit a cardinal modernist sin, that of appearing "foolish." Despite disquieting subsequent developments, the afterglow of 1989 continues to give foolishness a certain respectability that it has not previously enjoyed. Less than a decade ago the project of liberating the countries of Eastern Europe from both Soviet hegemonic influence and indigenous oppression certainly seemed utopian, and it would have remained so had not thousands and thousands of individuals acted out of moral and political conviction, regarding the integrity of the process as a justification that took precedence over calculations of the prospects for success or assessments of the relations of forces.

1

Throughout the chapters of this book, world order thinking is put forward as providing the vehicle for moving toward a more beneficial future for humanity. This approach is both humanistic and cosmopolitan, but it is also ecological and committed to the celebration and conservation of diversity. Following many years of self-clarification, the world order perspective is now solidly aligned with those social forces committed to grassroots globalism, and it is hesitant about promoting a postmodern alternative shaped by globalism from above. In this regard, the positive prospect rests on the further emergence of what is called "global civil society" throughout this volume. This construct of thought seeks to impart reality to the networks, belief and value patterns, and transnational undertakings that have in common an affirmation of human rights, democracy, and the preservation of environmental quality.

Modernism is by no means a spent force. It may yet persist in this next, globalist, phase of international relations, providing a technological unity for a planet administered from corporate headquarters and the office buildings of leading states. Such a globalism, as it encounters environmental frictions of a more and more serious character, is destined to become more and more coercive, especially toward the poor. The prolongation of modernism is likely to give rise to a variety of forms of control that share ecofascist orientations and to push North-South relations toward neoimperialist restructuring.

And so the fundamental tension addressed here is between a democratically conceived and constituted globalism and an autocratically conceived and implemented globalism. Globalism will ensue, but its nature and human consequences remain in the crucible of choice and struggle out of which the future will emerge.

PART ONE

The Postmodern Frontier of
International Relations

The three chapters of Part One examine the several interrelated facets of the contention that modernism in political life is being superseded, for better and worse, by a set of tendencies here characterized as "postmodern." The use of this terminology in the setting of international relations is controversial and is bound to be somewhat confusing, especially given the disparity between this use and the literary and cultural discourses that bear such a close verbal resemblance.

Chapter I sets forth the general position and links "the postmodern possibility" (for a preferred future) to the construction of a global civil society from the ground up and on the basis of a democratic ethos. This line of conjecture and advocacy is extended in Chapter II to address the new aliveness of religion as a generative source for politics. At the center of this aliveness is the reorienting of religious understanding by locating spirituality in the created order and through commitments to transform the social and economic structures responsible for impoverishment of body and soul.

Chapter III carries the same inquiry forward but considers culture as the matrix for assessment. As with religion, the renewal of values and visions depends on the widening of political concerns to include culture and to regard culture as a terrain whereon "the new" can emerge, if only at the margins of what is now regarded as the domain of "truth" and "reason." The cultural domain is also most adept at reconciling apparently contradictory tendencies and at aspiration, including this postmodern affirmation of both particularity (and difference) and generality or universality (and sameness).

Together, these three chapters seek to give a sense of the "exploratory" mode, and to establish "the citizen-pilgrim" as the postmodern explorer.

CHAPTER I

In Pursuit of the Postmodern

> For the Creator created not only the world, he also created the pos-
> sibility itself; therefore, he should have created the possibility of a
> better world than this one.
>
> Arthur Schopenhauer, *Essays and Aphorisms*

> Once the inevitabilities are challenged, we begin gathering our
> resources for a journey of hope.
>
> Raymond Williams, *The Year 2000*

MODERN AND POSTMODERN IMAGERY

THE CHALLENGE begins with terminology. The most extensive discussion of postmodernism appears in literary and cultural circles. In these
settings, the modern is generally associated with standards of science
and rationality by which to assess the progress of civilization and pass
judgment on its deficiencies, especially its emphasis on materialist and
technological achievement. The postmodern sensibility registers a strong
reaction by way of both taste and values. Postmodernism denies the capacity of language, mind, or spirit to establish standards in an objective
manner. It is radically deconstructionist, destroying, if it can, all illusions
that anything whatsoever can be singled out as truly significant. The postmodern mode is characterized above all else by a critical turn of mind,
both skeptical and ironic. At its best, this postmodern sensibility helps
emancipate us from the colonizing forms of knowledge associated with
both evident and disguised structures of domination: statism, nuclearism,
patriarchy, Western hegemony.

Now this cultural expression of the postmodern is quite different from
the spirit that animates these explorations. This spirit is reconstruction-

5

ist, optimistic, normative. It does not at all repudiate rationality and the benefits of modernity but seeks to supersede their negative features. A postmodern possibility implies the human capacity to transcend the violence, poverty, ecological decay, oppression, injustice, and secularism of the modern world. The failures of the modern world are here overwhelmingly associated with artificial and constraining boundaries on *imagination* and *community,* which then become springboards for conflict, inducing violence and massive suffering. The most menacing of these artificial boundaries are undoubtedly the borders of the sovereign state and the refusal of larger, more ambitious states to respect the autonomy of smaller, more vulnerable states. But additional false boundaries interact and intensify the forms of conflict associated with the state itself: those of race, class, religion, ideology, gender, language, age, civilization.

Closely connected with these divisions of the whole that have acquired emotive content are a series of divisions and categories that are integral to the specific efficiency of modernism, above all, the expropriating potency of specialization of labor, inquiry, and knowledge. Such specialization as organizing principle endows instrumental reason with a superior status in human affairs, creating the familiar hierarchical dualism of mind and body, spirit and flesh, reason and emotion, objectivity and subjectivity, thought and feeling, even virtue and vice. The modernist bias is to act-in-the-world as if these polarities express and exhaust the real structures of experience, providing both orientation and guidance. Postmodernism, by way of contrast, is trying to "reinvent" reality in more holistic, less hierarchical imagery.

The practical problems of modernity, but not necessarily the metaphysical ones, would be less severe if separateness could be consistently sustained by carefully delimited categories, but it cannot. It is the intensifying interdependence of the modern circumstance conjoined to this fierce sense of specific identity that makes the world so dangerous and frightening. Of course, these conditions are aggravated in the extreme by technology and by the cultural reign of mechanistic and reductionist understandings of science. Most obviously, nuclear weapons as instruments for struggle by part against part doom the whole and overwhelm any possibility of modernist sanity: insisting that my persistence as fragment validates ending the world as we know it so radically disrupts the relation of means to ends that any genuine form of collective happiness is precluded. Indeed, the prevalence of drugs, escapism, and mind-numbing popular music, especially among our young, is a warning that those inevitably entrusted with the future are tuning out of a world with no solidarity or promise.

Yet the challenge of modernity is much more than the need to overcome fragmentation and division. Wholeness, in other words, is not nearly enough. Part of our challenge has to do with the rescue of the spirit. Already toward the close of the nineteenth century, Nietzsche had delivered the startling message that god is dead, a message with prophetic consequences that continue to reverberate. If god is dead, then these partial identities almost inevitably become new absolutes, and totalizing approaches to politics and society are bound to emerge, and have emerged. Secular religions either become redundant rubber stamps for science and the state or become demonic historical forces, with idolatrous tendencies invisibly embedded in the whole edifice of modernism. Jean-Paul Sartre epitomized the absurdity of modern existence by associating it with nausea in the face of reality. The modern circumstance is groundless in the fundamental, ultimate sense of endowing our existence with a meaning beyond our mortality. When my death means everything, the death of others means nothing. The ethos of the terrorist becomes as natural as it is disruptive in such a world—whether those relying upon terror do so with kidnappings and hijackings, with covert operations and high-technology attacks on civilian targets, or with weaponry of mass destruction. The revolutionary and functionary relying on violent means tend to become mirror images of what it is they purport to deplore.[1]

The postmodern in this broader sense implies the rediscovery of normative and spiritual ground upon which to find meaning in human existence. It does not imply a return to the past, even to the early modern or premodern reality of a world given coherence and religious sanction by the acceptance of the great monotheistic religions with their faith bestowed on a centralized, hierarchical, patriarchal deity reigning over earthly matters from a heavenly throne. The postmodern horizon of spiritual recovery proceeds on a different basis: a dispersion of spiritual energy that is associated with the sacredness of the whole universe, and a related feminization of political life that finds power in *relations* rather than in *capabilities* for dominance and destruction—in earthborne more than in skyborne energy. Unity without centralization or hierarchy provides the only design imperative in conceiving desirable world order arrangements for the future.

To clarify this orientation I wish to comment upon two passages, each written by a prophetic postmodern voice. The first is taken from Martin Buber's *Paths in Utopia*:

> The vision of "what should be"—independent though it may sometimes appear of personal will—is yet inseparable from a critical and fundamental relationship to the existing condition of humanity. All suffering under a social order prepares the soul for vision and what the soul receives in this vision strengthens and deepens its insight into the perversity of what is perverted.[2]

Buber's rooting of vision in the actuality of suffering ensures that the essence of our political endeavors will be centered upon those who are most victimized by present arrangements. Unless we understand "the perversity of what is perverted," all the good will in the world cannot help. At the same time, it becomes critical not to reproduce perversity in our struggle against it; in questioning the role of violence in political life, we are reacting to the experience of betrayal that has been associated with so much revolutionary violence in our century. That is, a posture of struggle seems predicated upon perversity but includes a skeptical assessment of the place of violence—not necessarily its unconditional rejection—and imposes a heavy burden of persuasion on those who advocate a violent course of action and provide a line of exceptional, limited justification.

The second passage is from Lewis Mumford, *The Transformation of Man*:

> The emergence of New World culture, in completed form, in our time has produced in itself a world crisis. As far as records tell, this is the first planet-wide crisis that has taken place since the last glacial period. But the menace that then came from nature now comes from the busy hands and minds of men.[3]

The crisis of which Mumford writes is an outcome of technology and its appropriation for modernist purposes: that is, to promote the supremacy of certain fragments of humanity with the necessary consequence of subjugating others. Such patterns in pure form produce slavery but are also represented in more diluted versions by the relations between the West and the non-Western world, by the relations between white peoples and peoples of color, by the relations of industrializing societies to indigenous peoples, by the relations of men to women. The result of these structures is suffering, victimization. Mumford calls our attention to its new dimension—its global scale—yet does so in the patriarchal, patronizing idiom of modernity writing of humanity and personhood by reliance on the species-splitting rhetoric of "man" to denote the whole. Nuclear weaponry is both the culmination of modernism and a new circumstance suggesting that superior technology as a basis of dominance is now analogous to the once active threat of a catastrophic resurfacing of the planet by glacial formation. Nuclear winter is the sequel to the historical possibility of "glacial winter." A dramatic difference is that now we have fashioned our own jeopardy and might be in a position to overcome it whereas the natural forces of glaciers were—and still are—beyond our control.

CONTRA DISNEYLAND POSTMODERNISM

The first requirement for a curative response is confidence in the future. Such confidence involves both a vision of something desirable and a willingness to risk a great deal to attain it. Without sacrifice, commitment, and risk, it is impossible to confront successfully a well-entrenched system of beliefs, institutions, and practices. In this regard, it is important to appreciate the resilience and continuing success of the state as a focus for political loyalty, of nationalism as a mobilizing ideology, of the market as a basis for allocating resources, of war potential as the fulcrum of international stability, and of nuclear weapons as evidently having provided the only deterrence capable of avoiding world war between East and West, at least during the Cold War. We cannot achieve a postmodern reality without transforming the essential nature of these main pillars of modernism, and yet the pillars continue to be so firmly in place that they cannot be successfully challenged by direct action. This underlying situation has created a widespread condition of cultural despair, even if it is often unacknowledged. The failures of the United Nations and of disarmament and foreign aid efforts add to this despair, as does the general atmosphere of acrimony in international relations that has set the tone since 1945, the reliance by the superpowers on military means to uphold their global positions, and the incidence of warfare and poverty in many Third World countries, especially in circumstances of continuing population growth and heavy indebtedness.

To accept this difficult setting and yet to find a hopeful basis for understanding and action is what I think we need to concentrate our mental energies upon. Among several pitfalls are various categories of false hope: the utopianism of muddling through, the utopianism of a technological fix (such as SDI, Strategic Defense Initiative), the fundamentalism of an assured true path, and the fundamentalism of an unavoidable Armageddon. The identification of critique and jeopardy is far easier than the discovery of a direction for response. Amid American affluence, societal change might seem to require nothing more than the cumulative effects of personal will. It is necessary to be cautious, even skeptical, about such claims. To posit a New Age shift in civilization without any accompanying struggle invites a variety of misunderstandings, even deceptions.

My concern is this: There is a cultural disposition evident in certain circles, especially prominent in California, to suppose that we can successfully complete the transition to the postmodern by taking an appropriate psychological stance without ever engaging concrete sources of resistance, including human depravity and greed. I am suspicious on these grounds of "the Aquarian conspiracy," "the Hunger Project," "World

Beyond War," and many other well-intentioned navigational guides premised on seductive recipes for inner personal work and smooth sailing.
Epitomizing what I regard as misguided orientations toward the postmodern are the recent publications of the Ark Foundation, especially the
two edited volumes of soft advocacy put out by Don Carlson and Craig
Comstock.[4] I cannot conceive of useful knowledge that is not somehow
grounded on specifics, particularly on the dirty hands of our own governing process when it comes to such matters as the unabated legacy of
destruction directed at the indigenous peoples of our own continent, the
moral scandal of financing and promoting terrorism in Central America,
the still unacknowledged criminality of dropping atomic bombs on Hiroshima and Nagasaki and of preparing unabashedly for nuclear war, the
incredible discrepancy between our overall affluence and the growing
numbers of homeless and hungry persons scattered about our cities.

My reasoning here relies on the fused insights of Buber and Mumford,
in line with Gandhi, Tolstoy, Jesus, Martin Luther King, Desmond Tutu,
Henry David Thoreau, and all others who insist that moral concern is
serious only if it includes active participation in ongoing struggles against
injustice and suffering. Such a process may reject violence as a means
of struggle or reserve it for extreme situations and limited roles, but it
cannot dispense with criticism and explication of power structures or
with exposure and indictment of abusive elites. The contrary soft style of
peace advocacy searches obsessively for validation and encouragement
from established leaders, especially former heads of state and military
commanders, to demonstrate a supposedly uniform and shared commitment to rid the world of nuclear weapons or even of war. The implicit
intention is to suggest that power wielders are in good faith and share
the objectives of peace seekers, that a new world order can be brought
about merely by inner shifts in consciousness and by mutual recognitions
of good faith. No conflicts are inherent, and the posture of opposition or
struggle is regarded as superfluous and destructive of opportunities for
cooperative, curative efforts.

In their eagerness for support, soft advocates often seize upon rhetorical flourishes of established officials pulled far from the overall context
of their careers, beliefs, and convictions; frequently, peace-oriented assertions amount to rearview-mirror wisdom delivered from the largely
detached sanctuary of retirement from public life. Perhaps the most
notorious illustration of soft advocacy is the constant iteration of Dwight
Eisenhower's famous 1960 warning in his Farewell Address about the
military industrial complex. Over the years few have paused to ask why
Eisenhower waited until he was on the verge of retirement from public
life to deliver this warning and why he did so much to conventional-

ize the role of nuclear weapons in the armed forces while he led the country with the benefit of an overwhelming popular mandate. Rarely is it observed that those who gain access to militarized power structures cannot govern effectively unless they accept the overall legitimacy of the national security consensus, that co-option and careerism operate as potent conscience-numbing forces upon those who act prominently on behalf of modernist and highly militarized structures. It is not surprising, then, that glimmerings of conscience reemerge as individuals are released from these structures by retirement, but neither is it appropriate to regard such expressions of concern as related to prospects for change in the structures themselves or even as authoritative commentary. It is better to take wry note of such observations than to invoke them as demonstrative.

My view is this: Until we pronounce clearly upon these concrete issues of modernist illegitimacy, the quest and promise of a postmodern world is, despite all protestations, a disguised if unwitting expression of acceptance of the destructive character of modernity. This critical imperative entails an overall attitude of resistance or, at minimum, skepticism toward the policies and proposals of established structures and elites. For these reasons, I reject soft advocacy as misleading and diversionary, although its focus on shifting values and life-styles is a helpful emphasis, as is its implicit rejection of bloody revolutionary tactics. In essence, my critique comes down to an indictment of soft advocacy, or Disneyland postmodernism, that acts as a kind of opiate, promising an eventual salvation to be achieved without any transitional unpleasantness. In some ways, this critique is analogous to Marx's indictment of religion as "the opiate of the people" insofar as the Christian message involved patience for the rewards of the next world if one's lot in this life seemed demeaning or unfair.

At least five distinct problematic aspects of Disneyland postmodernism can be discerned:

- The abstract affirmation of a holistic, harmonious future as implicit or imminent operates as an evasion of the ethical injunction to engage concretely in the struggle to overcome suffering and to help sustain the life prospects of present and future generations.
- The integrative dynamics of such advocacy moves toward a homogenized, mercantile holism that ensnares the imagination and the human spirit. Whether we conceive of the future as acculturating music played in international hotel chains or in the manner of the Merrill Lynch bull that roams the world in search of investment bargains beneath the slogan "Your world should know no boundaries," such a future is eager to organize the planet globally, but it proceeds largely by colonizing logics (for example, the injunction "Think Global" highlighted in newsprint advertising on behalf of

the Scudder Global Fund, given spatial form by the logo of a global map girdled by double bands of ticker tape filled with stock quotations).

- The tendency to reinterpret science and natural reality as confirmatory of a spiritual grounding for human endeavors is useful as a basis for healing the cultural wounds of modernism, but it does not induce an overall transformation of the civilizational world view, at least not in accordance with a time frame relevant to the solution of the main world order challenges: war, famine, disease, oppression, environmental decay, alienation, poverty.
- The emphasis on holistic possibilities of encompassing conflict is not convincingly reconciled with the preservation and extension of diversity. Planetary ecology on any axis of concern is better served if diversity is seen as a resource to be nurtured simultaneously with the awareness of the wholeness and oneness of our identity as a species. A style of dialectical interpretation is needed to convey more convincingly the interplay of wholeness and diversity as positive elements.
- The detached imagery of postmodernism is largely an expression of the privileged status of the West that does not take suffiently serious account of the urgent preoccupations of non-Western peoples or of those who are "losers" in the West; as such, its claims possess a provincial flavor and risk dismissal elsewhere as frivolous diversions or new disguises for imperial ambition.

Taking heed of these deficiencies associated with Disneyland postmodernism enables the difficult search for political pathways that lead beyond the modern world in the direction of desirable destinations. This undertaking needs what Raymond Williams identifies as "the difficult business of gaining confidence in *our own* energies and capacities."[5]

A SECOND AXIAL UPHEAVAL

Karl Jaspers, Lewis Mumford, Paul Tillich, and Elise Boulding have called our attention to an initial axial age several centuries before Christ during which a series of great religions became established under diverse cultural and geographic conditions. The essence of the axial idea is a profound alteration in the shape of civilization and the content of human consciousness, and a reorientation of normative outlook and guiding values.

With the exhaustion of modernizing energies, and various normative reactions taking hold in opposition to specific forms of domination and destructive potential characteristic of the modern, it seems appropriate to conceive of the possible emergence of a second axial age. The tentativeness of such an assertion arises from the difficulty of interpreting inchoate social forces and contradictory types of evidence. The time interval for emergence is surely likely to be a matter of decades, if not considerably longer. Yet something helpful about the imagery of foundational reality is bound up with the axial perspective. It is also at the basis of the postmodern possibility.

To put it differently, if we are experiencing the early stages of a second axial upheaval, then this is what will enable establishment of a postmodern world. At present, the upheaval seems mainly an expression of oppositional imagery active only at the margins of modernism, a kind of critical reflection, little more than a snapping at the heels of modernism: initiatives contra violence, bureaucracy, centralizing technology, hierarchy, patriarchy, ecological carelessness. But it is also beginning to nourish some new modes of action: nonviolent practices, participatory organizations, soft energy paths and gentle technology, democratizing politics, feminizing leadership and tactics, spiritualized nature, green consciousness. The mixing of these axial elements in a variety of concrete embodiments as innovative forms of social action provides inspiration and heralds the possible approach of an axial moment: the Green party, Greenham Common, Ground Zero (Seattle), Lokayan, the Chipko Movement, Solidarity, the Great Peace Journey. Moving in history, these expressions of creative energy each works out tensions between different pulls, given the historical setting and felt urgencies of specific conjectures of time and space. Each initiative may wither, or succumb to mainstream modernist conventional wisdom about "winning" in "the real world." But each is worthy of study and help because it is informed by the postmodern possibility of a new axial breakthrough.

Let me be clearer. These axial gropings contrast with modernist impulses toward reform, whether initiated at the level of state action or the grassroots. Examples of modernist reform: the Nuclear Freeze movement, superpower summits, arms control negotiations, anti-apartheid struggle, law of the seas treaty, elimination of gross abuses of human rights. Each has useful, even crucial, elements that could contribute greater stability to our world, but each is dependent upon either violence or state power, or both, as the focus of its action. That is, violence of governmental initiative must be used as means, and a new configuration of state power is the main image of the goal. In other words, this style of action may uncover the normative potential of modernism, and even strengthen our capacity to make the transition to the postmodern world in a relatively gentle, less abrupt manner. Yet modernist politics, I argue, however effective as a holding operation, is incapable of overcoming fragmentation, technicism, violence, and statism; this incapacity ensures normative entropy and threatens the human experience with various forms of catastrophic collapse. The implicit distinction is between holding the modern world together and transforming it for the sake of the postmodern possibility.[6]

TOWARD A POSTMODERN ETHICS

The ground for action in the world is a combination of normative outlook and personal identity. The postmodern identity is constituted by a deep feeling of unity with others (what Erik Erikson regards as species identity) and with nature (a coevolutionary relation). It is also constituted by a sense of freedom and of responsibility for one's own behavior, and a refusal to accept as unconditional the authority of any external source of truth. These shared orientations provide a foundation for a postmodern ethics that is beginning to take shape in many distinct settings of challenge and response. Postmodern ethics has ancient roots that can be associated with the exemplary and mythic lives of Socrates, Jesus, the Buddha, even St. Francis, more as an embodiment in action than as an abstract precept of conduct. Some features can be identified:

- *reaction to the intolerable.* There is room for disagreement as to individual and societal goals, but there is no reason to accept avoidable suffering and every reason to oppose deliberate efforts to inflict pain, cause suffering, and deny truth. The concreteness of pain and suffering (psychic humiliation as well as physical torment) provides us with an assurance that our intentions and actions are beneficial.
- *refusal to lie or to manifest mistrust.* If any institution seeks obedience by insisting that lies be told, it is essential to resist even if doing so means confinement, pain. If a system of order implants distrust, it is essential to base personal relations on openness and truthfulness. Prior to 1989, Adam Michnik expressed this stance of sacrificial nonviolent defiance as the basis of an ethical life in authoritarian Poland, identifying the association of the state and the Communist party with an ethics of pervasive lying and mistrust. There is no way that an institution can deprive us of this capacity to be truthful and trusting, and so long as we are, a crucial domain of freedom is retained, however totalitarian the regime.
- *regard for personal relations as models of the good society.* The practices of everyday life reproduce and prefigure the patterns of more complex, impersonal relations. Our sense of order and authority is expressed by the way we live our life and arrange its activities at every level of social organization, starting with the family and clan. There is a close bond between desirable governance for the family and for the human family. A patriarchal social movement cannot contribute to the construction of a beneficial postmodernism.

- *acknowledgment of the primacy of conscience.* Trusting others depends on trusting and acting upon one's own sense of right and wrong. Such attitudes encourage nonviolent yet militant resistance, and expectations of accountability especially from those with institutional and economic power. There is also a burden to adopt a critical view of what is near, within the range of ethical reach. Criticizing one's own government is an especially valuable expression of patriotism in our historical epoch, particularly in an ascendant state that associates its security with superior military prowess and with the control of extraterritorial developments and makes use of a disproportionate share of the earth's resources. The disposition to project power and influence strengthens the impulse toward intervention and violent encounter.
- *action as if the future is now.* Within our zones of autonomous existence we can live as if our visionary hopes already exist and, by so doing, bring the desired transformation about.
- *readiness to journey to the future.* Although we can model the future, we must not deceive ourselves that it is in place already. Such a pretension overlooks suffering and structures of domination and distortion; it facilitates escapist flights of fancy. The unifying struggle that informs reactions to various modernist failures is dedicated to the establishment of a nonviolent, encompassing political community that allows distinct and diverse identities to flourish, overlapping and intersecting from individual to individual and group to group. It is not a specific project as such, in the manner of promoting nuclear disarmament or democratization of a given society, but rather a perspective that animates action to the degree that over time a cumulative dynamic of transformation gathers force and eventually displaces the old superseded order. It is not an event but a process—a sufficient shift in the ground of beliefs and values to overcome the prevalence of the modernist mind-set—that has been optimistically and probably prematurely identified as "the silent revolution." Interpreting the weight of new normative forms is virtually impossible, as much of what is significant seems to occur at unconscious levels of awareness or is subject to partisan perceptions that inflate or unduly minimize. The old order retains control over most flows of information, manipulates images from modernist perspectives, and may create an impression that the desired future is more remote than is the case. Experience with unexpected revolutions at the societal scale suggest that resentments often accumulate in latent form, creating illusions of stability that are discarded after the unexpected eruption takes place. There is the analogous ecological resilience of living systems (such as lakes) that "hide" their deterioration until the verge of collapse.
- *receptiveness to the vibrations of feminized consciousness.* Women as primary bearers of the feminine have a creative role, especially given the complex interplay of unity and diversity. Schopenhauer, despite reactionary and grossly sexist intentions, long ago intuited this generally unacknowledged vocation of women: "Because fundamentally women exist solely for the propagation of the race and find in this their vocation, they are altogether

more involved with the species than with individuals, and in their hearts take the affairs of the species more seriously than they do those of the individual."[7] This earthly sense of the whole provides a way of reanimating our political life.

■ *development of the ideal of the citizen-pilgrim.* The pilgrim is on a journey in space and time, seeking a better country, a heavenly one.[8] There are no illusions that the present is an embodiment of what is possible. The citizen pilgrim is loyal to this quest and is not bound by any sense of duty to carry out the destructive missions of a given territorial state to which she or he owes temporary secular allegiance.

■ *recognition that there are no messiahs.* The belief that only a charismatic presence can break the bonds of oppressive structure invites quietism and co-option. The movement makes its heroes more than heroes produce a movement. If we wait for a messiah, we wait; if we react to the challenges of present and future as responsible moral agents, as aspiring citizen pilgrims, then we act. When we act, a cumulative process unfolds, leaders emerge, and new horizons of realistic aspiration present themselves.

TOWARD A POSTMODERN POLITICS

This period of transition imposes particular demands on the level of political action. The quest: nurturing the new while muting the destructive features of the old partially superseded yet still prevailing political order. It is essential to reject a polarization of choice: repudiation of the old as decadent and obsolete, disregard of the new as utopian and hence irrelevant. The ongoing debate between realists and utopians implies a false either/or choice. Instead, we emphasize both/when, clarifying the province of reform and the domain of radical restructuring. At this stage, the political effort needs to be one of integration, first of all in the imagination: "Time present and time past are both perhaps present in time future" (T. S. Eliot). Even our separation of modernist and postmodernist possibilities is based on a dichotomy of convenience only. The displacement of modernism invites recovery of the premodern past as well as pursuit of the postmodern future. Or, as we conceive of postmodernist possibilities, it is helpful to infuse premodern understanding and wisdom. In many respects, the premodern anticipates the postmodern more helpfully than does the modern, especially by its implicit ecological world view, its sense of the religious life as embodied in the totality of individual and social practice, and its imagery of spirituality as often genderless and dispersed among feminine and masculine centers of energy (called gods and goddesses, or deities). The messy circumstance of action involves the implications of past and future in the present, not a sequence of lapsed premodernism, modernism now, postmodernism later. The process of moving toward a postmodern world requires that premodernist, modernist, and postmodernist forms coexist and interpenetrate within our lives and consciousness for the indefinite future.

SOME MODERNIST ACHIEVEMENTS

In our critical response to statism, war, and nuclearism there is a tendency to turn from present structures in disgust. Equally harmful is a tendency to suspend criticism because of an implicit or explicit conviction that these existing structures and their presiding elites are "the only game in town." To be at once critical yet receptive to normative opportunity seems the appropriate political outlook.

Modernist politics achieved some impressive gains over the decade of the 1980s; these can be enumerated for purposes of illustration, with the caveat that such positive policies are always subject to countertendencies and even to a process of policy reversal:

- China's success in mitigating imbalances in the relationship between its population and resources through a governmentally mandated policy of limiting family size to one child in most instances. The extraordinary adjustment achieved over the span of a single generation was possible both because of cultural conditions (ethic homogeneity; traditions of leadership; pride in unity and practical solutions; an orientation toward reality that can be summarized as "the Confucian advantage") and of political centralization and efficiency relative to divergent social forces in civil society. Achieving this degree of population control has contributed to the confidence of Chinese leaders to move rapidly, though reflectively, in demilitarizing directions (the innovative solution devised for the future of Hong Kong; the willingness to find a compromise based on renunciation of violence as the basis for setting the question of Taiwan's status; partial demobilization of the armed forces—by about 1,000,000; shift of production from arms to civilian goods; overall tenor of moderation). These achievements over the last two decades remain significant, although their quality is greatly tarnished by the response of the regime to the popular, student-led movement for democratization, climaxing in early June 1989 with the massacre in and around Tiananmen Square and, later, the persecution of activists all over China.[9]
- the success of India and Bangladesh in achieving self-sufficiency in basic foodstuffs. Relying on the modernization of agriculture, the Indian subcontinent has managed to avoid the specter of famine despite widespread, dire prophesies of doom made as recently as the 1970s. This success is controversial, partly because ecological side effects raise the whole question of

techno-agricultural manipulation and the abuse of soils and plant stocks, and partly because it is not clear how long such agricultural productivity can be sustained, especially given the continuing dynamics of population growth and urbanization.

- even without the full benefit of democracy, the Soviet Union's move to a leadership that is seriously committed to achieving a breakthrough in disarmament negotiations—at least to stopping the nuclear arms race and reducing, if not eliminating, the nuclear weapons dimension from East-West political conflict. Under Mikhail Gorbachev, especially in his early years, the Kremlin has taken serious unilateral initiatives (including a sustained moratorium on nuclear testing and the virtual adoption of U.S. official positions to circumvent negotiating obstacles) and set forth far-reaching credible proposals. At Reykjavik, Iceland, in late 1986 the leaders of the superpowers appeared to have agreed for some hours on a plan of total denuclearization to unfold over the course of the following decade: 50 percent reduction in nuclear missiles and warheads during the next five years, the remaining 50 percent in the subsequent five years (including balancing and reassuring adjustments in conventional force levels and a moderating of political antagonism). The breakdown of such a promising prospect should not blind us to the significance of its appearance. For a brief interval, at least, the leaders of the two most powerful states associated their security with the complete abolition of nuclear weaponry. Such a dramatic departure from security through nuclearism is something that not even the mainstream Western peace movement dared demand (neither the U.S. freeze movement nor European resistance to the deployment of Pershing II and cruise missiles ever posed such demands). Note, also, that both superpowers now are on record as morally repudiating nuclear deterrence, the United States purporting to place its hopes for a nuclear-free world on the drastic technical fix of the Strategic Defense Initiative, the Soviet Union appearing committed to a straight-line negotiated nuclear disarming process.

- a further tangible development was the intermediate nuclear forces (INF) agreement reached by the superpowers during the Washington summit of December 1987. The treaty instrument is notable because it actually gets rid of a class of nuclear weapons, and it removes all longer-range missiles of the Soviet Union and the United States from Europe. The Soviet commitment entails destroying about twice as many missiles in this category as the United States must do. Indeed, an American president who negotiated such an unequal treaty in the other direction would undoubtedly face censure, if not impeachment charges! The very absence of accountability gives Soviet leaders far more room for maneuver in disarmament negotiations, enabling arrangements to be agreed upon and implemented even in the absence of arithmetic equivalence in every context.

More recent developments extend these Soviet contributions but also introduce some new ambiguities into our assessment of the modernist situation. The Soviet withdrawal from geopolitics in the late 1980s facilitated the democratic revolutionary process of 1989, the ending of the Cold War, and a new preoccupation with domestic economic failure. Two new dangers, at least, emerged: the menace of civil war in the Soviet Union arising from separatist tendencies, and the heightened danger of regional warfare—especially in the Middle East—fought with advanced weaponry.

- the efforts of Greece, New Zealand, and the Philippines in various ways to limit their participation in nuclearism by challenging the prerogatives of the nuclear superpowers in specific ways. Under Corazon Aquino, the new constitution for the Philippines has a nonnuclear provision: "The Philippines, consistent with national interest, adopts and pursues a policy of freedom from nuclear weapons in its territory." In a harsh editorial the *Wall Street Journal* calls this stance "a real time bomb" and an "ostrich policy of declaring oneself a nuclear-free zone." [10] The most explosive aspect of this issue arises from the well-known "secret" that the United States government stores nuclear weapons at one or more of its bases in the Philippines.
- the transition of Argentina, Brazil, Uruguay, Chile, Haiti, and the Philippines from dictatorial and military rule to some form of constitutional order without having to go through a period of civil strife. Many democratizing movements in different countries are seeking to soften the relations between state and civil society, making the former responsive to the will of the latter. There is ample evidence, despite the fragility of each of these transitions, that the militarized state cannot permanently extinguish flames of public discontent, no matter how brutal its repressive means. Popular sovereignty is alive and well in many parts of the world, suggesting that the modern centralized state can be challenged and reformed by nonviolent mass action.
- the overcoming by several governments, including that of Bolivia, of triple-digit inflation. Hyperinflation, if unabated, destroys the social fabric of modernist arrangements, inviting nihilism and fanatical political response. To constrain inflation allows other constructive societal developments to gain strength.
- the willingness and capacity by several governments displayed to give up their reliance on hard drugs as a source of foreign exchange earnings, although the overall record of response remains mixed and inconclusive.
- the continuing existence of United Nations and its large family of more specific international institutions. Despite numerous difficulties, the UN remains intact, obtains quasi-universal participation, and is the beneficiary of a new surge of confidence, reinforced by the transformation of East-West relations.
- the continuously expanding intergovernmental frameworks of varying significance in areas of trade, money, pollution control, and antiterrorism, and the negotiation of a comprehensive global framework in the form of a treaty to regulate the use of oceans (although without the formal approval of several key states, including the United States).

Each of these instances of achievement has its shadow side, making assessment complex. Yet the evidence exists that governments have room

for maneuver and popular sovereignty can successfully challenge bureaucratic power and military/paramilitary styles of rulership. Positive modernist action remains possible and could be deepened and its field
extended by postmodernist pressures and perspectives. We do not yet
reliably know the outer limit or normative potential for modernist structures, but it is essential to keep probing.

POSTMODERNIST GROPINGS

> . . . because in 1985 blind faith in your leaders, or in anything, will
> get you killed.
>
> Bruce Springsteen (in concert)

Beyond the modern, a politics is emerging with a new dimensionality:
nonviolent, militant, feminized, transnational, grassroots, informal, and
often inspired by premodernist wisdom and insight. In an industrialized
democracy with a functioning constitution, this emergent postmodern
politics does not entrust the future to traditional forms of indirect participation: traditional parties, electoral campaigns, congressional lobbying,
representative institutions, enlightened presidential leadership. The emphasis is either upon a radical reorientation of traditional vehicles (for example, the Green party) or upon an "antipolitics" (involving extranormal
forms of collective expression).

A crucial organizing basis for postmodern politics is associated with
social movements of varying character:

- *the new social movements.* In the 1970s a series of powerful societal initiatives, frequently of transnational scope, resulted in movement activity: in
  the setting of opposition to nuclear power plants, on behalf of environmental protection, in opposition to specific weapons and deployments, on behalf
  of women, on behalf of sexually deviant groups, on behalf of indigenous
  peoples. These movements originated in normative grievances or fears, as
  well as in a sense of skepticism about the character of conventional political
  mechanisms of change and control. As they evolved, splits emerged paral-
  leling the modern-postmodern divide, especially as to the relation between
  process and substance. Beyond renouncing violence and shifting expectations for renewal and reform away from the political center, these efforts
  attached significance to finding practical ways of organizing that did not
  reproduce hierarchical, patriarchal patterns.
- *ascendant popular sovereignty.* There is a widespread yet uneven withdrawal of deference to the centralized state apparatus in all sectors of the
  world, although not in every society. The issue of legitimacy is being contested in many forms for both efficiency and normative reasons, usually

expressed as demands for democratizing reforms, including procedures enabling access to governmental authority and making leaders accountable for abuses of state power, whether economic corruption or repression of dissenters. Each struggle has its own specific character, but the overall claims of popular sovereignty are being asserted as existential demands; these cannot be satisfied by abstractions about a fictitious social contract vesting power in the state in exchange for public order or about the inherently liberating character of postrevolutionary proletarian rule. Neither liberalism nor Marxism-Leninism is presumed legitimate any longer, especially by those who reject the view that the national or class identity of a government is the decisive test of legitimacy. The appeal of premodern politics, especially when not hidden by layers of sentimental nostalgia, is its experience with holistic patterns of practice and with minimal institutional structure.

■ *challenges to secular supremacy.* In many settings, the almost religious deference to the state is also diminishing or being reversed, and secular doctrines of the separation of church and state are under attack from both fundamentalist and postmodernist outlooks. The association of religious convictions and solidarity with the poor provides a ground for mass mobilization against modernist orientations toward politics. "Liberation theology" in its many varieties aspires to a reunion of secular goals and spiritual identity. Regarding issues of nuclear weaponry and poverty, even mainstream churches are seeking to reclaim authority, at least to the extent of eroding the legitimacy of the state by counterposing contrasting normative imperatives that are addressed to the individual consciences of adherents, challenging modernist assumptions that obedience and respect for the state exhaust the meaning of good citizenship, that is, patterns of beneficial participating in a governing political community.

■ *the reclamation of law.* By invoking international law and personal conscience as justifications for violating domestic law, individuals and groups are calling into question unconditional notions of sovereignty and statist national security policy. An appeal to a global normative order suggests the importance of bonds among societies that take precedence over the state-and-society nexus. This postmodernist priority is emphasized by adherence to international human rights standards and, even more, by the Nuremberg Obligation, which holds leaders and policy-makers criminally liable for violations of international law in the war/peace area and imposes responsibility on individuals and even on citizens to implement the legal order against their own leadership; a freely elected government acquires no exemption from accountability. Another expression of this refusal any longer to regard law as belonging exclusively to the state is the establishment of judicial frameworks by informal and populist initiative: in many countries, "tribunals" set up by private groups hear evidence, interview witnesses, render judgments on issues of public policy. Several tribunals have been dedicated to a legal assessment of reliance on nuclear weaponry under varying conditions, on controversial uses of military force (Vietnam, Afghanistan, Nicaragua), on denials of human rights (South Africa, the Philippines under Marcos). Such a process of informal adjudication has been given institutional expression in the Permanent Peoples Tribunal (a project of the Rome-based International League for the Rights of Peoples), which carries out its assessment of public wrongs in relation to its own constitutional document: the Algiers Declaration of the Rights of Peoples.

- *transnational relief through cultural activism.* Rock concerts ("live aid") for overseas famine and disasters have created a new idiom for helping acute victims of calamity. Such events tend to be multiracial, multiethnic, multinational in character and create psychological bonds of solidarity that circumvent normal diplomatic channels and are not at all delimited by territorial boundaries.

- *transnational information.* The distrust of state motives, and the general state tendency to confuse information with propaganda has generated distrust of official sources. It has been established that during the 1980s intelligence agencies of the United States government intensified the Iran-Iraq War by a deliberate campaign of disinformation; a few months earlier a similar campaign of manipulation was uncovered designed to portray Muammar Qaddafi as an archterrorist, evidently to build the public support for punitive violence against Libya that eventually led to an air strike on Tripoli in 1986, costing many civilian lives. Our expectations of government have fallen so low that we tend to accept such disclosures as "routine" and to fault leaders not for what they did but for their failure to come clean or to step forward with a ritual apology afterward. In reality, the distortions that are part of this geopolitical power game—the negative pole of modernist politics—are quite lethal in their impact on life and community, either by building pretexts for military force (as with Libya) or by aggravating belligerency (as with Iran and Iraq).

- In view of this statist tendency to distort information, private associations with small resources but high integrity can help reshape public debate and perceptions. Amnesty International in the human rights area and the Swedish International Peace Research Institute with respect to the arms race and arms sales are two instances of successful efforts to provide generally reliable information in settings where partisan passions frequently distort or obscure.

CONCLUSION

The promise of a postmodern world depends on human initiative as well as historical tendencies. The prefiguring of the future in our imagination and lives gives each of us the possibility and also a responsibility to act—not merely by a leap in time but by bringing postmodern ethics and politics concretely to bear as therapy for the wounds that bring so much pain to those with whom we share the planet. Taking suffering seriously is the best indication that we care about the future in a way that matters.

Martin Luther King once told his congregation at the Ebenezar Baptist Church in Atlanta that "dissent and nonconformity" were the essence of "true Christianity."[11] Dissent and nonconformity are equally indispensable for an authentic embrace of the postmodern possibility. Unless we link our bodies and resources to the various struggles against the specific crimes of modernity we are not ethically and politically fit to cross that great divide linking the present to future. Contrariwise, if we become immersed totally in anti-modernist projects, however valuable, we lose contact with the most powerful set of liberating energies at work in our personal and public lives during this historical epoch. To be postmodern we need to develop the practices and nurture the consciousness that simultaneously inhabits premodern, modern, and postmodern realms of actual and potential being.

CHAPTER II

Religion and Politics:
A Second Postmodern Possibility

MANY OF THE confusions of the present age arise out of the reversal of the stereotypical roles associated with politics and religion. From politics we had come to expect radical challenges and a capacity for far-reaching societal innovation. From religion we had expected consolation and community but no tangible contribution to the public good; on the contrary, in Western liberal democracies the separation of church and state had been largely appreciated as facilitative of the modern world. Formalizing the confinement of religion to the sphere of purely private concerns was intended to facilitate governmental efficiency and rationality, as well as to provide the basis for a unified politics of the state in the face of religious pluralism and against a background of devastating sectarian warfare. Ostensibly, in the modern world, religious identity was declared irrelevant to the rational enterprise of administering the political life of society.

In countries under the sway of Marxist-Leninist governments, this process went even further as the state sought, additionally, to dominate the private sphere—thereby being aptly called "totalitarian"—and relegated religion to the domain of superstition, a premodern impediment to the true bases for hope: material progress, industrialization, the dictatorship of the proletariat, the elimination of class conflict, public ownership of the means of production, and so forth.

Although capitalism and socialism, with their continuing genuine differences concerning the role of private property and the market, as well as their contrasting views on the proper scope for individual conscience and political dissent, were in truth not so far apart when it came to the status of religion. Although the capitalists taunted Marxists for their atheism, secularism itself "killed" God by denying the relevance of spiritual perspectives to the conduct of public affairs. The consumerist spirit of

24

the West has been at least as materialist in its way as the Marxist-Leninist insistence on deifying the state as the only legitimate object of worship. Both East and West became unabashed champions of the modern project: to rest human prospects upon the expansion of productive efforts, relying on a continuous flow of technological innovations to make life better for a higher and higher proportion of humanity. The ideological debate between state planning and market allocation of resources was a tactical, intramural controversy carried on within the framework of modernist assumptions.

By and large, organized religion—with notable exceptions—rather timidly adjusted to its diminished influence, especially in the West, where its institutional prerogatives were largely respected in the private sphere. In the East, organized religion either acquiesced and became an enfeebled servant of state power or did its best to survive extreme coercive pressure, applied as part of the Marxist-Leninist dogma that religion is "the opiate of the people" and, accordingly, has no place in a revolutionary socialist society, especially given the relentless secularism of the modern project. Religion was effectively scorned as a relic or intrusion of the premodern, no longer needed as comforter for those exploited by capitalist-class domination. The momentum behind industrialism was the general conviction that modernization provided a universally valid solution to human torments connected with hardship and poverty. An extreme version of this view extended the hostile assessment of modernism to politics as well. In the society of tomorrow it was hoped on some fronts that the only issues for the leaders to decide would be technical in character, matters of allocating resources for purposes of efficient use, leaving decisions in the hands (or heads) of technical experts or, better, to computerized procedures.

The disappearance of politics (and politicians) in the wake of the disappearance of religion (and religious divines) was premised on the acceptance of efficiency and instrumental rationality as the main unfinished business of organized societal life. This technocratic optimism about human capacities to overcome problems of scarcity and the resistance of nature assumed extreme forms that now seem ludicrous. Herman Kahn, now dead but earlier an influential futurist (besides being a notorious nuclearist), turned his formidable intellectual powers to what he conceived as one of the greatest challenges likely to emerge in the next century—the menace of boredom arising from an abundance of leisure time!

In the course of some twenty years, these circumstances have changed in a number of crucial respects. The inevitability of modernization has been openly challenged from diverse directions by those sharing the conviction that religion (and politics) was somehow relevant once again to the core issues of the current human situation. On the one side was a series of shifts within the religious domain which called for active participation by devout Christians in struggles for liberation from oppressive economic, political, and cultural conditions. Especially in Latin America, priests and theologians broke out of their roles as upholders of the established societal order and increasingly associated the mission of the church with an active involvement in overcoming the suffering of the poor. The emancipatory perspective insisted that the essence of religious practice was solidarity with the poor rather than attendance at church or the display of religious devotion through financial contributions. Even a nonprofessing Christian was given a better purchase on salvation than a professing Christian who lent his muscle or resources to an oppressive political order.

Such a theologically shocking claim was bound to stir things up in the Vatican, as indeed it did. "Liberation theology" is the name most often given to these diffuse Third World tendencies to emphasize the role of religion-in-the-world, a role that drew directly upon the main nonreligious source of social and political radicalism—namely, Marxism—for its sense of the direction appropriate to the practice of revolutionary politics. The sublime realization that religion, in order to rediscover its ground of vitality, needed to enter into coalition with its most determined ideological adversary has yet to be widely appreciated in the North. What is more, the receptivity of radicals to the participation of priests and theologians in their shared political enterprise represents a drastic reformulation by secular revolutionaries and radical reformers of the nature of their struggle, as well as an altered vision of justice. Remember—religion had previously been an enemy and obstacle for revolutionary socialism, as well as a source of resistance to it. Now, all at once, Christianity has emerged as a revered ally of transformative politics.

The revolutionary triumph in 1979 and subsequent twelve years of Sandinista government in Nicaragua involved the most significant fusion of Marxism and Christianity that has yet to achieve an embodiment in history. It was such a troublesome phenomenon for conventional Western thought that its reality was largely denied. American mainstream commentary on the Nicaraguan political system has generally explained developments since Anastasio Somoza by reference to familiar East-West categories: Daniel Ortega's government in Managua was labeled Marxist-Leninist and largely portrayed as a Central American replica of Fidel Castro's Cuba. For pragmatic reasons, liberals in this country did not contest these assessments; even those ardently opposed to helping the contras were eager to insulate themselves from accusations of Marxist sympathies or of displaying insufficient fear of Soviet strategic penetration in Central American affairs. Yet dispassionate witnesses and commentators consistently noticed the real and persisting importance of religious convictions and vocation to the Sandinista leadership in Nicaragua and to its political style. The 1990 electoral defeat of the Sandinistas remains difficult to interpret impartially. Those who supported Ronald Reagan's interventionist pro-contra policies interpret Violeta Chamorro's victory as one more proof that socialist approaches to development will be rejected as soon as the citizenry can vote. Those who were impressed by Sandinista achievements were stunned by the election results in 1990, but tended to view them as a cry of popular despair by an impoverished people being squeezed for more than a decade by the weight of superpower coercion. From the perspective of religion and politics, the Sandinista orientation remains instructive in a number of respects.

At one stage in the mid-1980s Foreign Minister Miguel d'Escoto, one of four ordained priests among the nine top Sandinistas, requested a leave of absence so that he might fast in protest against the extension by Congress of further aid to the contras.[1] Even if such an act is discounted as a gesture, it was a symbolically significant reflection by a supposedly radical, Marxist-oriented political movement of its renewed willingness to join arms with those who find religion at the center of their personal and revolutionary being. Such a premodern form of political expression by a high government official alters the public understanding of political language, creatively implying the potency of nonviolent and religiously sanctified instruments of protest and resistance. One can hardly imagine a comparable American official making a response that so engaged his personal being and body and included a comparable avowal of religious conviction.

The United States government refused to acknowledge this religious component of the Sandinista experience, stressing instead the anti-Sandinista strain evident in the clerical hierarchy, represented especially by Miguel Obando y Bravo, one of the few Central American churchmen ever elevated to cardinal—evidently a recognition by the Vatican of his role in stemming the tide toward this reconciliation between Marxism and Christianity, as well as an expression of approval for his active involvement in supporting contra violence. In effect, for ideological reasons the United States did not wish to cope with a world in which Marxism and Christianity are allied in form and substance, preferring black/white polarizations as a way of rationalizing intervention against the Sandinistas in the familiar currency of the Cold War.[2] If our adversary were no longer godless, it would be far more difficult to vindicate our resort to force and to uphold the traditional image of ourselves as a fair and generous people that gained its own political independence after a harrowing armed struggle.

Whatever we may wish, the fact is that all over the Third World a

Christian presence has emerged at the center of radical opposition politics. In South African townships it is generally religious leaders who have given direction and transcendent passion to the anti-apartheid movement. In South Korea it has been the Christian churches, along with students and workers, that have joined ranks with democratic forces and opposed a militantly anti-Communist governing coalition. And in the Philippines, at the crucial moment in 1986, it was the tilt by the leading prelate of the Catholic Church in an anti-Marcos direction, despite warnings from the Malacanang Palace that the Communists carrying on an armed struggle would benefit, that enabled the triumph of the moderate yet then intensely democratic movement led by Corazon Aquino. Significantly, ideological affinities have given way to normative affinities: the Christian commitment, admittedly with notable exceptions, has increasingly involved siding with the poor, regardless of ideological implications. And political radicals have reciprocated, welcoming and revering Christian leaders who join their struggle, feeling validated by such an affirmation. Both religious and political perspectives have also converged spontaneously on a nationalist creed that seeks above all to wrest control over resources, culture, and the state away from foreign hands and to transfer governmental control to the representatives of the people.

And it is not only in the Third World that such a pattern of religious and political interpenetration has occurred. In Poland the Solidarity movement, although initiated by workers, has been consistently inspired and protected by priests and officials belonging to the Catholic Church. The main Solidarity figures, including Lech Walesa, presented themselves all along as devout Catholics. Of course, the Polish church has quite a conservative background, making its support of the movement part of a long-standing battle against Soviet influence; but it has been, possibly unwittingly, swept along in a political movement that was antiauthoritarian, motivated by a democratic ethos that itself seems quite at variance with the hierarchical and antidemocratic notions of authority long associated with the history of Catholic tradition and practice in Poland. Whether this ethos can and will be sustained in post-emancipation Poland is highly uncertain.

Extending this survey to Western Europe and the United States, one finds a less focused yet definite reassertion of religious presence on many political battlefields. In the peace movement, religious personalities have been at the forefront. The U.S. sanctuary movement has enlisted several hundred churches of all denominations in a challenge to the primacy of state power over a crucial realm of public policy: control of the dynamics of immigration, especially deportation. The willingness of religious communities to extend "sanctuary" protection to "illegal" refugees from Central America, especially El Salvador, is impressive, given the prospects for prosecution and even imprisonment. A surprising number of Americans during the supposedly placid 1980s engaged in nuclear resistance, invoking Nuremberg notions of personal accountability to explain and justify their duty to disobey state policy in the war/peace area, although the consequence for such individuals was likely to be criminal indictment and imprisonment. The main justification for such stands is an altered sense of citizenship and patriotism, but the underlying motivation is generally a religious conviction, often arising out of a collective form—a communal or semicommunal circle of believers who profess a radical version of Christian faith that seeks, above all, to be attuned and responsive to suffering in the world. In this critical respect, religion from below and radical politics converge on the idea of taking suffering seriously.[3]

It would be a grave error, however, to assume that all religious ventures in the political domain are motivated by progressive purposes or imagery. Quite the contrary: There has been also a remarkable surge of fundamentalist religion in the last few decades. The most vivid instance is undoubtedly the Islamic revolution led by the Ayatollah Ruhollah Khomeini in Iran. Iran's undertaking to banish alien modernism in favor of a restored, rigorous theocratic polity shocked the Western secular sensibility while mobilizing many of its own poor and stimulating many in the Islamic world, especially among the youth. The fundamentalist appeal has demonstrated its capacity to exact sustained and extreme sacrifice, and it can do so without offering materialist inducements. When Iraq attacked Iran in 1980, smart modernist thinking anticipated a rapid and decisive Iraqi victory, underestimating the capacities of fundamentalist Iran to resist despite the substantial collapse of its military capability under the Shah. The fundamentalist tidal wave emanating from Tehran has introduced dangerous elements of instability in a series of Islamic countries.[4]

But again, the fundamentalist breakout is not confined to the Shi'ites in Iran or to Islam. The emergence of American fundamentalism in the form of "the Moral Majority" and evangelical Christianity has represented a determined assault on the modern life-style of secular modernity, especially as embodied in big cities. This sort of fundamentalism reconciles many Americans to their pessimistic expectation of nuclear doom by converting this dreaded catastrophe into an expression of the divine plan. There results a "blessed assurance," to quote one writer who was astonished by the widespread yearning for the rapture of Armageddon that she found in Amarillo, Texas, the city dominated by the Pantax factories, responsible for assembling America's entire arsenal of nuclear bombs.[5] The AIDS epidemic has operated as a kind of objective confirmation of the fundamentalist critique of modernism, with its permissive ethos of private— especially sexual—relations.

In the meantime, fundamentalists are preoccupied with punishing the

infidels—those who refuse to heed the true faith. Their harsh exclusivity
fits well with the old ideological stereotypes of the enemy in Moscow embodying an evil that contrasts with the essential goodness and innocence
of Americans. Of course, such a moral dichotomy is anti-Christian, re-
viving the Manichean heresy that envisioned as the climax of history a war
between the forces of light and darkness, with victory going to the former.
The rejection of Manicheanism by the early church was a consequence
of the heretical tendency to banish evil from the self and, hence, to deny
effectively the basic doctrine of original sin with its notion of indwelling
evil. The Manichean claim was a manifestation of deadly pride, considered
a fundamental vice since medieval times. It is ironic that the Cold War
hardliners brought Manicheanism back into the churches in the guise of
unremitting anti-Communism[6]—and with it, a religious assertiveness on
matters formerly assigned to secular control: for instance, the determined
efforts to reestablish prayer as part of public education. Among potential candidates considered for appointment to the U.S. Supreme Court by
President Ronald Reagan, J. Clifford Wallace, a Mormon jurist with lower-
court experience, is said to have attracted positive attention in the White
House because he didn't believe in the separation of church and state.

How are we to interpret this tendency toward religious self-assertion,
whether in a liberating or fundamentalist mode? Is it coincidentally associated with various local circumstances of conflict and tension in the
world? Or is a wider pattern of secular and modernist discontent inducing
a variegated religious revival?

My hypothesis is this: The complex modern project to apply science
and technology to human problems has encountered several severe challenges that are undermining both its legitimacy as a creed and its coherence as a basis for action. Simplistically put, modernism as practiced has
given us nuclearism and an overwrought encounter between human activity and ecological viability. Normative and spiritual blinders have not
well served the human species, at least not in this century. Of course, the
modernist logic continues to lure many of us with its promises to overcome *with* technology the difficulties that technology has created: more
modernization for the Third World, computerized democracy, electronic
weaponry. But the crisis of modernism is generating nonmodernist responses as well. To cope successfully, we are urged to look backward (a
heroic premodern antecedent) and to strive for a far greener future (a
heroic postmodern prospect).

Religion provides the materials out of which to fashion either type of
response and thereby to recast politics. Marxism—as a radical politics attractive to the oppressed—increasingly fails to mobilize mass support in
the cultural circumstances of Third World and non-Western societies. A

religious radicalism has far greater mass appeal, especially given the over-all disenchantment with the Soviet model and the collapse of ideological and economic support from Moscow. Liberalism—as a moderate politics attractive to those with humane values and middle-class interests—can-not ground its convictions (which, aside from procedural beliefs in due process and fairness, are generally little more than calculations) in ter-rain strong enough to support radical societal restructuring or normative risk-taking of any consequence. A religious grounding deepens and ex-tends struggle, enabling a resistance that incurs risks and accepts sacrifice, insists upon an agenda of radical restructuring, and yet does not aban-don normative discipline.[7] The secular mentality tends to depersonalize suffering, whereas the religious mentality generally regards seriousness about suffering as central to its undertaking.[8] Of course, religious funda-mentalism drives out modernists, but in a bloody manner that reproduces suffering in a variety of nonmodernist forms.

A RELIGIOUS COUNTERTRADITION

But there is another dimension of the religious awakening. An exciting new energy is intent on remaking religion and, with it, politics and cul-ture. Such remaking can either breathe life into inherited symbol systems, establishing its path by invoking a counter-tradition long marginalized by the mainstream, or go back to a moment in the past prior to passage of a religious tradition across some Rubicon of ecclesiastical and doctrinal decay. In Christianity, reference can be made to the Franciscan counter-tradition, with its understanding of the sacred web of life, and to the earliest centuries of Christianity, those extraordinary Christian commu-nities that flourished in the Mediterranean region prior to the conversion of Constantine, in which the ethos was mainly pacifist and of the poor. This remaking can also occur by the weaving of a new relational web of symbolic significance: for instance, by celebrating the arrival of a new goddess religion, a new religion can arise that is animistic without being pagan. The doctrinal and institutional form of this religious remaking re-mains uncertain and inchoate, but the intense striving toward it has been evident in recent decades.

Whatever the new religion, it seems grounded in the earth (as dis-tinct from descending out of the sky) and richly relational. An influential passage from New Age guru Gregory Bateson captures the ecological viewpoint that lies at its center: "What pattern connects the crab to the lobster and the orchid to the primrose and all four of them to me? And me to you? And all six of us to the amoeba in one direction and to the back-ward schizophrenic in another? What is the pattern which connects all the living creatures?"[9]

Another scriptural text of postmodernist religion is contained in a poem by Gary Snyder, "Revolution in the Revolution in the Revolution." Cleverly parodying Marxist-Maoist rhetoric about the drift of revolutionary energy, Snyder converts the secular rhetoric and sensibility of Communist ideologues in an unexpectedly ecological direction:

> Revolutionary consciousness is to be found
> Among the most ruthlessly exploited classes:
> Animals, trees, water, air, grasses.

Snyder can be read as saying the Marxists cut off their analysis too soon and didn't push their revolutionary fervor deep enough, into the earth itself; or Snyder can be heard more cynically as dismissing Marxist materialism in favor of true revolution, that of the spirit, which includes giving our blessings to the whole of nature and finding power not in the barrel of a gun but, as he reveals later in the same poem, in Buddhist meditation:

> & POWER
> comes out of the seed-syllables of mantras.[10]

The new religious sensibility endows all of nature with a sacred, privileged status. It becomes worth dying or making a human sacrifice for the sake of dolphins, whales, perhaps even rivers, mountains, and forests.[11] A symbolic occurrence is the *Rainbow Warrior* incident, in which French intelligence agents sank a Greenpeace ship on July 10, 1985, while it was docked in Auckland, New Zealand, killing a member of the crew, staff photographer Fernando Pereira. The ship and its multinational crew were seeking to protest and disrupt French nuclear testing in the Pacific. The political violence initiated by France represented a modernist effort to destroy the postmodernist kind of challenge being mounted by Greenpeace: it was clearly an act of war by modernism against postmodernism. There was muted response on the part of most governments, apparently caught in a swirl of statist emotions: after all, France was upholding the primacy of the state in external relations, but it was doing so by an illicit and terroristic violation of the sovereign rights of a white, predominantly Western state (the violent deed being done in New Zealand without permission and in defiance of that country's antinuclear stance). Even governments hostile to France were discreet, possibly giving subconscious expression to a growing anxiety about attacks upon the statist framework as the basis of international problem-solving. The interplay of forces released by the *Rainbow Warrior* affair suggests not only the persistence of the modernist framework of state power but also the legitimacy of the postmodernist impulse, which was eventually validated by an $8.1 million damage award issued after hearings before a panel of international law specialists.[12]

Postmodern religious revisioning may assume such shaky forms as, for instance, the emphasis placed on the "harmonic convergence" of August 1987, which was to enable the earth to obtain a "cleansing energy" from a rare alignment of planets. This alignment was supposedly of sufficient magnitude to overcome a period of catastrophic events predicted for the earth by several ancient calendars. Such "readings" of the cosmos are assuredly a kind of antimodernist backlash but do not lead us to enter the process of transformation in any serious or sustainable way. To gather at sacred sites around the world at a given time may be exhilarating for the participants and offer an irresistible potential for media hype, but it does not address the real issues of power, depravity, danger, and destruction in our world. Nor, I might add, do most of the New Age expressions of religious sentiment that promise their adherents growth and tenderness *in vacuo* or, what amounts to the same thing, on sunny beaches and breathtaking mountain heights. That too may be enjoyable, but it is not politically serious to place our trust in any appeal that does not concretely and courageously respond to the actuality of suffering (past, present, and future) in our world.

It is certainly a sign of ethical sensitivity or more astutely of political cynicism (the legacy of Bitburg) for American leaders to visit the carnal houses of the Holocaust, as George Bush did a few years back, perceptively writing in the Visitors' Book at Birkenau: "In remembrance lies redemption." But truly, to remember the atrocities of others is not redemptive at all. To visit the diseased survivors of Hiroshima might be redemptive for George Bush, if this occasion of the first atomic attack on a human settlement were then and there acknowledged without qualification as a crime against humanity. In fact, most American political figures have stayed away from Hiroshima, probably neither daring to look back nor willing to dedicate themselves to the pursuit of a nuclear-free world or even to confront the full range of ethical consequences of an atomic attack.

The path from a religious renewal to a political renewal is complicated, controverted, and still quite difficult to discern. As I have suggested, there are several assured features: an ecological feeling for the wholeness of experience as primary; a decentering of anthropocentric presuppositions about the divine plan and the locus of the sacred; a grounding of religious and political life in the challenge of suffering, not only of humans but of animals and even of nature as well; a conviction that the creative and imaginative locus of energies is passing from those who currently preside over established hierarchies of state and church; a trust in the cooperative potential implicit in human nature as well as a distrust in a variety of "realisms" that claim human nature to be ineradicably aggressive and entrapped within current behavioral patterns and organizational enclosures; and closely related, a repudiation of violence as the path to security, justice, revolution, transformation.[13]

Among the controversies are those about whether to connect the postmodern with left or progressive modernist causes, with organized labor or with the extension of rights. Is the postmodern a continuation in a different direction, or a new start?[14] A specific cluster of disputes concerns the degree to which the postmodern ethos accepts the outlook of the "deep ecologists," those who would altogether withdraw a privileged status from human aspiration and share resources on the basis of some sort of parity with animals, plants, and even rocks and mountains. For deep ecologists the issue as to whether a rock feels pain is of great consequence, but most postmodernists, while reacting to the modernist disregard of nature, refuse to go nearly this far.

Neither religion nor politics has as yet crystallized around a definitive embodiment of the postmodern. To be sure, fascinating explorations are being undertaken in response to particular felt urgencies of time and space. I would encourage careful scrutiny of the Green party movements in various countries—perceived both as the emergent postmodern and as the waning yet still formidable modern.[15] The inner tensions of Green politics represent different ways of deconstructing the modern at a given historical moment and in a particular place. Closely related instances of grassroots activism in Asia, especially India, are intent in a Third World circumstance to revitalize democracy by reversing the flow of energy from periphery to center.[16] In a more explicitly modernist religious frame the *communidades de base* (base communities) throughout Latin America, initially the seedlings of liberation theology, more recently persist as exploratory frameworks of new styles and formats for politics.[17]

Similarly, the new social movements associated with feminism, peace, and the environment, which have ebbed and flowed since the 1960s with a distinctly transnational reach, are best understood as quests for comprehensive renewal and societal transformation rather than as issue-specific and programmatic efforts.[18] In contrast, organizations seeking reforms—such as International Physicians for Social Responsibility and Amnesty International (each certified by the receipt of the Nobel Peace Prize)—are quintessentially modernist, working to nudge existing institutional frameworks into minimal decency without posing a transformative challenge.

The postmodern posture can be identified by its necessarily challenging and provocative character. The otherness it seeks can be grasped by a crude contrast with the modern: the postmodern reveres nature and the cosmos and finds sacred and mysterious energy embedded in life itself.[19] From this embeddedness a new religiosity is beginning to take specific shape, but its distinct form and credo are not yet quite discernible. Only glimpses appear on still distant horizons. Enough is happening so that Bethlehem is once again on alert!

CONFUSIONS OF TWILIGHT

The secularism of modernist civilization has lost its capacity to respond to fundamental challenges in the contemporary world—nuclearism, ecological decay, mass misery. As a result, a dynamic of cross-penetration is under way between politics and religion, producing a series of developments that can be either constructive (liberational) or destructive (fundamentalist). Politics is being reinfused with religious symbols and claims; religion is being summoned to the trenches of popular struggle, even lending support in some circumstances to violent tactics. This breakdown of the separation and antagonism between politics and religion represents an effort by modernists to handle a new agenda of societal demands. What is most revealing is the reconciliation of Marxism and Christianity in a series of Third World settings, a process that is one of mutual enrichment without any necessary effort to subordinate one to the other. The United States government with its unwavering mandate to suppress Marxist tendencies in the Third World has refused to acknowledge this reconciliation, and continues to attack leftist governments on the premise of their godlessness.

These concerns at the core of current world conflict and ideology remain entrapped within an essentially modernist framework: that is, distinct territorial states look forward to an expansion of their productive capacities as the primary means by which to relieve the misery of their peoples. To find more effective and humane means of mobilizing peoples to pursue these ends is a challenging, hopeful development the full potential of which remains untested.

At the same time, there is emerging a postmodern political sensibility animated by an entirely different world view. It too is a kind of religious politics or political religion, but not one growing out of the mainstream of established world religions, especially those of a monotheistic character. This postmodern orientation is ecological at its foundation, finding spiritual coherence in the processes of nature itself. Safeguarding the blessings of the created order (that is, the whole of nature) against violence and destructiveness becomes the most critical religious undertaking, especially given our growing realization that natural life-support systems are under severe strain.

The human species has a special coevolutionary capacity and responsibility. Unlike other species we are aware of our roles in the world and bear the burdens of awareness of having disrupted the ecological order to such a dangerous and unnecessary degree. As humans, we can respond to the pain of the world by devoting our energies to various kinds of restorative action, building institutional forms and popular support for such a dramatic reorientation of behavior. This "conversion" from secularism is under way but to an uneven degree, and virtually not at all in relation to the powerfully entrenched governmental and market structures associated with the modernist enterprise.

The premodern anticipates the postmodern, although historically it gave way to the modern. The postmodern draws on the distant past but cannot reproduce it. The acute sense of jeopardy, complexity, and technological unfolding and the sheer density and interpenetration of peoples and cultures assures that the postmodern is a way forward, not a recovery of the past and certainly not a repetition. It needs to be both a political way (to deal adequately with resources, relations among societies, group identity, human and nonhuman needs and aspirations) and a religious reawakening (the release of spiritual energy associated with this readjustment of role and mission). Whether Green politics, new social movements, reemergent indigenous peoples, or small communities of faith and resistance are vehicles of this postmodern possibility remains to be seen. Assuredly, each of these tendencies is expressive of a reaction against modernist encroachment and a partial revelation of what a fused religious and political consciousness imagines that an alternative, preferred world might be. Such imaginings are being given a preliminary concreteness in the form of many discrete explorations. Nothing, as yet, has jelled into a pattern that can claim for itself the insignia of postmodernism or can monitor initiatives to decide whether or not their contribution is genuinely postmodern rather than merely antimodern. We remain at a stage of postmodern consciousness in which our discernment of negations has formed a consensus but our imaginative attempts at alternatives remain at the experimental stage, hence fraught with controversy and disillusion.

CHAPTER III

Culture and International Relations:
A Third Postmodern Possibility

THE EXCLUSION OF CULTURE

INTERNATIONAL RELATIONS as a discipline has generally neglected to recognize culture as relevant or appropriate to its concerns. The most influential forms of inquiry have analyzed interactions among states which rest upon power and wealth. The prevailing realist interpretations of international relations, even as softened by neorealist emendations, are preoccupied with issues of conflict and capabilities treated as matters of "security" or "political economy" on the basis of the primacy of sovereign state actors. Ideology is conceded to be a factor but normally treated as bearing only on the motivation of political leaders at the state or bloc level and as connected with their capacity to mobilize resources—including support for foreign policy, especially in relation to war and peace, and being most tested with respect to morale and legitimacy in the face of defeat. Leadership, like ideology, is considered mainly as a dimension of political strength that bears upon the power dynamics of relations among states. From Thucydides to Henry Kissinger the core inquiry of international relations theory has examined how major political actors pursue their interests and ambitions, given the absence of either government, community, morality, or law at the international level. As a consequence, the history of international relations is dominated by the records and spectacles of wars and ensuing peace settlements.

Cultural variations and influences can be assimilated by such a realist understanding of international relations but only in a restricted way. Different cultural legacies can be regarded as relevant to the internal and external effectiveness of a political actor, or as shaping the style of government and leadership. The ascendancy of the West has often been explained in cultural terms associated with the liberation of reason from the grip of superstition and religion—a process that can be traced back at least as far as ancient Athens, though it took several centuries to bear its full fruit: it was during the Renaissance that reason as the engine of societal innovation, principally by way of science and technology, generated a dynamic of accelerated development in the leading West European countries. Culture, then, underpins differences in civilizational capabilities, especially if these capabilities are measured by the materialist criteria of progress associated with modernism. Yet intangible criteria of fulfillment connected with social solidarity and a sense of personal well-being may be diminished by the very forms of efficiency required to produce material progress.[1]

Those who emphasize the cultural basis of political action often tend to regard the appropriate unit of analysis as civilization rather than the state.[2] As a consequence, cultural identity is more decisively associated with a multistate notion such as "the West" than with any particular territorial actor, although a continental country with an experience of its own, such as the United States, will have a strong, distinct version of Western civilization. To this extent, we can better understand why international relations theory, with its interest in conflict among states, will find it not useful to study cultural factors that seem to point toward the interplay of civilizations. Since civilizations as such rarely engage in warfare, however, their life stories seem connected more with art and religion than with politics. It is a primary goal of this chapter to challenge such conceptual traditions of foreclosure.

The framework of modernism associated with the rise of the West is the main intellectual background against which thought about international relations developed. As I have argued elsewhere, the transition from feudalism to modernism from the eleventh through the seventeenth century was expressed within the West by a shift in jurists' emphasis from natural law to legal positivism: that is, from a system of overarching principles and standards resting on revelation and authority to a system dependent upon the direct (treaty-making) or indirect (custom-making) expression of consent by territorial states—the only type of political actor entitled to full membership in international society.[3] In fact, despite the generalizing tendencies of international relations specialists, it seems evident that the early phases of statist diplomacy were an expression of European regional development. The globalist rhetoric was misleading in many respects, including its tendency to disguise patterns of interstate hegemony, especially between Europe and the rest of the world.

Lurking within this Western cultural legacy, as nurtured and evolved over the centuries by dominant religious institutions and traditions, were several dangerous ideas that continue to exert powerful influences upon political consciousness. There was, above all, in this legacy a deeply embedded sense of "chosen people" as privileged vehicles of progress entitled to exert dominance by some underlying appointment, which is then turned back to an original covenant between Yahweh and the Jewish people. However this biblical myth is interpreted, it provides a basis for both a cult of superiority and a mandate to impose one's cultural forms upon all those that resist, whether they are inside territorial space (inquisitions) or outside (holy wars). Symbolism based on the ravaging character of the evil other can be secularized and given many different forms. The evil that is to be eradicated has become godless Communism or heartless capitalism in the opposing materialist calculations of values. The early emphases of religious heresy have given way, at least on a literal basis. Similarly, the good may be the blessings of "democracy" or of "socialism," or the alternative ideas of "the market" and "property" versus state planning and socialism. Or, as has happened recently, ideologies may converge on a shared commitment to "modernization," although such convergence is challenged to a degree by fundamentalist political undertakings.

Another side to this Western cultural heritage is also embedded in its origins: a disposition to question and challenge authority. Going back to the Jewish prophets and Socrates, we notice a tradition of thought in the West that assigns a subversive role to individual conscience, reason, and moral passion. This sense of individual autonomy as a precious attribute to collective human experience has inspired the politics of the West at each principal stage of its evolution. It is evident in the rise of the common law of England as a restraint upon royal authority; in the central claims of constitutional order contained in the French and American revolutions, especially as expressed through notions of the "inalienable rights" of citizens; more recently, through the affirmation of welfare rights; and, generally, by the gradual establishment of an elaborate framework of international human rights during the course of several decades. The extension of criminal liability to German and Japanese leaders after World War II represented an official acknowledgment that the state cannot shield an individual from his or her responsibility to uphold international law. This experience was generalized in the form of the Nuremberg Principles, which bind all leaders to uphold international law on matters of war and peace and regard the failure to do so as criminal. Subsequently, as a result of the interpretation given the Nuremberg Principles by many activists, a claim was posited to validate citizen resistance in the face of crimes of state, a process that has come to be known as the Nuremberg Obligation or Nuremberg Action.[4]

In this century, the Western, modernist cultural frame has been split into two main historical streams since the Bolshevik Revolution of 1917, but the civil war raging within the West on issues of class rule and property rights has accepted as common ground the central idea that the progress of human society depends upon the more and more efficient mobilization of productive forces. Marxism-Leninism carried the capitalist line of materialism a step further by centralizing authority within the socialist state, but attitudes toward growth and nature were indistinguishable. Both ideologies sought rapid and maximum economic growth, and both ignored the externalities of industrialization. Both ideologies generated "realists" in international relations, whether the language was that of capabilities analysis and balance of power or that of the correlation of forces. And both accepted the state as the fundamental political actor in international relations for the foreseeable future. In this sense, capitalism (or liberalism) and socialism (or Marxism) present the non-Western world with the two main faces of modernism as developed by Western civilization.[5]

This selective overview of the Western cultural legacy helps focus an initial set of generalizations about international relations as an account of the behavior of territorial sovereign states. First of all, there exists a suppressed tension between individual integrity and collective goals that becomes evident as soon as cultural factors are introduced. This tension works dialectically and may help explain both the resilience and creativity of the West as a cultural space. The character of this tension arises from the societal interplay between expansionist drives that are implicit in cults of superiority and the critical backlash against unrighteous behavior that arises out of a cultural commitment to conscience and reason and, by extension, affirms the place of the individual. In this regard, the Western role has been a contradictory one in relation to non-Western societies, both hegemonic and antihegemonic, transmitting as a result of its dominance the very ideas that can be reinterpreted to provide the normative foundation for resistance by those victimized. One small instance: children in North Vietnam were made to memorize the Declaration of Independence of 1776, despite the U.S. intervention, because it was one of the inspirational sources of Ho Chi Minh's struggle against colonial rule.

Second, the West itself is not necessarily trapped indefinitely within the modernist frame, as its underlying cultural experience antedated the rise of the state system and seems capable of adapting to poststatal images of world order. At the same time, such a possibility must overcome the momentum of modernism, which is mainly responsible for the various ecological and geopolitical threats to the viability of *any* form of planetary existence. Apologists for modernism, embattled now to offset the pressure of its limitations, are engaged in a massive exercise of deception and pacification, relying on a heroic confidence that rationality within the modernist framework remains both necessary and sufficient, despite the evidence to the contrary provided by nuclearism, interdependence, and ecological decay.[6]

Third, the non-Western forces of resistance have mounted a formidable challenge to Western hegemony on a political plane but less so on an economic plane. The anticolonial struggle has involved an extraordinary movement in history, made possible by the potency of various movements of nationalist resistance. Almost everywhere this process has achieved for the political community formal independence and a status entitling it to participation as a full-fledged member of international society (symbolized by access to the United Nations). Almost nowhere, however, has the process of anti-colonial resistance been able to wrest effective control from the West on matters of economic policy. Multinational corporations and banks, as well as various forms of indebtedness, accountability to international financial institutions, and currency dependence, have sustained an overall pattern of Western technique and practice—in Japan, for example, and newly industrialized countries (the so-called NICs). In short, there are degrees of economic independence, but the more successful examples, whether capitalist or socialist, seem dependent on a cultural adoption of modernism: that is, the Western cultural stance toward reason, science, and technology. This adoption is explicit in the case of capitalist countries and, in later developments, several socialist countries; most notably, Gorbachev's Soviet Union and post-Mao China (with its "four modernizations") affirm their modernism far more confidently than their socialism.

A different sort of challenge to Western hegemony has been mounted by the Islamic revolution and other forms of fundamentalism in the Islamic world. Again, the definition of what is Western is at issue, as Islam arises out of the Judeo-Christian experience and contains and extends monotheistic claims of assured truth and divine mandate to a particular anointed fraction of humanity. Yet the Islamic world has never adopted the modernist path with any great success; experiences of disaster in the Shah's Iran and Anwar Sadat's Egypt suggest how treacherous is an unabashed turning-West for cultural inspiration. In this respect, the fundamentalist and traditionalist backlash, by its intensity and reliance upon indigenous culture as a shield against modernist penetration, is a more thoroughgoing repudiation of the colonial experience than has been achieved by even radical secular politics. Insisting on traditional dress, disallowing Western music, and some delinking from the world economy carries the drive to self-determination quite far, though not necessarily in a sustainable fashion or in a manner that is popular or beneficial for the people. To stand apart from modernism often means to be cut off from capital, technology, markets, and ideas, and this has meant an inability to address the reality of mass misery. Recourse to some varieties of traditionalism can lead to gross abuses of human rights, to the denial of any democratic prospect, and to militant expressions of chauvinist politics.

What seems evident is that on the one hand, a strong cultural identity can play a vital role in securing the full independence of non-Western countries in the post-colonial period but does not necessarily do so in a beneficial fashion, at least as measured by widely shared international standards of human rights and democracy. On the other hand, effective restraints upon repressive elements of tradition can create a cultural vacuum that opens up a country to easy penetration, including the crude retention or reimposition of Western "rule." The response of "culture" to the weight of international relations is vividly illustrated by the various phases of Iran's history since World War II, including the struggle to overcome a heritage of Western domination.

To elaborate upon the relevance of culture to the weight of international relations, the subsequent sections of this chapter explore modernism as a cultural vehicle for the hegemonic project of the West and then consider two interrelated forms of possible alternative development: first, a postmodern Western sequel, and second, a series of antimodern enclaves of resistance.[7]

THE RESILIENCE OF MODERNISM

Regarding the civilizational unit as more critical to the contours of cultural identity than the sovereign state causes some confusion for the interpretation of international relations (that is, relations among sovereign states). Yet the confusion is unavoidable. States can act as vehicles for the spread of culture outside the civilizational unit and are undoubtedly the most important actors in many non-Western civilizations. Western civilization's own internal dynamic led to the formation of strong territorial states as the principal political actors. Beyond this, the state became the guardian of an emergent industrial capitalism that contributed to the overseas drive to obtain and protect markets, resources, and investment outlets. This drive was also a moving force behind the colonial outreach, leading the West to provide an anchor for the first phase of a global political order initially managed from Europe. Postcolonial arrangements have shattered the political dimension of colonial globalism but have strengthened its economic dimensions and, arguably, its ideational dimensions as well.

This Western hegemony is now based on predominance in relation to capital and technology, as well as on the dissemination of information and aspirational imagery, although reinforced, as necessary, by military intervention. The multinational corporation, transnational bank, and the transnational news agency are manifestations of this global order; each is based on Western culture and seems likely to persist. Non-Western countries have shaped their own plans and ambitions by reference to a Western image of already realized modernization, which includes an expanded middle class and a variety of consumer goods. The meaning of life is overwhelmingly associated with material satisfactions, and notions of collective gain derive from economic growth as an overall indicator of "progress." Technology makes this modernist world view plausible, apparently providing ever new possibilities of extracting more from nature for less, thereby improving economic performance and enabling relative and absolute gains in international status via an expansion of overseas trade.

Further, the cultural artifacts of the West have been widely interpreted around the world as literal embodiments of modernism, especially those of the United States, which provided the earliest and most spectacular success story. These expressions of attainment are often spontaneously adopted by local people to hasten the advent of a future with which they identify. The spread of jeans and rock music, of fast food chains and discos, of Holiday Inns and Hilton Hotels illustrates the missionary penetration into non-Western countries of a globally packaged Western orientation. In such a normative atmosphere, those states in the Third World that build rapidly expanding middle-class markets and industrial sectors are looked upon as "successful," and those that are unable to do so are viewed as "failures." From the perspective of modernist cultures, it is less important to assess ecological and demographic pressures, protection of human rights and democracy, satisfaction of the basic needs of the poor, and signs of happiness and social integration. Here, the Trilateral Commission countries of North America, Western Europe, and Japan provide some negative imagery. The United States is the most modernist country but also the most hospitable habitat for social distress (crime, suicide, divorce), militarism, and ecological decay.

Yet the darker side of modernism does not mean that the cultural energy underlying this vision of the future is as yet a spent force. Within modernism are a variety of "checks" designed to prevent its excesses from producing catastrophe. Technology can be deployed on behalf of environmental protection, peace and justice, even human rights. The efforts to halt reliance on chlorofluorocarbons (CFCs) is illustrative: governments seek to respond by imposing restraints that are essentially dependent on voluntary compliance, and some of the most flagrant commercial uses are being phased out by voluntary cutbacks beyond those mandated by treaty because benign substitutes that are commercially viable have been developed. Materialism can also be softened by religious revival, artistic activity, and societal initiatives. Whether these checks are by themselves sufficient to reverse destructive trends seems highly doubtful at this stage of history.

In the 1970s such studies as *The Limits to Growth* and *Blueprint for Survival* presented strident warnings about the sustainability of modernist reliance on economic growth for progress.[8] These studies argued that there were limits on population density, arable land, capacity to absorb pollution, and resource stocks and that according to available data these limits were being approached at an accelerating and alarming rate. Apologists for modernism emerged to reassure the West and the world that pessimistic assessments were exaggerated and premature, that growth could go on indefinitely, especially if self-evidently prudent regulatory steps were taken; furthermore, automatic market adjustments by way of costs would turn behavior in desirable directions long before the onset of catastrophe. Indeed, the alleged prophets of doom had overplayed their hands on a literal level and in the short term. The world system was more resilient than they had anticipated, though far more threatened than the reassuring voices would have had us believe.

The 1980s saw, in turn, a discrediting of the apologists for open-ended growth. A new wave of concerns often reinforced by authoritative scientific studies—on "nuclear winter," ozone depletion, greenhouse effect, climate change, acid rain, ocean pollution, desertification, deforestation, water shortages, demographic pressures—reintroduced the question of the sustainability of modernist life forms into the political sensibility. There is a less alarmist concern about the ecological future of the human species in the 1990s, but there also appears to be a sense of resignation, a view that the process of disintegration has gone too far and that the Green social forces needed to build a sustainable future are not serious contenders for power.[9] Unlike the first wave of ecological concern in the 1970s, the second has produced neither dissent nor, as yet, any serious prescription for adjustment. The mainstream political leaders have apparently reached a tacit agreement to ignore this crisis agenda of planetary management, concentrate their alleged environmentalist concern on local matters and the easier global issues, and continue to be preoccupied with the best tactics for addressing the traditional statist agenda of national security and economic growth.

Here, then, is the central relevance of culture to the major world order challenge facing human society: Industrializing, growth-oriented, technology-based modernism has shaped the world economy, mainly in a market-directed fashion. This orientation has also supported the formation of strong, militarist territorial states as a means of reconciling nationalism with aspirations for economic development. Modernism, in this regard, is preoccupied with harnessing productive forces. Whether organized around the guiding ideas of Adam Smith or those of Karl Marx, it is insensitive to the limits imposed by nature.

Can this legacy of modernism be overcome or decisively redirected over the course of the next several decades? The adaptive potential of modernism seems far less than what is necessary to address the magnitude of the challenges facing organized societies around the world or menacing the system as a whole. Is there a postmodern possibility? Before offering a response to that question, I discuss briefly some society-scale responses to modernism in the Third World, look at traditionalist repudiations of modernism, and consider the resources of non-Western cultures that disclose partial alternative patterns of action to modernism.

TRADITIONALIST REVIVAL AND THE
ROLE OF NON-WESTERN CULTURE

As earlier suggested, the Iranian repudiation of modernism since 1979 has been bound up with a rejection of Western culture as brought to Iran in a particularly corrupt and deformed manner by the Shah in the two decades after 1953. Associating the U.S. life-style and political role with evil and Khomeini and Islamic fundamentalism with good suggested one path by which to escape from Western cultural hegemony, at least temporarily, as well as to purge Iran of foreign influence. Only Islam, as revived and interpreted by a charismatic figure, has seemed strong enough to enable a society to overcome the combined weight of Western political, economic, and cultural pressure, and even this deviation from modernism may turn out to be temporary and partial.[10]

In the postcolonial era of international relations, opening up too quickly to the West can lead to a cultural backlash, especially among Islamic countries. Sadat's move to the West in the mid-1970s—by way of an accommodation with Israel, attracting foreign capital and corporations, and embodying Western life-style—unleashed a backlash that included regional alienation, domestic unpopularity, and a virtually unmourned death by political assassination carried out by Egyptian fundamentalists. Yet whether traditionalism is a viable alternative to Western hegemony even in the Islamic world is by no means established. It is a strong force, especially in the hands of an efficient and ruthless ruler, but by itself it provides no basis for development, for meeting basic human needs, for providing human rights and democracy. Its emphasis can be negative, a descent into a form of pre- or antimodern darkness.

Possibly, at a subsequent stage, an integration of Western technique and indigenous cultural world views can produce a viable basis of action-in-the-world. Arguably, such an integration has occurred to an impressive degree, though in a variety of forms, in some Asian countries—those in which modernism has built upon rather than displaced Confucian and even Buddhist traditions. From the perspective of international relations, this kind of integration may contribute a new emphasis on the mediation of conflict. China, for instance, has exhibited creativity in recent years, working out a model for the future of Hong Kong that enables the dynamic of decolonization to proceed without rupturing the internal structure of this model of Oriental prosperity premised on liberalism and market economics. Yet in light of the antidemocratic persecutions of 1989 and subsequently, new doubts exist as to whether the Chinese government can be trusted to respect the autonomy of Hong Kong (which is the essence of the arrangement negotiated with Great Britain) when it becomes fully operational later in this decade.

To an uncertain and controversial extent, China has relied on its traditional cultural emphasis on harmony, rational leadership, moderation, and unity to work toward a demographic policy that brings resources and population into manageable balance. In contrast, the more individualistic and communal priorities of Hindu culture deny India such an option based on larger scale identities. Culture matters in establishing limits and options in state-and-society relations, and these relations are of utmost relevance to participating in regional and global politics, as well as to addressing world order problems. The war system thrives on internal discontent, governmental incapacity. Culture can be either a valuable resource or a formidable obstacle for conflict-resolving and conflict-transforming solutions; this variance is not fixed but contextual. That is, if the priority is a large-scale practical solution, then Confucian cultural forms, especially as evolved in Chinese thought and action, are well adapted. But if the priority is democratic practice and individual liberty, then Confucianism is ill adapted and Hinduism well adapted. Such a grossly oversimplified generalization does hold up to a superficial extent: with the brief, confirming exception of the Emergency (when in the mid-1970s Indira Gandhi suspended civil liberties), India has since independence sustained democracy and human rights, despite poverty, continuous strife, and frequent warfare, but has had almost no success in a variety of attempts to provide centralized, state-initiated solutions for population pressure, poverty, and caste and communal violence. China has traditionally had remarkable success in providing unified leadership, especially of a sort that imposed a call for moderation and harmony, but almost no positive results from its democratization campaigns, and it crushed the one spontaneous movement of democracy shortly after it emerged in 1989. The stability of Marxist-Leninist governance in several Asian countries can also be partially attributed to their Confucian background, whereas one of the most turbulent experiences in recent Asian history arose from the Maoist excesses at the core of the Cultural Revolution, which significantly included a harsh and direct repudiation of Confucian—that is, traditional cultural—identities.

In sum, international relations reflect the character of leading sovereign states, which in turn incorporate variants of a small number of world civilizational traditions. These states cannot operate successfully in the postcolonial period unless they nourish their cultural roots, roots that influence the choice of governing and developmental options. Each cultural tradition has a wide range of alternatives, all authentic expressions, from which to choose. Islam can support more democratic and secular paths, and the current potency of the fundamentalist path may be a temporary overreaction to a failure by more moderate forms of Islam to prevent destructive varieties of cultural penetration by the West. Nor is the fundamentalist option the only politically disturbing tendency in the region. The radical secularism of Iraq under Saddam Hussein has turned out to be far more dangerous to international peace and security than the fundamentalism of Iran under Khomeini. Revealingly, in the course of the crisis and war generated by Iraq's 1990 invasion of Kuwait, Hussein appealed to Muslim solidarity and cultural identity rather than to nationalist aspirations in justifying his actions. Confucian China and Hindu India, while penetrated and corrupted by the West at the periphery of their societal existence, retained the integrity of their cultural identity during the colonial ordeal.

It seems evident that an appropriate cultural ground for a strong sense of identity is indispensable for constructive participation in international relations. The converse is also convincing: A repudiation of cultural identity disrupts civil society and produces turbulent results that generate violence and discontent at home and abroad. This discussion concerning non-Western societies pertains with almost equal force to the more backward parts of the West itself, as the postwar experience of Poland so painfully exemplifies; the imposition, by means of foreign military occupation, of a Marxist-oriented modernism disrupted Poland's societal belief system, which was centered on traditionalist Catholic experience. The extraordinary extent of collective Polish resistance, embracing virtually the totality of society, was an expression of cultural self-assertion defying the violation of Polish identity by pseudo-Marxist rule from within and by crude Soviet intervention from without.

The cultural factor in international conflict is vital in relation to explanation and prediction, suggesting the need for its incorporation in the study of international relations. Such an assertion may seem obvious, but it runs against the main realist emphases on capabilities, changes in relative power of states, and the implications for warfare of technological innovation.

GLOBALISM AND POSTMODERNISM

At present, it is mainly the consequence of the globalization of Western cultural influence, including its commitment to modernization, that has produced a world order crisis of multiple dimensions: nuclearism, industrialism, materialism, consumerism. Whether the issue is ozone depletion, greenhouse effect, oceanic or atmospheric pollution, ionized radiation, the main causative agents have evolved and their use has been concentrated in Western countries, especially in the United States. True, this Western pattern of development has been enthusiastically adopted by most of the non-Western world in the postcolonial period. Available methods of interstate cooperation to mitigate the detrimental effects of modernism, whether through treaty standards or institutional arrangements, characteristically lack serious coercive mechanisms and rarely challenge entrenched economic interests. Reliance is placed on moral suasion and voluntary patterns of compliance, if suitable standards of regulation can be agreed upon at all; without the willing participation and consent of the offending state(s), there is virtually no capability to protect the global public interest.

Globalism informed by modernism is leading to an integration of the planet under the aegis of technological capacity, shared images of materialist success, and the idea of an optimal market for the allocation of resources and the sale of goods and services. Such a globalism is not necessarily destructive; although it brings with it traditions of maximizing profits and production, dumping wastes, and overlooking human misery, environmental consciousness is now a feature of the modernist mind-set, an adjustment of reason to a new set of material conditions.

This globalist tendency in international life is generating a new political order in which the role of states and war is likely to be diminished, although persisting as prominent and even decisive features for decades to come. Relevant to the focus of this chapter is the central role of "culture" in preparing attitudes and beliefs for a much more integrated system of relations among political communities, with economic actors and arenas assuming greater significance, as well as functional regimes for environmental protection and practical administration especially of the global commons (oceans, atmosphere, space, polar regions).

This cultural overlay, disseminated by television images, rock stars, and advertising logos, may not displace the specificities of cultural identity associated with diverse civilizational and ethnic traditions. As earlier discussed, the cultural pretensions of modernism will be severely challenged (and dismissed as spurious and corrupting) by fundamentalist appeals of various sorts. Especially to the extent that "the culture of modernism" does not deliver materially, impoverished masses will become ever more susceptible to appeals based on the need for purification and for the revival and assertion of indigenous cultural traditions, first of all, as a defense against foreign (that is, Western, which itself is further deconstructed to be seen as American) penetration and domination—which has become more sinister in the postcolonial era because presented in a universalist container. In this regard, cultural identity depends on defending indigenous tradition against modernist encroachment.

Can there be a reconciliation? Must modernism occupy the entire territory of cultural imagination? Is it possible to accept the benefits of the new globalism without extinguishing specific cultural traditions? Can the new globalism become a moral force, providing hopes for the poor and offering prospects for a safeguarded environment? Put differently, is a compassionate and ecologically sound capitalism a real political possibility at this stage of international history? Such questions now need to be posed with utmost seriousness, though they yield no assured answers.

Yet there is one line of more constructive assessment. A second, contrasting type of globalism coming into being that offers some grounds for optimism, both to moderate the bad effects of modernism and to provide an alternative vision of the future. This second type of globalism is informed by the postmodern possibility to an extent parallel to the first type of globalism being informed by modernism. The comparison may suggest too sharp a contrast, for the postmodern possibility incorporates portions of modernism, including aspects of science, technology, reason, and such institutional features as constitutional governance and the rule of law.

Postmodern globalism emerges from below on the basis of societal initiatives of transnational scope and dimension. Movements for democracy and human rights, for environmental protection and Green politics, for feminist reinterpretation, and for a peaceful world are vehicles for disseminating these new images of solidarity and connectedness that both spring from and give rise to a sense of shared human destiny and, with this sense, feelings of species identity that complement feelings of local, national, and civilizational identity. The aggregate of such transnational gropings can be associated with a political postulate: the emergence of *global civil society* as a background against which history unfolds. The realization of this postulate is uneven, deeper in some regions than others, more urban than rural, further evolved in some substantive issue areas than others.

Just as civil society is a construct without spatial dimensions, global civil society is a construct of the mind and imagination, a device for recording initiatives of transnational scope and global implication and for acknowledging normative aspirations to build the inevitable globalism of the future on democratic foundations, thereby resisting and regulating the globalism from above that arises out of the technocratic elitism of modernism.

In effect, then, international relations are being reshaped in the crucible of cultural ferment, here stylized as the encounter between the "cultures" of modernism and postmodernism.[11] The interaction of these tendencies, presented as opposites, will yield a future that is globally constituted. States may retain their decisive role for an extended period, especially through their continuing capacity to wage war, but their own very persistence will depend on their sharing the stage with other actors working in larger formats. The integrative energies of modernist globalism are evident in the restructuring of European economic life, as are the complementary energies of postmodernist globalism, which have generally opposed and resisted Europe 1992. Adherents of the globalism of postmodernism may, in some settings, prefer the statist framework of relative decentralization to modernist programs for restructuring capital, markets, and institutions on more integrative and totalizing bases. The postmodern anxiety in these contexts involves the conviction that modernist projects for partial globalization, as in Europe, have the primary effect of reducing the political space available for democratic and grassroots transnational activism and innovation.

International relations theory, as birthed by the central Westphalian idea of autonomous territorial states, was premised on a politics of fragmentation. Culture was conceived, if at all, as an *internal* factor largely extraneous to the functioning of international relations. In contrast, the collision of emergent globalisms draws on opposed cultural emphases, both originated in the West but both aspiring to provide the basis for a more integrated future existence on the planet. Modernism is almost completely an outgrowth of Western civilization, whereas postmodernism is more eclectic, having its origins in a reaction to modernism within its main Western home but drawing inspiration from the lived existence of all the peoples of the earth, including premodern enclaves. It thereby evolves in an eclectic fashion that is constituted by various specific cultural experiences, yet finds, as well, common humanizing elements that can provide the belief and mythic foundations for progressive thought and action beneath the banner of postmodern globalism.

PART TWO

Planning the Journey Ahead

*This second cluster of chapters represents an effort to connect a con-
cern with civilizational context to the tradition of thought associated
with world order studies and, more concretely, with the more recent
work of the World Order Models Project and with the Peace and Global
Transformation Project of the United Nations University. As such, these
chapters shift the world order emphasis from an agenda of global concerns to an assemblage of global initiatives that are expressions of a
nascent transnational dimension of movements of democratization.
The cumulative effects of these movements seem to ebb and flow with
shifts in geopolitical pattern, but their importance for the next century
seems beyond reasonable doubt.*

*Chapter IV considers global reform from this orientation of grass-
roots globalism and puts forward some suggestions for more systematic ways of assessing different kinds of initiatives and developments.
It stresses not only the bottom-up democratizing perspectives but also
the substantive importance of the environmental agenda. The 1980s
established definitively the depth and breadth of this agenda and the
degree to which international relations will need to devote growing
attention to the global commons. Functionally relevant as well is the
extent to which economic integration at regional levels and interdependence at global levels are redrawing the meaningful boundaries
between political actors in a manner not communicated by a map of
sovereign states.*

*Chapter V goes on to focus on the process of transition, moving
toward the desirable deliberative, determined, yet nonviolent means.
More ambitiously, this chapter seeks to provide a politics for transition
that interprets the extraordinary exploits of transnational initiatives*

and connects these exploits with the process of constructing a global civil society that encompasses without encroaching upon the autonomy of distinct and diverse societies in a plural world. Chapter VI is complementary, emphasizing the agency of social movements in the politics of transition and offering some examples.

CHAPTER IV

Solving the Puzzles of Global Reform

AS LONG AS there has been serious political speculation, thinkers and prophets have put forth images and ideas about a world based on harmony, unity, and happiness for all. Yet the history of organized political life is dominated by narratives of war, fragmentation, and misery for most inhabitants of the planet. This tension between possibility and actuality has become almost unbearable in contemporary circumstances, where the dangers of species self-annihilation have become persistent themes of popular culture and dream life.

The political order of the world is premised upon the interplay between sovereign states, more or less coordinated by diplomacy. These states are of diverse size, resource endowment, geographic circumstance, developmental state, cultural heritage, ideological outlook, and governing style. The dominant states set the tone of the international system and give it a hierarchical character, as well as raising or moderating tensions, stabilizing or destabilizing economic relations, and establishing, or not, acceptable kinds of leadership for the world as a whole. Between 1945 and 1989 this hierarchy (in actuality, somewhat varying hierarchies in distinct settings) informed the most significant dimension of international security in bipolar terms: the administration of the war system beneath the shadow cast by two antagonistic superpowers each with immense arsenals of nuclear weapons, and the ideological rivalry of the two blocs for the hearts and minds of non-Western peoples liberating themselves from the oppressiveness of colonialism.[1]

Yet in both these contexts the superpowers failed the tests of leadership. A nuclear arms race imperiled human survival, diverting vast quantities of resources and undermining the sovereign rights of all political communities; and superpower diplomacy in the Third World was neither benign nor effective, producing a continuous flow of interventions, facilitating militarization at high levels of modernization, and promoting models of development that have not successfully addressed problems of poverty or population growth, or encouraged democratic forms of popular participation in political life. These failures of leadership generated a movement toward non-alignment in the Third World, an effort to insulate sovereignty from the dangers and costs of superpower hegemony, and to build countervailing power on the basis of solidarity. Of course, the failures of superpower diplomacy also threatened the developed states of the North. As an autonomous unit legitimated by upholding security within its territory and by achieving democratic participation, the state here has become virtually a mirage. Because of the bloc system, these states have lost control of their destiny on issues of war and peace. And in the nuclear age, such loss of control reduces the citizens of bloc countries to the status of hostages, a situation well captured by the slogan of the European peace movement: "No annihilation without representation."

Still, matters could have been far worse in the Cold War era. World War III was avoided. Enough political space was cleared, partly as a result of bipolar rivalry, to enable decolonization; both superpowers, despite their opportunism in practice, acted at least partially out of their differing anticolonial traditions. United States control over international economic policy was generally enlightened and intelligent, exhibiting postwar generosity, providing a stable currency, building up trading partners and markets, and enabling sustained growth for all sectors of the world capitalist economy. Similarly, United States influence also lent prestige to institutional efforts at global and regional levels to strengthen most cooperative aspects of international life. These positive features of U.S. leadership were greatly diminished during the Reagan years, producing despair about future prospects for world order.

In fact, geopolitical and economic crises occurred throughout the Cold War period of recent history, disclosing in a variety of settings the fragility of the world system and conveying a sense that the structure could collapse altogether. Beginning in the 1970s a new kind of international concern emerged in the form of ecological anxiety, centering on doubts about whether the mix of population growth, pollution, and resource depletion were compatible with the carrying capacity of the earth. Compounding this anxiety was a rather manipulative reliance on sophisticated computer models, temporarily lending an objective imprimatur to prophetic warnings that industrial civilization on a global scale was running out of growing space. The ecological preoccupation of the early 1970s began to recede late in the decade, only to return ten years later in a more sober and sobering manner that induced political leaders across the spectrum to proclaim themselves "environmentalists."

These concerns amid the complexity of international life engendered a global awareness of "one world" in key respects. Thus, Bhopal is not just a city in India; it is a city that was the scene of an unprecedented industrial disaster in a world of integrated consciousness. Its victims evoke empathy everywhere, and their efforts to receive adequate compensation raise key issues of transnational responsibility for the multinational corporation, an actor that is a curious blend of the territorial and the non-territorial and, for this reason alone, hard to pin down; as was the case with Union Carbide at Bhopal, the main corporate actor distances itself organizationally by operating through a subsidiary (the word itself implying subordination) and gains further protection through the complicity of governmental authorities at local and federal levels.

As the stresses and strains on the state system have cumulatively intensified over some four decades, so too have militaristic responses. But reactions of a creative sort are also becoming more prominent. A struggle is shaping up to determine the future of specific peoples and civilizations and of the species and its habitat. This struggle goes mainly unreported in the daily media, although episodes and symptoms may surface from time to time, usually in some turbulent form, whether it be a mass demonstration, a campaign of resistance, a world leader who questions the logic of nuclearism or militarism by a concrete act, a declaration of intent by some movement for societal renewal, or evidence disclosing the further deterioration of some critical dimension of the global environment. Once our perceptual lens became attuned to struggles between alliances and states, between forces from the "left" and "right" or, at best, between "top" and "bottom," the struggle to remake our world called for new categories, new frameworks, and a new political language. And the tools are emerging, especially as a result of the activities of social movements addressing some facet of oppression or arising to deal with immediate problems by relying on grassroots and local resources. These new forms represent what Green party cofounder Petra Kelly calls "gentle subversion."[2] The word "gentle" is at least as important as the word "subversion."

What is striking for our purposes is the resilience of the state system in the face of all these subversive happenings. There is no doubt that the state system has been challenged by the persistence of modernism, but it has evolved and responded and, if anything, strengthened its hold. The essence of a state is a function of two quite distinct elements: its capacity to coordinate and exert control, and its legitimacy as a guarantor of nationalist identity. According to Ernest Gellner, the former has been important for the evolution of postagrarian or industrial societies: the coordinating capacity was continuously modernized and reflected the increasing mobilization of science and technology as instruments of state power. And the latter has reflected the intensity of nationalist sentiment—a faith to die for. Paradoxically, it should be noted, states oppress and destroy hostile or subordinate nationalism within their boundaries. Gellner estimates that there are 200 states and at least 800 movements of effective nationalism—plus 7,000 potential nationalisms if ethnic identity is taken as the premise.[3] The disparity explains why the state is necessarily both a vehicle of dominant nationalism and a coercive instrumentality in relation to subordinate nationalism. In fact, from the point of view of global reform, statism overwhelms whatever stirrings of globalism can be identified. This is because the emergence of militant subordinated nationalism threatens the viability of the state from within, as well as producing a certain globalist solidarity among these struggling movements.

This chapter explores the terrain of gentle subversion in relation to state power. The first section makes some observations about why the outcome of World War II created a surprisingly unfavorable context for global reform of an antistatist character, as compared with World War I. Such observations challenge the conventional view that there has been a linear growth of internationalism over the last century or so. Rather, my contention is that the main energy for global reform in the postwar world—namely, the anticolonial movement—was statist in character, though, to be sure, there was also the United States effort to establish and administer a global economy of mutual benefit in order to avoid the kind of destructive economic nationalism that was widely regarded as a major cause of the breakdown of international order in the 1930s and the slide toward world war.

The second section examines the contradictory side of the ledger of political struggle. It discusses both the denuclearizing and demilitarizing initiatives that have periodically surfaced and defensive moves designed to uphold the existing situation against threatened deterioration. The more radical reformist thinking has a blind side: the neglect of tactics and struggles to prevent these further deteriorations (as distinct from the pursuit of enhancements). Nevertheless, I make the assumption that within existing structures of world order there is positive political space to be occupied, as well as space to defend against encroachment.

The third section reaches out to consider the search for the promised land. Here the inquiry centers on the invention of a new politics that is compassionate, globalist, localist, and spiritual at its core and that refuses to assess the person or the group by reference to militarist prowess or capacity to administer the apparatus of state power. A first act of allegiance to this radical alternative politics would be to declare ourselves citizens of the invisible political community that is to be our promised land, a polity based on justice and ecological reverence. Such "citizenship" implies a commitment to pilgrimage, not membership in an existing polity, but such a break with present political configurations would dramatize the importance of resisting illegitimate claims of established political orders and would symbolize the exercise of a new form of human freedom animated by the imaginative quest for a peaceful and just world.

THE ILLUSIONS OF IMMOBILISM

If we analyze prospects for global reform by traditional means, we find little ground for hope. The scale of the reforms required to realize a world of peace and justice seems decisively blocked by the orientation and dominance of sovereign states and by a host of other obstacles, including especially a mood of skepticism about any project for human betterment that interferes with the operation of markets. What is worse, the faint glimmer of hope associated only a generation ago with incremental reforms fashioned by states acting together on behalf of shared interests and of their peoples has been virtually extinguished by the cumulative drift of more recent developments.

Further, it is not widely appreciated that the period of maximum antiwar sentiment occurred not after World War II but rather after World War I, when substantial sectors of democratic societies were deeply disillusioned by the devastation and inconclusive geopolitical results of the 1914–18 period of intense warfare, and more generally by balance-of-power approaches to security premised on the military capabilities of sovereign states. It was early in this interwar period that the most dramatic efforts to achieve collective security and disarmament were pursued, as was also the quest for peaceful settlement procedures as diplomatic alternatives to war.[4]

That the failure to avert World War II was widely attributed to this drift toward "peace" led to a popular reaction abhorring "appeasement," as epitomized by the concessions of the liberal democracies to Hitler at Munich in 1938. But other elements have also helped increase the warproneness of the state system. First, there is the unacknowledged realization that only the war pulled world capitalism out of the Depression and that Keynesianism, in order to work during peace time, must operate in the *as if* atmosphere of a war economy, requiring a heightened sense of continuous international political tension to justify high levels of peacetime expenditures on military preparedness. Second, there is the recognition that new military technology requires permanent mobilization of opinion and resources, an adjustment dramatized by the (supposedly) surprise attack launched by the Japanese on the isolationist and slumbering United States at Pearl Harbor and by the obvious capabilities of long-range bombers and missile-firing submarines—even without the added spur of avoiding a potential knockout blow from missile-guided nuclear weapons. Third, there is the ideological notion that preparing for war is a better assurance of "peace" than is disarmament, especially given the view held during the Cold War years of an irreconcilable East-West tension, with the leaders of each side demonizing those of the other; in this respect, theorizing about deterrence is really the crystallization of a deeper reorientation toward security, premised on a permanent enemy and on a readiness to fight a war of colossal scale with only a few minutes' notice. Fourth, there is the moralizing view that a willingness to fight can be necessary and worthwhile no matter what the costs of war, an outlook captured by the chilling phrase "better dead than Red." And fifth, there is the view that it is better to engage the enemy in peripheral space, such as the Third World, in order to avoid the destruction of one's homeland and to sustain the war system without inviting the mutual catastrophe of yet another world war—this one fought with nuclear weapons.

The point is that the state system survived the challenge of the 1920s and 1930s and emerged stronger after the experience of the 1940s, however destructive it was and seems to us in retrospect. Of course, peace in 1945 brought a temporary surge of war avoidance: the horrors of the recently concluded war were raw memories; anxiety about atomic warfare surfaced; the United Nations was founded; some military demobilization occurred for a brief period; and disarmament proposals were put forward. But memoirs and historical studies, especially on the Western side, have shown that these engagements with global reform were cosmetic, meant halfheartedly and even reluctantly, undertaken mainly as public relations gestures.[5] The positions of influence within the most powerful states, East and West, were dominated by "realists" convinced that a balance of power built on the logic of containment could alone keep "the peace." That is, war as expressed through its threat became the means to achieve peace, or, more fairly, lesser war was the price to be paid to avoid greater war. We now have prominent writers of security matters who are quite convinced that "deterrence," even with nuclear weapons, is the best "peace system" a world of states can ever achieve and a great improvement over the prenuclear world of "rational" war-making. Underlying this view is the assumption that the state system is ultra-stable, or at least so highly resilient that to consider alternative world orders as anything other than a flight of literary fancy is naive and irrelevant.

The initial focus on war here is not meant to imply that this concern overshadows problems of poverty, repression, or ecological balance. As discussed elsewhere, these normative concerns are fused in such a

way that reordered responses can hope to succeed only if they deal
with the whole range of unevenly felt grievances of the various peoples
of the world.[6] Rather, the emphasis on war at the outset is a reflection
of the narrative history of global reformist thought and action. As well,
the distribution of war-making capabilities at the state level is what ultimately stabilizes the existing world order system of bounded territorial
units claiming sovereign status (defended space). What will destabilize
this system in a creative manner—that is, without generating general war,
economic collapse, or ecological catastrophe—is the grand puzzle that
needs to be worked out by world order activists. What forms of political
and cultural destabilization are likely to lead in the direction of demilitarization? Developing "defense systems" for use in space, for example, is
an undesirable variant of political and economic destabilization because
it contributes to further militarization. Similarly, terrorist tactics designed
to shock the public, penalize representatives of state power, and create
an atmosphere of chaos and uncertainty involve another type of comprehensive destabilization that intensifies and even legitimizes militarization,
especially when directed toward behavior within civil society.

   The disappointing record of superpower geopolitics during the Cold
War has generated a general mood of helplessness about reforming international political life. The original expectation during World War II, held
by Franklin Delano Roosevelt, among others, envisioned virtually a Concert of the World ("the Four Policemen") administered for the sake of
international stability by the most important victor states after the defeat
of fascism. This idea has been revived in various forms—including the
briefly tantalizing idea of "a five-power world" operating in concert that
surfaced toward the end of the 1960s—and was given prominence by
Richard Nixon and Henry Kissinger during their years of greatest influence and at a moment of difficulty for the United States as a consequence
of the failure of its Vietnam policy. Such a conception of the leading centers of state power acting collectively on behalf of world interests did not
elicit interest in Moscow, or elsewhere, because the momentum of the
Cold War remained too strongly entrenched. Even Nixon and Kissinger
soon relinquished whatever attachment they might have had to a shift in
geopolitical emphasis from conflict to coordination.

   During the Cold War, collective undertakings reflected the geopolitical fracture between East and West: meetings of NATO or the Warsaw
Pact, gatherings among the nonaligned. Such expressions of militarization
and conflict at the global level generated oppositional coalitions of various
sorts, and within these coalitions one found hierarchies dominated by the
strongest states. Occasionally, periods of tension were broken by super-

power summits, which, when successful, fostered a public awareness that geopolitical encounter was not endemic or necessary.

Even within zones of ideological affinity, there is very little disposition to engage in meaningful forms of cooperation beyond the scope of alliance politics, and even there the cooperative aspects seem to reflect mainly the dominance of the respective alliance leaders. More revealing for our purposes is the exclusively managerial outlook that these leaders entertain. Except for sheer propaganda purposes, as at annual speeches in the United Nations, the serious preoccupations of power-wielders are meeting challenges and threats posed by "enemies" and smoothing over the differences and tensions that emerge among "friends." There has seemed to be no conception of a potential political community, embracing friends and enemies, that is capable of dealing with collective needs and aspirations in a more creative manner. The impoverishment of political imagination during the Cold War, a time of great human danger, was tragically notable, and the situation has not significantly improved in the immediate aftermath. Although there is now almost no prospect of superpower antagonism spiraling out of control, there is also little disposition by the United States, at least, to give greater weight to law, institutions, peaceful settlement, and diplomacy in settings of international conflict. And since the United States is operating as virtually uncontested superpower, this new circumstance can cause large-scale war dangers, as occurred in the Gulf War of 1991.

Another line of positive expectation in the period after 1945 was associated with promises made on behalf of competing ideological conceptions of development. Even if the international system could not be unified, or modified, at least it seemed possible that the processes of decolonization would produce a series of encouraging models in state-building and economic development at the societal level. Of course, controversy and variation abounds as to the results achieved, but what seems evident is that neither socialist nor capitalist models have yet worked successfully, if the assessment is made from the perspective of world order values. Socialist societies, with their commitment to basic needs and to societal fairness, have encountered a variety of practical and normative difficulties; most seriously, the emergent state tended to be repressive and inefficient, and found itself tied to a circumstance of Soviet dependency. The alternative breakaway experience of either China or Yugoslavia illustrates the difficulty facing a socialist society within the predominantly capitalist world economy. Even those socialist states that have managed an independent path in foreign policy seem saddled with a governmental apparatus that distrusts and hence stifles the creative energies of its own people. Now, with the disclosure of Soviet bloc economic failure, the socialist model has been widely discredited.

The experience of capitalist-oriented postcolonial states is only superficially better. Although some of these states have managed impressive records of growth, especially in East and South Asia, they have done so by burdening their poorest citizens and by imposing "discipline" in the form of repression. As well, these states have been often linked into the wider patterns of militarization in international life. Others, less successful in the economic sphere, have also experienced militarization (within and without) and find their economies deeply mortgaged to international creditors and their polities beset by enemies. To survive as viable economic entities, these states accept a variety of "conditions" imposed by the International Monetary Fund (IMF) with an eye toward credit-worthiness, thereby further increasing the privations of the poor and frequently augmenting the repressive tendencies of government in the face of resistance from those who are asked to bear the burdens of adjustment, generally the poorest strata of society.

Nor has the Third World produced successful models of its own, although several notable attempts can be observed. Gandhi's great achievement in mobilizing India around the tactics and principles of nonviolence continues to serve inspirational purposes, but its promise was deeply compromised at the moment of Indian independence by the outbreak of massive, collective Hindu-Moslem violence and by the emergence in India of a militarized state that has behaved in its region like a traditional great power. Nevertheless, a resonance from the Gandhi period remains genuine and sets India part, giving it some credibility when it calls for a halt to the most destructive patterns of superpower conduct and strengthening the Indian will to resist foreign economic penetration. There are also various Third World experiments in self-reliance that seek to extend nonalignment to the economic sphere and thereby invent and adapt the meaning of "development," rather than have it derive from either capitalist or socialist antecedents in the North—West or East. Such a path seems difficult, especially given the strength of materialist conceptions of progress and the pressure to link economic policies to the wider world economy. China's evolution since 1949 is a microcosmic expression of the impulse to forge an independent path toward socialism, followed by a definite flirtation, at least temporarily and to an uncertain extent, with the capitalist ethos. Emblematic, perhaps, are reports that the latest shifts in China's approach toward its own future included in the 1980s a relatively heavy inflow of Japanese investment capital.

These tendencies are not linear, or invariant. Severe militarization in South America during the 1960s and early 1970s, for example, encountered a variety of problems associated with making the economy work. As a result, and in reaction, promising if fragile programs of democratization are under way in several critical countries. In others, repression has engendered a growing tide of opposition. The learning experience of failed militarization (along with the dark consequences of fundamentalist revolution in Iran) has induced the search for moderating alternatives that will sustain the prevalent structures but ease up on their most repressive features. Whether the search for a moderate center in these (neither left nor right) polities is an exercise in self-delusion remains to be seen.

The main features of the global situation do not give rise to an encouraging assessment. On a geopolitical level, despite fiscal constraints and the end of the Cold War, the arms race seems likely to continue and to enter dangerous new domains such as space and nonnuclear weapons of mass destruction (biological and chemical warfare, and "the revolution" in conventional weaponry), and neither a relaxed geopolitical setting nor popular protest nor the powerful symbolic warnings implicit in "the nuclear winter" findings seem able to reverse the destructive momentum. In fact, the mind-set of U.S. leaders twists warnings into rationalizations for yet further militarizing initiatives; alleged moral reservations about deterrence and evident political concern about public protest stimulated the endorsement of "star wars" technology in the early 1980s. At a time when not a public dollar was being invested in disarmament initiatives, a deficit-conscious superpower enthusiastically proposed an understated minimum of $24 billion to proceed with a new range of military technologies that can only add to current forms of instability, as well as plunder still further the resources available for the alleviation of misery at home and abroad. The misallocation of global resources and the dangers of global-scale catastrophe worsen too, of course, the life prospects of future generations. The program has been continuously revised and given new rationalizations as the global setting has changed, but several nations continue to devote substantial funds to the militarization of space.

The world economy in the period ahead is likely to be bound still tighter in a highly stratified structure reflecting a hierarchy of technologies. On the capitalist side, a triumphal confidence in market mechanisms, combined with antagonism toward governmental programs associated with social issues and large deficits in key donor countries, has greatly weakened earlier welfare tendencies. Domestic and international adjustments by way of concession, compromise, or compassion are less likely to occur in these circumstances, except possibly to soften the effects of such outright disasters as periodic famines in Ethiopia, Sudan, and Bangladesh. This renewed posture of First World indifference is certainly facilitated by passivity and disarray among the constituencies of victim countries throughout the Third World, as well as by the absence of geopolitical rivalry for influence and prestige.

There is, further, only a weak disposition to reverse the deteriorating maelstrom in which the United Nations finds itself. The failure of negotiations for the law of the seas to produce a ratified treaty—quite explicitly a result of the statist outlooks adopted by several of the richer countries—temporarily, at least, diminished otherwise bright prospects for functional internationalism. Of course, this dark mood could be changed rapidly by an about-face on the part of a leading government or by one notable internationalist success. But at present there is very little positive energy being invested anywhere in this traditional type of reform. What is more, the institutions and procedures that do exist are being demoralized and weakened through neglect and, in some instances, outright hostility. The repudiation by the United States of the International Court of Justice in the course of its dispute with Nicaragua in the mid-1980s was a notable example, representing both a refusal to allow its interventionary statecraft to be constrained by international law and an expression of blatant unilateralism on the part of the state that had earlier done the most to shape postwar expectations about the desirability of law-oriented statecraft. A similar blow was struck earlier in the 1980s by the American withdrawal from UNESCO, the international agency which, for all of its failings, remains more closely attuned to Third World priorities than do other actors in the UN system.

At the state level, despite interesting innovations in both socialist and capitalist states, there is little foundation for optimism about prospects for humane governance. For one thing, the problems confronting most governments are overwhelming, given the instruments at hand. In this regard, the burden of population growth is especially significant. Its dynamics are multidimensional: the drift to the cities from overcrowded rural areas is one expression; pressure to undertake illegal and hazardous immigration is another; and hiring oneself out on some indentured basis as "a guest worker" is still another. But clearly, in all these instances, the quality of life is diminished by the direct and indirect effects of "surplus" population.

At the same time, all states are caught up in the persisting dynamics of nuclearism and militarism, as well as the less spectacular but not less serious hazards of ecological deterioration. Governments are the expressions of the state mechanism, whose bureaucratic orientation reflects the mix of special interests (from within and without). The obsolete canon of "realist" thinking continues to place regime security (at a state level) on a pedestal of such great height that the well-being and even the survival of domestic society is mindlessly jeopardized. Nothing takes precedence over the survival of a particular governmental regime, even in its most bizarre manifestation as a remnant of the ruling group locked away in some far-underground vault during a hypothetical nuclear war. The societal substance of the human experience is offered as "a sacrifice" to the avenging gods of technological prowess. The earlier republican notion of government as a conditional and limited delegation of societal powers has been completely submerged by these modern security arrangements, given the nature of technologies of mass destruction. Besides, for most states—really, for every state—there is no reliable way to opt out of the larger orbit of geopolitical disaster in the event of escalation above the nuclear threshold. During the Cold War the actuality of sovereign rights became hostage to the whim and wisdom of whoever was presiding in Moscow and Washington at a given time and, to a degree, even to the conduct of other governments possessing nuclear weapons. The two giants locked themselves in a perpetual death embrace. No amount of investment in "defensive" military technologies could alter the stark reality that they lacked any prospect of defending their territories against annihilation. At most, it could reshuffle the tactics of the offensive use of nuclear weapons. Gorbachev's Soviet Union has unilaterally opted out of such a destructive security system to a substantial degree, more or less by abandoning an assertive foreign policy.

It seems likely that direct efforts to achieve global reform will not soon be forthcoming from state leaders and, to the extent attempted, will yield only trivial results that are not responsive to the real challenges of international life. Further, states as now constituted are very unlikely to achieve great normative gains internally for very many of the peoples of the world, although there will be a diversity of balance sheets by which gains and losses are computed. The relevant point here is that we cannot, at present, view reigning ideologies as capable either of governing effectively and humanely or of providing a liberating challenge to the established authority structure. Indeed, as has been argued, the political competition now taking place in most countries does not include a serious option of liberation, even if the rhetoric of liberation is often relied upon by political challengers. The most likely result of a successful revolution is a reproduction, on occasion even in a less restrained form, of the failures associated with the old regime, especially in the broad domain of human rights. The torments of political prisoners in Iran during the 1980s is emblematic: "One day in Khomeini's jails is like ten years in the jails of the Shah!"

Maintaining the quest for global political transformation, then, requires looking elsewhere than to state action, although an innovative leader, especially one heading the government of an important country, can make a significant difference. The Soviet internal and external shifts loosened the bonds of oppression in a manner regarded as inconceivable less than a decade earlier. Yet it is not "realistic" or "sufficient" to invest our energies in the outworn belief that enlightened self-interest will lead to a pattern of global reform. We need to learn from mistaken expectations. It seems vital to include on the political agenda of movements for change and visions of the future at this historical time the transformation of the state by nonviolent means, with the objective of reconstituting political community on the basis of a program dedicated to peace and justice: demilitarization as method, as process, as goal, and as the keystone of political ethics. Any *principled* reliance on violence, as in the Marxist tradition, has a reproductive logic and record, making reliance on political violence generally unacceptable. It is important also to note that certain situations justify conditional recourse to violence, as during the most difficult stages of the anti-apartheid struggle. Political violence may still be justifiable in a context where the only choice available is between liberating and oppressing violence and where recourse to liberating violence is conceived tragically, is taken with utmost reluctance and in a minimizing spirit, and is an option that possesses some reasonable prospect of success at a proportional level of human costs.

The ongoing struggles of the oppressed offer opportunities, both by widening our understanding of oppression and by establishing networks of solidarity that are not restricted by international boundaries. Such struggles may create some tension between solidarity and a commitment to nonviolence, but a purist stance does not seem warranted. The anti-apartheid struggle, which has so often sought to proceed nonviolently and seemingly does so again in light of the dramatic developments of 1990 and 1991, justified support even when its method of struggle included instruments of violence. Perhaps outsiders can diminish the role of violence and insist, as possible, on avoiding violence against "the innocent," although the identification of innocence in the South African setting is itself immensely complicated.

It is important to identify those social forces that can act on behalf of the oppressed. Such forces may involve reinventing culture or, rather, recovering and strengthening those dimensions of culture supportive of new forms of order, authority, security, and fulfillment. The idea of "the oppressed" needs, at this time, to be extended to embrace the world of living spirits, human and animal. The entrapment of all peoples in ordeals threatening the various dimensions of survival is a potential foundation for unity. Because the peril extends to nature, it establishes the basis for an ecological partnership between human society and other living beings. This wider ecological outlook, involving a solidarity between human society and nature rather than the disruptive hierarchical relationship characteristic of modernism, also reinforces a wider planetary ethos of strength-through-diversity. In addition, such an outlook provides a self-concerned basis for the protection of marginal peoples and cultures. This is vital because universalization of communications, trade, and knowledge flows should not be allowed to become a recipe for the homogenization of world culture, a tendency that has had ethnocidal consequences for indigenous peoples everywhere.

Finally, the encounter between the state and civil society in all its multiple forms needs to become and remain a central normative focus. Such an encounter will take on the character supplied by each distinctive setting informed by tradition, economic endowments, and political experience. The normative stakes will vary greatly as well. There would be no room for dogmatism, though the state might on occasion intervene to protect the victims of communal forms of oppression and defend a social contract that assures decency (that is, basic human needs, including liberties and rights) to all elements of society. The issue of policy and appraisal, then, is one of situation and context. Structural relations do not by themselves sort out normative priorities, and therefore even the connections between state and civil society cannot be specified as if invariably oppressive. It is appropriate in this discussion to focus on those situations where the state is an object of concern.

In some settings, the objective of societal action is a change of policy and personnel to assure an end to patterns of gross abuse of human rights, individual or collective. In others, a more comprehensive concern with the public good challenges prevailing forms of security, resource policy, and conditions of work. Or the encounter is about the character of the state itself, its leadership, restraints on its abuse, its ways of gaining revenue, and its uses of information—matters of bureaucratic scale and balance, and procedures for accountability to the citizenry.

The tactics of encounter will involve a disposition to seek non-statal solutions for societal problems such as unemployment and environmental pollution: in other words, to rely for capital, knowhow, and legitimacy on grassroots, local, and regional frameworks; in effect, to reshape the state and reconceive its role by discovering that man's societal problems can be better solved without reliance upon it. More radical than the withdrawal of dependence and the creation of grassroots alternatives is citizen resistance in various nonviolent forms, from declining to participate as a soldier or military technologist to engaging in some form of tax refusal. What joins these various postures is a general dissatisfaction with the state as a normatively acceptable vehicle for the realization of human values, even if that realization were to be restricted geographically to the peoples living within the boundaries of a given state. Given the actualities of interdependence, such images of autonomy are misleading and artificial. The central focus of this commentary on local and citizen initiative is on the complex internal dynamic of state and society; but given the interlocked character of the modern world, the external dynamic of state-to-state relations is also necessarily at issue—especially in the war/peace area but also with regard to food prices for the poor, to the availability of basic services and jobs and credit, and, of course, energy and its use and price. External effects are also unavoidable, given the technologies now at the base of social practice almost everywhere. The Chernobyl meltdown demonstrated in a chilling fashion that nuclear safety is not a local or even a national issue, and not a matter that can be entrusted to regulation by a particular state. There is simply no successful way to seal off the world from either the formation of national policy or its effects on most matters of critical policy.

At this stage of international history, then, direct paths to global reform should be pursued but seem insufficient to meet the dangers. In this regard it is beneficial to let go of illusions that global leaders (top down) can be persuaded to make radical adjustments, and to adopt instead an emphasis on mobilizing "the people" (bottom up). True, existing global leadership mainly reflects entrenched interests and overwhelmingly adheres to a world view arising out of several centuries of experience within the state system; at present, despite some notable defections—especially the Soviet shift—the leadership of states is not expected, nor does it have the capacity, to handle the world order agenda or to promote humane values on a planetary scale. It should be noted, as qualification on this generalization, that leadership style at the state level can make an enormous difference: Gorbachev's success in reorienting Soviet foreign policy during the late 1980s is remarkable in this regard; the loss by assassination of a relatively visionary leader such as Sweden's Olaf Palme leaves a gap in the global setting that cannot easily be filled and alters the political discourse on critical issues of policy and choice.

Likewise, "the people" as a whole, despite all diversities, carries no such vision at or near the center of its experience. The preoccupations, although uneven and covering a wide range of variations, tend to be immediate, but not necessarily secular or materialistic. The larger concerns of peoples tend to be historically conditioned and are prominently associated in the current period with nationalist or sectarian religious fervor, two forces that intensify the fracturing of the human community, although possibly responding to specific oppressive circumstances and thereby furthering antiimperial and even human rights goals. There are many intense conflicts in the world between a dominant nationalism that controls the apparatus of state power in a particular territory and peoples without states who seek to establish conditions for the realization of their nation-hood. In the developed countries, popular concerns with global reform, if they exist at all, are often very ephemeral, associated with surges of anxiety about war or economic collapse and of fear directed at enemies. And as national revolutions in a variety of settings have exhibited, the oppressed can quickly adopt the role and even the literal trappings of the oppressor. Indeed, recent empirical studies suggest that mass opinion is generally supportive of hierarchy and violence in political life, not very committed to democracy and human rights, especially for others.[7] The simplistic politics of "power to the people" provides no normative assurance that a better civic order or a more enlightened view of international relations would emerge.

At the same time, those mass movements animated by purely normative concerns, such as the various peace movements of recent decades in Western Europe and North America, have quickly fizzled and appear to lack either the tactics of sustained struggle or a sufficiency of commitment. If we examine successful social movements that have transformed unfavorable power balances, we find they possess certain common features: a vision of a promised land; a leadership dedicated unto death; a set of tactics that produced illuminating and symbolic encounters with the established order and that generally resulted in some kind of blood sacrifice; a widely endorsed moral passion; economic and political developments that weaken the old order in decisive respects and make its maintenance appear impractical or illegitimate to an expanding constituency of its former upholders. Movements against slavery, royalism, colonialism, and, more recently, the Communist regimes in Eastern Europe are illustrative of this pattern, as are such struggles as culminated in the Russian (October) Revolution, the establishment of the state of Israel, and the victory of the Islamic revolution in Iran. The anti-apartheid movement is currently proceeding along the path to success. By and large, peace movements and movements avowedly dedicated to global reform have been formed out of a conviction that a better system is possible, desirable, and necessary. Such concerns have had only limited impact, however, as commitment to them has been largely abstract or superficial, not eliciting blood sacrifice or even a willingness on the part of many adherents to take serious personal risks. World federalism is a typical instance of a failed social movement, fashioned by reason and constrained by deference to the legitimacy of the existing order.

There are two constructive forms of political activity, rooted in the same transformative consciousness, that represent different time frames and, often, distinct political sensibilities. The first is concerned with testing the political space *within* and *among* states by imaginative challenges designed to defend against encroachment, to roll back existing encroachments, or to discover liberated space. Characteristically, this emphasis regards the existing arrangement of states as the framework within which politics as the art of the possible must be practiced, though it does not preclude a more transformative perspective to inform action in the here and now, either to avoid catastrophe or to embody the future in the present. Also, some who direct their energies at existing arrangements subscribe to a theory of gradualism positing that shifts in quality are usually best promoted by a series of shifts in quantity.

The second form of activity is concerned with creating a new setting for politics based on the predicates of a citizenship of pilgrimage: that is, an allegiance to a political community not yet established but expressive of ideals, values, and goals. Its basic claim is that a civilizational sea change can occur and is occurring at the level of behavior and culture, thereby providing a new ground for future political arrangements.[8] "Freedom" for individuals and groups is historically exemplified by renouncing the *constraints* of membership in a state, not membership itself, and by acting as if one already enjoyed the rights and duties of a citizen of "the promised land" and insisting upon their embodiment now.

Figure 1 summarizes and schematizes these thoughts in a crude and preliminary fashion. It attempts to draw a dividing line between working within the existing framework and acting within a new one appropriate to a pluralist yet global civilization. Yet it is clear that acting on either side of the line implies engagement on the other. To act effectively against militarization in the current context implies a commitment to the nonviolent possibility of eventual peace and harmony; by the same token, commitment to the future will be empty unless it produces concrete deeds in the here and now, even if only of the imagination but connected concretely to the present ferment of contradictory forces. It should be emphasized that a "field for action" is conceived of here mainly with respect to the vital political encounter between the state and an array of social movements, and then only in an illustrative manner.

SOCIAL MOVEMENTS AND THE BEHAVIOR OF STATES

Aside from studies of the international implications of national revolutions, there has been surprisingly little academic attention devoted to the interplay between social movements and the overall behavior of states.[9] Work has been done, of course, on a sectoral basis, through the study either of a particular organizational vehicle for a social movement (for example, Amnesty International in the area of human rights) or of the

	Normative Space in the State System	Predicates of a Citizenship of Pilgrimage
Resistances to Encroachment	✔✔✔	✔✔
Reversals of Encroachment	✔✔	✔
Enhancement	✔	✔✔✔
Revitalization of Democracy	✔	✔✔✔✔
Revitalization of Religion and Culture	✔✔	✔✔✔✔✔
Imaging the Future	✔✔✔	✔✔✔✔✔✔

✔ = unit of emphasis

FIGURE 1   Fields for Action

impact of a social movement on some given international problem (such as the effect of the environmental movement on the use of pesticides or on the establishment of ocean standards to regulate the discharge of oil on the high seas). But none of these inquiries has been conducted in relation to a wider concern with global reform, either its process or its substance. Some of the neofunctionalist writing does set forth a conception of global reform but not in the setting of social movements. Marxist theorizing about conflict and change is also relevant as background, but it does not include any systematic effort to link mobilized social forces with world order.

This section sets forth some preliminary ideas on countervailing societal tendencies that are challenging the state and the state system on a variety of terrains. These normative challenges can be categorized either by reference to world order values (peace, economic well-being, social and political justice, ecological balance, and humane governance) or by reference to "D-5" (denuclearization, demilitarization, dealignment and depolarization, democratization, and development).[10]

I use the term "social movements" in a nonrigorous way to cover the range of normative pressures mounted against the state and societal policies and practices from within civil society, whether or not the behavior achieves organizational persistence and identity by becoming a social movement in a rigorous sociological sense. The emphasis can be further explained by what have been identified as normative initiatives originating in the "Third System."[11]

My approach relies on alternative exploratory perspectives. The principal perspective is one of enlightened citizenship in both a particular territorial polity and the emergent global civil society. Here the question posed is what can be done within a specific state, and in the state system as it has evolved, to moderate dangers and mitigate injustices. In a fundamental sense, this perspective is "another realism," different from that of entrenched power-wielders, adopting a different calculus of values and perceptions to assess short-term and long-term "national interests." But this other realism should not be confused with the deliberately utopian perspective of the citizen-pilgrim who acts here and now on behalf of an invisible community or polity that lacks spatial boundaries, is not yet, and may never be. The citizen-pilgrim ethos can operate as the foundation for very concrete action, but its commitment is radical and essentially religious in character, not depending on any validation by the prospect of immediate results. The interplay and tension between these two radical perspectives express a dynamic that is experienced inwardly by each of us to some degree, a dynamic of contrast between the logic of thought and action in the state system with its short time horizon and bounded territory, and the logic of thought and action in an emergent but still inchoate global polity generally lacking in institutional embodiment.

A distinction between social movements above the line and those below the line in Figure 1 is intended to express both a difference in emphasis and a potential complementarity in undertaking. The terrain of movements is so vast that discussion of each category is intended only in a heuristic spirit. More careful systematic work is needed to follow up on all these issues. Figures 2 and 3 summarize the overall terrain as far as it relates to activities by those whose primary political identity remains rooted in the territorial state. Positive initiatives (discussed separately below) cannot always be restricted to a particular value zone. And there are often value tradeoffs, as when arms control negotiations or political accommodation are promoted at the evident expense of self-determination and human rights. Peace forces—perhaps mistakenly, at least in retrospect— were so eager to end the arms race and reduce the threat of general war that there was a definite reluctance to enter objections to the oppressive Soviet domination of Eastern Europe. In the mid-1980s, however, there occurred a notable change, and peace groups, especially END (European Nuclear Disarmament), were at the forefront of social forces supportive of the struggle for democracy and political independence in the Soviet bloc. As the developments in 1989 and afterward suggest, under certain conditions the pursuit of peace, human rights, economic well-being,

Value \ Initiative	Peace	Economic Well-being	Social and Political Justice	Ecological Balance	Humane Governance
Resistances					
■ governments at state level	Dutch deferral of cruise missile deployments	Ethiopian disaster relief			support for Nicaraguan government
■ organized international community (UN)		← Non-Aligned Movement →			
■ social movements; individual and group initiative	Greenham Common Ground Zero (Bangor, Washington) N.Z. refusal of docking privileges		Sanctuary Movement for Latin American refugees / Amnesty International campaign against torture	toxic dumps / nuclear power plant sitings	cultural survival for indigenous peoples
Reversals					
■ governments at state level	5 Continent Initiative	← family planning program (China) →			
■ organized international community (UN)		← support for liberation movements →			
■ social movements; individual and group initiative	ABC (Manila) / Pacific NFZ freeze movement in U.S.A.	← liberation theology →		Greenpeace campaign to save whales	
Enhancements					
■ governments at state level		← Law of the Sea negotiations →			
■ organized international community (UN)		← UN support for aspirational declarations and standards →			
■ social movements; individual and group initiative		← Lokoyan (India) →			Green party

FIGURE 2 The Scope of Political Space

Initiative \ Normative Process	Denuclearization	Demilitarization	Dealignment	Democratization	Development
Resistances					
■ governments at state level					
■ organized international community (UN)					
■ social movements; individual and group initiative					
Reversals					
■ governments at state level					
■ organized international community (UN)					
■ social movements; individual and group initiative					
Enhancements					
■ governments at state level					
■ organized international community (UN)					
■ social movements; individual and group initiative					

FIGURE 3 D-5 and Societal Action: Normative Processes

and environmental quality can be combined in a coherent movement for radical political change.

As Figure 3 depicts, social movements and societal initiatives act directly and indirectly. Their indirect effects may be to constrain or shape government policy. The Australian peace movement seems by 1985 to have induced Prime Minister Robert Hawke, against his preference, to withdraw his earlier willingness to allow the United States to monitor MX flight tests from a site located on Australian territory. Pressures can operate in adverse directions as well. Felipe Gonzalez campaigned as a Socialist for election in Spain beneath the banner of nonalignment, yet as head of state, apparently bowing to external economic pressures, he swung over to support Spanish membership in NATO.

RESISTANCES

Governments have political space to resist encroachments of various kinds.[12] A dramatic instance was the refusal in the mid-1980s by New Zealand to permit the United States to use ports for naval vessels powered by nuclear energy or carrying nuclear weapons. This refusal reflected the influence of the New Zealand peace movement on the Labour Party and its leadership. Prime Minister David Lange, an antinuclear activist, resisted U.S. pressure exerted on behalf of the coherence of the ANZUS alliance. The United States responded by excluding New Zealand from further participation in ANZUS.

The United Nations, on the other hand, has seemed remarkably insulated from the pressures brought to bear by social movements. Its undertakings are severely restricted by the most militarized sectors of international society. True, the General Assembly "resisted" with rhetoric such encroachments as those associated with the extensions of Israeli sovereignty over the occupied territories, the latest excesses of South African racial oppression, and such international outrages as the Soviet invasion of Afghanistan. Even this activity, manifesting the ethical consciousness of the world, generally caused a backlash during the Cold War years, including severe accusations of partisanship from its most powerful members, as well as withdrawals of support. As of 1990, however, the United Nations seems far more capable of mounting a consensus among its principal members, as during the Kuwait crisis, although this impression may disappear in light of the failure of the Gulf War to restore peace and security.

Direct resistance activities by civil society are of greatest interest for our purposes. The conventional expressions of resistance are those undertaken within the framework of legal action, which amount to appeals to the authorities. In the United States, lobbying Congress or mounting an authorized demonstration is illustrative. More interesting and significant are those initiatives that pose the challenge in more serious terms, defy the authority of the state to varying degrees, and act out of the reoriented consciousness of the citizen-pilgrim. This sort of resistance is a symbolic surrogate in a time of danger for the real commitment to a transformed and, as yet, hypothetical societal order. The occupation by English women of the area around the cruise missile base at Greenham Common for several years during the 1980s is an excellent illustration.[13] That activity was also an expression of radical feminism, exemplified by the way decisions were taken within the group and by the women's commitment, manifest in the daily round of their encampment, to an entirely different conception of authority and power.

A similar resistance consciousness has been mobilized by the small community in Bangor, Washington, that calls itself Ground Zero. The members' particular project was to blockade a naval base on the Pacific coast whenever it added a new Trident submarine and to obstruct the trains carrying the nuclear warheads for the Trident, which the group believes to be a first-strike weapon and, as such, especially objectionable from legal, moral, and religious viewpoints. The Ground Zero activists have gone to jail repeatedly and have altered the outlook of important symbolic figures such as Archbishop Raymond Hunthausen of Seattle, a county prosecutor, and several workers at the base. Their position is an amalgam of early Christianity and Gandhism, strongly reinforced by a conviction that the Nuremberg Principles are authoritative guidelines for citizens and leaders alike.[14] Like the Greenham women, these militants are citizen-pilgrims who in their lives and activities work to build the normative foundation for what amounts to a new civilization. Their specific acts of resistance are directed against particularly objectionable encroachments upon civil society by the militarized state, but their concern is to reinvent politics and community. They lack any confidence in representative democracy, political parties, and elections as these function in the modern liberal states of the West. Their initiatives are assertions of freedom at the grassroots level, and center upon using the tactics of nonviolent defiance and love to expose the illegitimacy of and planetary menace posed by the violent state. The Ground Zero ethos seeks, above all, to enact in political settings the transforming power of love.

There are other substantive settings, of course, where normative initiatives are being undertaken. An initiative of particular interest in the United States is the so-called "sanctuary movement" organized by a series of churches in the Southwest and elsewhere to provide sanctuary for "illegal" aliens, especially from El Salvador, who would face persecution and often execution if returned to their country. Religious concern with protection of the weak and vulnerable has led these churches to defy the state and its cruel polities by offering individuals an alternative haven, secure against deportation.

A major resistance context that now exists in many states involves movements for the protection of indigenous peoples against the seizure of their lands and resources and the destruction of their cultural identity. The weakness and helplessness of such groups have led to increasing efforts on their part, with help from various benefactors, to build networks of solidarity across state boundaries. The organized international community, especially UNESCO and the United Nations Commission on Human Rights, by way of a Working Group that has met annually in Geneva in recent years, has helped create an expanding societal awareness of the extent of grievance and the urgency of organizing rapidly some kind of effective resistance. As with nuclearism, the decisive issue here is one of survival for the ethnic unit. The cultural orientation of many indigenous peoples is quite antagonistic to the modernism that has been the implicit ideology of the state system. And even if their avowed goal is the recovery and nourishing of revered tradition, an additional objective is to provide humanity with models and images of humane governance that have sensitivity to nature and the long experience of species survival on earth. In this critical regard, indigenous peoples are prime victims of the existing order and living witnesses to the actuality and possibility of alternative orders.

It is not appropriate to romanticize the experience of indigenous peoples, for their record includes cruelty, human and animal sacrifice, and instances of ecological disaster. Moreover, because they possess a range of orientations toward nature and intergroup violence, it is a mistake to posit a homogeneous world view or mind-set and attribute it to indigenous peoples *en bloc*. At the same time, the story of indigenous peoples is generally one of a struggle to survive the onslaughts of modernism, and an often forgotten element in this story is the preoccupation of premodern cultural experience with accommodating the uncertainties and constraints of nature—as we must do in consequence of the ecological challenge. The preoccupation today is assuredly not a matter of returning to premodern modes but, one hopes, of extending modernism or initiating postmodernism with the benefit and inspiration of premodern wisdom and experience.

REVERSALS

The distinction between resistances and reversals is not a sharp one. Particular initiatives often have features of both or can be understood from different angles. The two terms are intended to differentiate be-

tween opposition to concrete extensions of negative processes (such as
a given policy of a particular government) and undertakings designed to
oppose and undo the process itself (such as war or nuclear power in
general). Resistances refer, then, to "incidents"; reversals, to "processes."

By these definitions, the nuclear freeze movement of the early 1980s is
a clear instance of reversal. Its main political message to the superpowers
was "Stop!"—referring, of course, to the nuclear arms race. The freeze did
not devote its energies to prevent specific destabilizing weapons systems
from being added to the weapons arsenal. Its tactics, although encompassing grassroots organizing, were mild,—as if the state and the procedures
and institutions of representative democracy could be made suitably responsive to swings in public sentiment on basic national security issues—
and thus almost ineffectual. By challenging the modern state through
formal mechanisms for achieving change, the message of the freeze was
filtered and diluted and, hence, less compelling—the final proposal calling
for a mutually negotiable freeze. Leaving aside the merits of emphasizing the momentum of an arms buildup rather than its most destabilizing
elements, the pursuit of a negotiated freeze calls for a bargaining process of monumental complexity, one vulnerable to bureaucratic ambush
in domestic politics by militarist critics of peace initiatives. The deeper
point here is that reversals, as distinct from resistances (canceling a destabilizing weapons system) are almost impossible to achieve at this time,
at least by reliance on mainstream procedures.

Similarly, influence exerted by a few leading members of the United
Nations makes it difficult for this principal set of international institutions
to break free of the logic of highly conflictual and egocentric politics.
The cynical evasion of "the common heritage" principle during the Law
of the Sea negotiations—a result registered long before the appearance
on the negotiating scene of the Reaganites—suggests how difficult it is to
promote the common good, or even an enlightened view of longer-range
state interests, under the auspices of the United Nations.

The anti-apartheid movement does suggest some normative capacity
on the part of the United Nations to promote an initiative that would
qualify as a reversal. And certainly societal pressures and a variety of anti-
apartheid voluntary associations have helped establish a political climate
in which governments opposed to apartheid can occupy virtually all the
moral space on the issue within the United Nations. The political and
economic space, however, is much more difficult to penetrate, much less
occupy. South Africa's ideological alignment with the West, its strategic
role in relation to sea-lanes and vital minerals, and its participation in
the world economy by way of providing trade and investment havens
have made it difficult, but not impossible, to move beyond censure and

rhetoric to a posture of sanctions. The gap between a rhetoric of denun-
ciation and an operational code of acquiescence, even accommodation,
helps discredit the United Nations on all sides. For conservatives, it provides evidence of "politicizing" the organization, both because apartheid
is emphasized while the allegedly worse practices of totalitarian states of
the left are ignored and also because the whole history of producing a
stream of resolutions is indicative of the UN's hypocritical and ineffectual role as a center for the dissemination of Third World propaganda. On
the other side, liberals and progressives grow equally disillusioned because the members of the organization with leverage to act do as little as
possible to make the moral repudiation of apartheid effective in political
and economic spheres; on the contrary, they obstruct efforts to close the
rhetoric-reality gap.

Of course, the anti-apartheid movement can be viewed more optimistically. Even the United States and Great Britain, despite conservative governments, were induced by domestic and transnational pressures
to legislate and uphold a program of limited sanctions during the decade of the 1980s. It is difficult to assess the impact of sanctions on the
white rulers in South Africa; but it seems impossible that independence
for Namibia, the release of Nelson Mandela, the legalization of the African National Congress, and the dramatic moves toward multiracialism in
South Africa could have occurred in the absence of a global anti-apartheid
campaign. Whether these steps can be carried forward in the 1990s to
the achievement of constitutional democracy and human rights for the
whole population of South Africa remains uncertain, but far less so than a
decade earlier, which is by itself an extraordinary reversal.

Social movements and individual and group initiatives are also
thwarted when it comes to lending support to *reversals*. The more activist elements in society, being skeptical about traditional procedures for
reform, concentrate on resistance against concrete threats at the local
level: for instance, protesting the presence of nuclear weapons or nuclear-
powered ships at a local port. Explicit concern about global reform is
restricted to matters of war and peace, human rights, and environmental
policy. To the extent that broader agendas of reversal are promoted, the
initiatives make little headway because they lack an appropriate political perspective and are entrusted to voluntary associations with limited
resources and no capacity or disposition to mobilize personal forces in
opposition to state policy.

The more radical expressions of resistance are also often motivated
by deeper and more comprehensive visions. When individuals risk their
lives to stop "the white train" carrying Trident warheads or to block entry
into port of a Trident submarine, for instance, the animating political con-

sciousness is strongly conditioned by the outlook of the citizen-pilgrim, even if not articulated precisely in these terms. More explicitly, this sort of symbolic action of defiance, often taken at considerable personal risk and cost, is serious politics even if it has no prospect of overturning state policy. Its "success" is measured by the religious element of witness to the choice between good and evil, by the political element of delegitimizing statist approaches to the pursuit of national security, and most of all, by the pedagogical element of insistence that human freedom includes the capacity and responsibility to say "no" not just with words but with one's body. The operating premise of Ground Zero is a common humanity and a vision of the future that centers on the eventual establishment of a political community that shares a vision of peace and justice *in time.*

One set of recent societal initiatives that seek reversals comprises multi-national blue-ribbon commissions on central problems of international life. Among the most prominent of such initiatives are those associated with the names Willy Brandt (on North-South economic relations), Olaf Palme (on East-West security relations), and Gro Harlem Brundtland (on global environmental policy). It is characteristic of these commissions to make a radical statement of the normative problem but then to formulate an action program that consists of a very modest series of steps. This tendency to tone down policy implications reflects the practical view of commission members that there is no point in losing credibility with existing power-wielders, and that there is no way to achieve even modest ends except by persuading elites to induce voluntary actions on the part of leading governments. Unhappily, the results have been disappointing to all constituencies, mass movements tending to find the action programs technical and marginal, and established leaders tending to find them overly ambitious and in the end less satisfactory than the status quo.

For instance, in the "Principles for Action" of the Palme Commission we find support for radical ideas of reversal and even for enhancement: replacing deterrence through armaments by a doctrine of common survival premised on a commitment to joint survival; support for general and complete disarmament. Proposals for concrete recommendations, however, are framed in terms intended, in the commission's own words, to pursue "realistic and attainable objectives" (code for "achievable by way of leading governments amid Cold War pressures in accordance with current outlooks").[15] The objectives formulated in the early 1980s were divided into short-term and medium-term measures. Recommended in the short term were ratification of the SALT II Treaty, preservation of the Anti-Ballistic Missile Treaty, nondeployment of "mini-nukes" and neutron bombs in Central Europe, and so forth—measures that were at the time important but restricted forms of resistance. Medium-term objectives included substantial reductions in the strategic forces of the superpowers (deepening the SALT process), the establishment of ceilings at reduced levels of parity for NATO and Warsaw Pact forces, agreement on substantial reduction of battlefield nuclear weapons in Europe, and so forth.[16]

My intention is not to belittle these proposals but to contend that they are too sweeping for statists and too marginal for transformers. As well, since blue-ribbon commissions tend to be dominated by enlightened statists, whose own prominence is based on statist credentials, they have a natural preoccupation with appearing "realistic" and eschewing confrontational tactics. As a result, their contributions help to shape public discussion but not to restructure governmental policy. Both in composition, outlook, and working procedure (witnesses, staff), these commissions are hostile to the revisioning of the future that forms the core attitude and political style of citizen-pilgrims. They give no consideration to civil disobedience, to the implementation of the Nuremberg Principles, or even to the promotion of democracy in the setting of reshaping national security policy.

ENHANCEMENTS

Like the previous two categories, enhancements are somewhat arbitrarily identified. The intention is to consider under this heading those social movements, goals, and projects that attempt to make a positive contribution to improving the quality of international life.

Because reversals seek to shift the energy of negative processes and enhancements seek to introduce new positive elements, important and extensive overlaps exist. Thus, whether the various global efforts to establish the unconditional immorality and illegality of nuclear weapons should be regarded as a reversal or an enhancement is largely a matter of judgment. Is the importance of such efforts by religious and professional lawyers' groups mainly a matter of negating the existing role in national security planning of the nuclear powers, or is it the positive establishment and implementation of the norms of prohibition? To conceive of a prohibition as an enhancement means to see it as part of the process of establishing a postnuclear world order.

Part of the reason to discuss "enhancements" is to emphasize the constraining character of the state system and its corresponding range of political identities. As long as one works within the formal, legalist framework of the state, even in a country that nurtures ideological diversity and political democracy, the inhibitions on normative innovation are powerful. For one thing, there is a general acceptance of the view that the militarized status quo is so powerfully entrenched that it can be challenged only symbolically and at the margins. For another, so many countries are linked to the world economy by ties of debt, aid, and trade that their sense of freedom of maneuver seems tightly restricted. But the pursuit of enhancement presupposes a different calculus of action, one that proceeds from the world view identified here as that of the citizen-pilgrim: that is, an overriding commitment to the possibility and necessity of building a future political community that serves the well-being of all peoples. Citizen-pilgrims are loyal *now* to that future possibility.

For example, commitments to general and complete disarmament (that is, radical disarmament) and to the establishment of international regimes for the implementation of the right to food are illustrative of substantive goals that are "impractical," given the character of the state system, but essential elements of an invisible global community organized to realize principles of peace and justice regardless of territorial identities. When these goals are pursued by "conventional" political sensibilities and through orthodox tactics, frustration ensues, along with either disillusionment or self-deception. The sharp split between ends and means creates a rather pietistic impression that such societal initiatives for enhancement are not serious, lack any appropriate politics, and, finally, foster the view of most experts that only tinkering with the present order by fulfilling its more enlightened potentialities is worthwhile.

In contrast, citizen-pilgrims embodying their future vision in their lives and politics tend to be joyful and hopeful, despite their acute awareness of the militarized power of the state and the menace it poses. They adjust means to ends in terms of both tactics and consciousness. Such an adjustment does not assure success, nor does it rest on any overly optimistic interpretation of social forces. Strength and vitality arise from the spiritual character of the commitment and from the realization that normative politics cannot be practiced through calculations about the likelihood of success or by relying on the procedures of representative institutions. In that regard, there is a natural spillover between the pursuit of enhancements and the revitalization of democracy. Indeed, the revitalization of democracy is itself an enhancement, as well as an indispensable instrument for the transformation of the state and the state system. The adoption of core Nuremberg Principles as the basis for establishing accountability and seeking redress from the state on matters of war and peace has an increasing appeal to those militants who qualify as citizen-pilgrims.

An interesting illustrative instance is found in efforts to make political parties vehicles of state transformation. In Great Britain a group of intellectuals within the Labour Party attempted a decade ago to reformulate socialism in more communitarian terms so as to give the party leadership a new basis upon which to appeal to its electorate. Of course, opposition parties are forever seeking reformulations of their political appeal, but what is of immense cultural importance is the extent to which this enterprise of reformulation centers on altering the role of the state by way of strengthening the more dispersed and local capacities of civil society to shape political destiny. It is regrettable that Margaret Thatcher's England swept aside such creative attempts to rethink socialism. Similarly, it is significant that conservatives and neoconservatives often seem dedicated to the same agenda, although their prescriptions tend to augment the state's military role and diminish still further its welfare role, whereas progressive critics call for precisely the opposite scale of priorities. Culturally, then, redesigning the state is at the center of the politics of renewal at this stage, whether the perspective is left or right, and ideological debate is about the aptness of demilitarization as a focus for political renewal.

Enhancement can take other forms. In a more modest sense, institution-building at the regional and global levels is illustrative. The creation of the United Nations Environmental Program (UNEP) as an aftermath to the UN Conference on the Human Environment at Stockholm in 1972 is an example of adding something new to world order on a problem of normative relevance to the operations of the state system. Especially in retrospect, UNEP seems like a very minor enhancement—not without some negative side effects by way of pacification—that does not begin to give the world the kind of capacity needed to protect the environment against dangerous activities and practices. UNEP, with a tiny, restricted budget and the handicaps of operating within the UN system, can do little more than disseminate useful information on environmental threats and protection, and even this function must be performed gingerly to avoid antagonizing the very powerful statist and financial interests that pose the most severe dangers to the environment. Whether the conference planned for Brazil in 1992, on the twentieth anniversary of Stockholm, can expand the global response to the environmental challenge is uncertain at this point of fiscal constraint, economic growth, and renewed anxiety about world energy prices and supplies.

Arms control arrangements and human rights treaties can also, on occasion, be looked upon as enhancements. For instance, the Biological Weapons Convention of 1972 spelled out a comprehensive and unconditional regime of prohibition that has been accepted by all leading governments and has probably inhibited a biological weapons race. Whether it can succeed in preventing such an arms race, without other adjustments in international life, is increasingly being drawn into doubt. Similarly, the 1950 Genocide Convention helped focus world public opinion on a particularly outrageous form of statist behavior. Again, the legal arrangement on its own does little more than register the outrage and provide some legitimated foundation for mounting a political campaign against a violator in this area of human rights.

In sum, the subject matter of enhancement involves the internal and international practices of states. Results are meager because the establishment procedures are themselves controlled, and virtually nullified, by states. This reflects in part the absence of democratic participation in internal and international settings, and in part the militarization of statist outlooks at a time when the overriding enhancement mandate is demilitarization. As a result, on the left of the vertical line in Figure 1, there is not much political space for enhancement, while on the right of the line, there is insufficient power under present conditions to do more than mount symbolic, educational challenges. For these reasons, staying above the horizontal line induces pessimism if one is fully aware of the severity of the problems associated with the operation of states in the present world setting.

TRANSFORMING THE STATE AND THE STATE SYSTEM

Acting below the line (see Figure 1) shifts the emphasis to the right side of the proposed taxonomy. It implies the embarking of the citizen-pilgrim on a political journey of exodus and liberation in search of a promised land of renewal. The foundation for this kind of politics is hopeful, because the mere act of embarking on the journey—not just reaching its destination—itself assures self-esteem and transcendence. Action premised on imagining a better world order avoids entrapment within the confines of territory and violence associated with statism. The implications in territorial time and space of such a posture for the individual is militant, demilitarizing struggle: that is, active participation to achieve change by taking stands in tangible local settings that involve matters of justice, peace, and environmental defense. Such a posture is in sharpest contrast with citizenship and conventional politics in the modern militarized state, where political participation even in democracies is being reduced to ritual performances of voting, demonstrating, and petitioning. True, these rituals retain vitality in many states, ranging from Greece to Argentina, especially those countries that have eliminated or restored the forms of representative democracy in recent years. That is, the wide range of disparity in political circumstance is normatively important with respect to the extent of internal militarization within the territorial grid of the state system.

The degree to which a particular governmental apparatus adopts a militarized stance toward its own population causes enormous differences in the quality of everyday life for various elements of the citizenry. As indicated earlier, no matter how vigorous societal democracy appears to be, the global dynamics of nuclearism (as well as of environmental decay and economic waste and exploitation) introduces unacceptable limitations on the capacity of civil society to exert its will. In powerful states the doctrine and mechanisms of "national security" override the democratic ethos; in weaker states, either by way of delegation (for alliance members) or by way of vulnerability (for nonaligned states), there is no democratic potential with respect to overriding issues of well-being. A similar dynamic exists, via the world capitalist setting, with respect to human survival and basic needs. The availability and distribution of food surpluses at affordable prices—as distinguished from an ability to pay artificially high market prices—are treated as matters of charity or geopolitics (that is, instruments of influence) by the granary states. The various dimensions of environmental decay are also results of an interplay of elements that are rarely correlated with the effective reach of the police powers of a given state.[17]

The entire flow of analysis suggests that below the line, states and the organized international community are resistant or immobilized with respect to our normative agenda, whether it is expressed by reference to values (Figure 4) or to processes (Figure 5).[18] The field of meaningful action is increasingly influenced by social groups acting to a growing extent out of the consciousness here associated with that of the citizen-pilgrim. This consciousness is also expressed by the slogan "Think globally, act locally," a dialectical call for nonterritorial orientation and a grassroots embodiment. Its inversion, "Think locally, act globally," although less evident, seems equally valid; we need to inform local responses with global implications, building networks and links of solidarity as part of our commitment to the fragile reality of global civil society. The perspective of the citizen-pilgrim also draws upon ideas of the ecological ethos, the primacy of species or spiritual identity, and the internalization of holistic thinking in science and culture. Implicitly, these developments produce a direct challenge to the exclusivity of the juridical concept of territorial citizenship: "Think and act in subordination to the state." The citizen-pilgrim is less a *member* with rights and duties than a *participant* and *voyager* with transterritorial goals and aspirations.

Given the range of actual circumstances throughout the world, the embodiment of the deterritorializing of political energy will vary greatly in form from setting to setting. There is a natural disposition in the North to focus on nuclearism and the war/peace agenda, in the South to concentrate on the development process as a way of overcoming the daily ordeals

Value Initiative	Peace	Economic Well-being	Social and Political Justice	Ecological Balance	Humane Governance
Revitalization of democracy ■ governments at state level					
■ organized international community (UN)					
■ social movements; individual and group initiative					
Revitalization of culture & religion ■ governments at state level					
■ organized international community (UN)					
■ social movements; individual and group initiative					
Imaging the future ■ governments at state level					
■ organized international community (UN)					
■ social movements; individual and group initiative					

FIGURE 4 Transforming the State and the State System: Values

Normative Process / Initiative	Denuclearization	Demilitarization	Dealignment	Democratization	Development
Revitalization of democracy ■ governments at state level					
■ organized international community (UN)					
■ social movements; individual and group initiative					
Revitalization of culture & religion ■ governments at state level					
■ organized international community (UN)					
■ social movements; individual and group initiative					
Imaging the future ■ governments at state level					
■ organized international community (UN)					
■ social movements; individual and group initiative					

FIGURE 5 Transforming the State and the State System: Normative Processes

of poverty, indignity, and repression endured by the overwhelming majority. Yet there are also important unifying strands: the various struggles in different parts of the world are oriented toward survival, but not survival conceived only in physical and material terms. Although fundamentalist politics often includes a call for more equitable economic policy and a strong indictment of foreign economic exploitation, the several surges of fundamentalist passion make clear the actuality of nonmaterialist motivations even for the very poor. The search for solutions involves recreating or circumventing the state; the attainment of a transformative power is not primarily connected with the acquisition of military prowess, yet it is deeply associated with mobilizing for militant struggle. When South African militants carry spears and clubs into encounters with South African officialdom, they manifest both vulnerability to firepower and a will to sacrifice in the course of prevailing whatever the cost.

Whether the participants in these survival struggles are implicitly part of an emergent social movement for global reform is a question of judgment and interpretation. My position is that the most helpful interpretation acknowledges what exists but does not overstate the case; the designation "emergent social movement" expresses the actuality of what is occurring without claiming that the state or the state system is being challenged in a manner comparable to the ways in which the South African and Polish regimes are being drawn into combat with hostile societal forces organized for coherent action. The organizational vehicles used by citizen-pilgrims are generally not yet connected in visible and familiar patterns, except by way of convergent lines of macrohistorical interpretation. Active connections across time and space do not yet exist even on the level of awareness. Strikingly, for instance, the small communities of nuclear resisters that have taken shape in major cities of the United States during the last decade are often out of contact with one another, despite their shared agendas and similar tactics. Each group tends to produce its own newsletter and distribute it to widening circles of sympathizers and devotees who are heavily clustered around the particular locale. There is as yet very little effort to form even a national network, although some leading personalities (Daniel and Philip Berrigan; James Douglass) have wide, significant followings. Revealingly, also, the national media virtually ignore this activity even though it is widespread, producing in the 1980s more criminal trials and far longer imprisonments than occurred among protesters during the Vietnam years.

At the same time, there is a nonterritorial (or at least nonstatal) growth of awareness. The European peace movement of the 1980s, although clearly differentiated on a state-by-state basis, evolved strong mechanisms for transnational solidarity and identity, especially on a regional scale, perhaps most significantly within the framework of European Nuclear Disarmament. Toward the end of the 1980s END gradually began to expand its own identity to incorporate the superpowers and the Third World. More significantly, it shifted its fulcrum of concern from resistance struggles (above the line) to revitalization of democracy (below the line) and extended solidarity to democratizing tendencies in the Soviet orbit as well as to the promotion of demilitarizing and democratizing struggles in Western Europe. This expansion of concern is also important from the perspective of conflict resolution. The statist mode of response, whether left, right, or center, is to blame either "the self" or "the other" for the perpetuation of conflict, risks of war, and reliance on violence. A new radicalism, neither strictly left nor right and as yet without a coherent ideology, emphasizes the anachronism of statist structures and militarist outlooks, that to indict and negate a particular actor, thereby polarizing the field of action.

The mainstream American peace movement, which has evaporated in the early 1990s, was overwhelmingly above the line in spirit and inclination during the 1980s, restricting its agenda in a literal sense and hence easily becoming disillusioned by the unfavorable relation of entrenched forces operating within the formal arenas of representative democracy. This "backwardness" reflects, in part, the one-party character of politics in the United States, especially when it comes to fundamental questions of property rights and social justice, as well as the related sterility of political discourse in a culture that rarely addresses matters of choice except in the pragmatic terms of exerting short-run influence on the government.

Each of the three categories of transformational (below the line) politics—revitalization of democracy, revitalization of culture and religion, and imaging the future—has developed characteristic ways to approach the relevant concerns.

REVITALIZATION OF DEMOCRACY

For our purposes, the revitalization of democracy is not concerned primarily with the reform of representative institutions. As acknowledged earlier, restoring some role for elections and parliamentary activity, as well as establishing a climate supportive of political parties and oppositional freedoms, can grant significant degrees of relief from the most oppressive aspects of state structure. My argument, however, rests on the wider perception that given the character of geopolitics, the nature of modern warfare, the distribution of resources and needs, the hegemonic patterns of economic penetration and interaction, and the deteriorating ecological setting, there is only a limited distance that most governments can go, even if their disposition is positive. Interdependence generates a powerful network of interlocking constraints that bind the spirit and limit the will of political leaders to the familiar pathways of political imagination.

Our sense of "revitalization of democracy," then, emphasizes an agenda arising out of the realization that the state and the state system must be transformed so as to constitute a new problem-solving framework for international life. Manifesting this realization by creating alternative problem-solving or, even more modestly, problem-stating frameworks is the essence of this more ambitious understanding of revitalization. When Worldwatch Institute issues its State of the Globe Report, summarizing the dangers of current trends in food production, environmental decay, population growth, and resource depletion, it is filling a knowledge vacuum created by the refusal of governments and international institutions to face the explosive consequences of their own far vaster collections of data. In this so-called information age, it is ironically often those actors with the best computers and data sets whose effective use of information is politically disabled. Potentially useful information is restricted, even suppressed, by the problem-solving frameworks and interest patterns of statist structures.

It is this need for access to information as a precondition for democratic participation that makes the issues of secrecy, disinformation, and propaganda so important and dangerous in our world. Espionage, a preoccupation of the mainstream, is actually the most trivial dimension; amounting to little more than reciprocal patterns of information exchange among statist rivals, it is a process that is generally stabilizing and, like most sources of stability, is treated by governments as "illegitimate" or even criminal on the part of adversaries. Reliance on spies acting on behalf of civil society and humanity is implicit in Johan Galtung's speculations on these matters. Daniel Ellsberg's release of the Pentagon Papers in 1970 and, subsequently, documents on nuclear strategy was a symbolic action of historic importance, expressing the need to violate state secrecy laws to enable civil society to know what is *real*. Incidentally, Ellsberg's initial impulse was to revitalize representative institutions and procedures by releasing materials to important, sympathetic members of Congress, but they turned out to be so co-opted or intimidated by the national security consensus that they demurred. Hence, it was necessary for Ellsberg to induce major newspapers to undertake the task, which they did with great reluctance, despite their supposed independence and the eminent newsworthiness of how the government shaped its Vietnam War policies.

And recently in England, Clive Ponting won an extraordinary legal victory when a British court endorsed his claim that sharing information about the sinking of the Argentinian cruiser *Belgrano*, with a Member of Parliament, was not a violation of the Official Secrets Act. Like the incensed reaction of Nixon and Kissinger to Ellsberg's initiative, Margaret Thatcher's response was to treat the whole affair as an outrageous betrayal: " 'I have never seen the Prime Minister in such a fury,' one of her closest advisers said last week. 'Like a woman possessed, she could talk of nothing else and think of nothing else.' "[19] Ponting, like Ellsberg, had resigned from government service and was stripped of his security clearance. That citizens have no constitutional right to know the truth about war/peace issues rests upon statist interpretations of national security doctrine; the position hardened throughout the Cold War and is likely to persist, regardless of how insistent the state may be about its commitment to democratic constitutionalism.

It is by challenging the denial of knowledge and information that revitalization is stimulated. For this reason, the various sets of disclosures by former CIA, and now former KGB, operatives are important. Not only have such witnesses brought valuable insight into the workings of the modern state, especially those located in the two superpowers during the height of the Cold War, but they also dramatize the ineffectuality of the procedures of representative democracy to assess controversial public policy. Also, recent exposure of the suppression for years of nuclear health hazards for those working in power plants or living nearby suggests a much broader problem than the insulation of controversial foreign policy from domestic criticism: even democratically constituted and legitimated states are not trustworthy in relation to the basic conditions of well-being for their own citizenry. The failure of this reality to provoke anger and mass protest is itself deeply worrisome, indicative of civic weariness and impotence, a sure sign of surrender by civil society to state and corporate power. Participation in democratic control cannot occur without the transformation of the internal bureaucratic power bases of states. In the meantime, it is at least a step forward to get rid of illusions as fully as possible and to challenge the most extreme prerogatives claimed by the state, such as engaging in covert operations at the discretion of the head of government. With the Cold War over, one major justification for the national security state has been removed, making it easier to mount criticism.

The struggle to reassert democratic control over statism is not only a matter of defiance; there are also creative possibilities to convert law into a societal instrument. Two quite distinct settings can be mentioned. In one, citizens and legal specialists drawn from many statist backgrounds came together in Rome and Algiers in 1976 to establish the "Permanent People's Tribunal," operating normatively within a framework of law contained in its "Declaration of the Rights of Peoples." Since its establishment the PPT has organized more than fourteen sessions on such diverse matters as Indonesian aggression against East Timor, repression under Marcos in the Philippines, Turkish genocide against the Armenian people in 1915, Soviet aggression against Afghanistan, and U.S. aggression in Central America. The governments accused are invited to participate, but they invariably refuse; nevertheless, their arguments are put forward as competently as possible by skilled advocates and by documentary evidence. A tribunal of jurors, numbering from seven to twelve, listen to the evidence and produce a reasoned judgment, usually supplemented in time by a volume of documentation. The publicity attending the event, as well as the political education associated with the written materials, gives a certain prominence to an array of abuses that the state system perpetrates and ignores. Because the authority of the tribunal derives from a portion of civil society (the people), not the state, its weakness (and strength) is that its judgments cannot invoke any coercive apparatus of the state system, not even of the United Nations, and that the claim of representativeness on a populist basis is always controversial and difficult to investigate. The tribunal form was emulated by the Green party at Nuremberg in 1985 and very effectively, later the same year, in the form of the London Nuclear Warfare Tribunal.[20] These various activities express, among other things, a loss of confidence in the existing machinery of government to address the normative failures of statism, as well as the legitimacy of spontaneous additions to "government" by societal initiative. In effect, the state is losing its monopoly over law-making, both to expressions of conscience (moral domain) and to counterstate lawmaking (political domain). This aspect of revitalization, currently quite marginal, offers possibilities for further growth.

A complementary effort involves activating formal institutions to challenge the excesses of the state. Here the terrain is difficult, as the state exerts considerable control over its component parts, even those that enjoy "independence" and whose fidelity is supposed to be directed toward norms and the well-being of society. An ideology of subordination is one expression of militarism, taking the form of excessive deference to whatever is claimed in the name of "national security." As with any other strong tendency, some countervailing pressures emerge. A variety of efforts are under way to induce more judicial and parliamentary activism, whether it be to keep foreign policy within the confines of domestic and international law or to establish some kind of oversight for the secret or covert activities of government. A case in Vermont some years ago involved a group of protesters disturbed by U.S. interventionary policies in Central America during Reagan's presidency. Charged with criminal trespass against the office of their senator, they defended their actions, in part, as *necessary* to induce their representative to take steps to end a course of foreign policy they believed to be illegal. Invoking the Nuremberg Obligation, the judge charged the jury members that if they believed the defendants acted out of a sincere conviction that what they were doing was reasonably related to violations of international law, and necessary to end them, then they could be acquitted. They were acquitted, and the outcome was celebrated even by the leading conservative newspaper of the state as a kind of victory by Vermont over Washington. Such an outcome is a small spark, but it expresses a weakening capacity on the part of the state to obtain the services and resources of at least some of its own institutions or of the citizenry to carry out its dirty work.

Revitalization also depends on new forms of self-reliance at all levels of society and in most sectors. Such a generalization does not question the reality that intervention by the state may sometimes reduce or even overcome local forms of oppression, especially certain extremist forms of social behavior that may enjoy pockets of local strength (for instance, the emergence of neo-Nazism in West Germany). In mounting a critique of modern states, one must not become oblivious to the often greater oppressiveness of certain local circumstances and practices. Yet from matters of environmental policy to those of human rights, revitalization depends on initiative at or beyond the boundary of the law. When Kim Dae Jung returned to his native South Korea in the early 1980s, an accompanying delegation of prominent Americans acted not only to deter abuse against him but also to disclose, beyond any ambiguity, the crude character of Chun Doo Hwan's regime in Seoul, despite elaborate public relations efforts to sell it as engaged in a liberalizing process.

When individuals or groups break the law to oppose dangerous weapons deployments, they are doing more than resisting. They are exploring new forms of citizen participation under conditions of altered oppression. As well, they are turning their back, for these purposes at least, on the forms of normal participation available to citizen opponents and expressing the societal need for more effective modes of redress.

At this stage, ending deference to unconditional state authority is itself of great importance. It is the essence of freedom and responsibility for individuals and groups. Freedom emerges because it becomes evident that secretive initiatives for confronting and dealing with the worst of problems exists, and because freedom is discovered, responsibility follows. To the extent this orientation spreads, the climate for a movement of democratic opposition and renewal will take shape. It is now in that stage of waiting to be born.

CULTURAL AND RELIGIOUS REVITALIZATION

The deeper foundations of governance are established by cultural and religious forces, and if these forces shift their ground, the political (and economic) foundations can be decisively shaken, shattering structures of apparent power and authority. The illusion of dominance and stability associated with the Shah's Iran is an important illustration of this dynamic of change. It seemed hardly plausible as late as 1978 that the unarmed, tattered followers of Shi'ism, demonstrating beneath the image of a then obscure ayatollah who had been living in exile for years in a remote village in Iraq (until banished to Paris a few months before the downfall of the Shah), could in a matter of months successfully challenge the modernized and extensive apparatus of military, paramilitary, and political power developed by the Shah's regime to keep all elements of opposition weak, divided, intimidated. Of course, if such a challenge is mounted, as in Iran, by a violence-prone and bloody-minded fundamentalism that seeks to invert and even intensify the oppressive relation of state and society, then the success of the popular uprising is no victory for democracy, and much less for human rights.

In all major civilizations at present, I think, social movements of varying strengths and perspectives are raising basic doubts about the adequacy of the normative groundings of statism. A broad dedication to an expanded view of human rights is central to the more specific agendas of particular constituencies of victims and benefactors. Four such clusters of commitment are especially important because their agendas call for the general reconstruction of state-society relations in a positive direction: women, indigenous peoples, those seeking racial liberation, and those active on behalf of ecological balance. It should be noted, of course, that vast differences of style, tactics, and goals are represented within the bounds of what I describe here as distinct social movements. It is reasonable to question whether the concerns in each activist setting possess sufficient overall coherence and self-consciousness to warrant the title of "movement."

Women. Women in the West, in order to comprehend their oppression, have been led to reconsider and then to recreate the basic myth structures of the civilization. To the extent that sexism arises from a profound and deeply rooted hegemony woven into civilization at all levels, it justifies the critique of patriarchy as underlying diverse forms of exploitation and a hierarchical manner of establishing and exercising authority. The cultural demands of feminism extend, then, far beyond reformist steps to achieve equality within the existing order; they question the most basic forms of violence and abuse, especially as embodied in "the war game." The prominence of women in recent stages of the peace movement, as well as expressions of feminine creativity, suggest that the most radical women are moving beyond strictly gender issues to provide an alternative vision of order, security, and conflict resolution to that contained in the realist dogma now providing ideological sustenance for the state system. The tactics and social forms evolved by the women at Greenham Common reveal that this drive includes a broad cultural revisioning as the core identity of the women's movement. Of course, sectarian and even fundamentalist energies are also at work, making it uncertain whether this source of cultural creativity will be sustained by women.

There have also been efforts, removed from activism and militancy, to explore the implications of women's awakening in works of the imagination, a burgeoning of such literature from many diverse viewpoints. One challenging exploration is Ursula Le Guin's *The Dispossessed.*[21] Bearing the subtitle "an ambiguous utopia," it compares the patriarchial planet earth with a matriarchically conceived alternative society set in the harsh geography of a habitable moon where resources are limited but political violence has been eliminated from societal experience. The utopian elements are not overdrawn, nor is the alternative existence romanticized. New painful and unpleasant encroachments on human freedom emerge; but in the end a normative choice is clearly made by "the hero" of this exploration, a physicist caught between the two worlds, in favor of the new civilization born of feminine imagination.

These literary gropings toward a new order both reflect and influence the shape of social activism among women. There are many varieties of citizen-pilgrim, although each is bound to a quest for a promised land organized on principles other than that of the state system, an invisible community beyond time and space calculations. As a result, each withdraws energy from territorial modes of identity and loyalty, thereby weakening the claims of the state in general and disclosing that other constellations of power, authority, and community might be brought into being and deserve our loyalty.

Indigenous Peoples. The deeper quest of indigenous peoples too are only beginning to be understood as interconnected and as having significance for the self-appraisal of the entire modern experience. So far, the issues have been treated mainly as matters of social policy and human rights, not as fundamental cultural revisionings. And yet, as indigenous peoples form their own networks of social action, there has gradually taken shape a transnational social movement with far-reaching shared goals that run counter to the logic of statism. Again, the movement is very segmented, divided between the specificities of short-term goals of resistance and the more common commitment to longer-term goals of self-determination.

Throughout the history of the state system, indigenous peoples have been principal victims. Their lands have been seized, their populations killed or assimilated, their cultural patterns derided and challenged, and their overall normative status deprecated as "inferior" or even "barbaric." Dominant social forces operating through the coercive framework of the state have regarded the life-style of indigenous peoples as a natural casualty of "progress." Yet they provide us with images of alternative civilizations that are generally, though not invariably, more nurturing toward nature and perhaps more consonant with species survival in the post-industrial epoch. Their world view is less materialistic and possessive than what has evolved in industrial civilization. Preserving indigenous peoples is also part of a broader commitment to cultural pluralism and, as such, an aspect of human rights.

The goals and orientation of indigenous peoples are usually antagonistic to the criteria of efficiency and development that shape the outlook of most government officials. The struggle over land use and ownership is severe in many parts of the world. In most settings, behind the specific demands of indigenous peoples is a search for assurance that their way of life will be protected against further encroachment. This protection seems secure only if it includes the authority to administer their own communities without interference from states or corporations. To the extent that these positions can win acceptance, political communities other than territorial sovereign states might begin to have an independent status in the world, augmenting trends toward the assertion of kindred forms of local autonomy (for example, nuclear-free cities and zones; municipal foreign policies for cities and local communities).

Race. As has often been noted, the structures of hegemony associated with the state system correlate closely with racial variation: within rich countries, whites tend to dominate nonwhites; among rich and poor countries, the rich are mainly controlled by whites (Japan is treated as and acts as if "honorary white"), the poor by nonwhites. As well, the nuclear deadlock has increasingly shifted the geopolitical conflicts of whites onto nonwhite battlefields, resulting in the concentration of warfare in nonwhite settings. Of course, the turbulence of decolonization has generated conflicts on its own, but interventions and arms sales by the superpowers have often increased dispositions toward war, as well as the magnitude and duration of political violence.

Whether the drive toward racial equality and liberation carries with it wider normative implications is difficult to say. The mere access of nonwhite leaders to existing power and wealth systems has not yielded encouraging results, possibly because cultural liberation has not been achieved. To the extent that non-Western cultural attitudes toward technology and human relations gain prominence, there might emerge a greater sense of choice with respect to the organization of the future.

Ecological Balance. The spreading realization that modern society cannot take nature for granted has called attention to the normative and functional limits of the state (and the market) as a problem-solving and policy-making framework. As famine spreads across Africa, there is growing evidence that a downward environmental cycle of population growth, deforestation and soil depletion, drought, and food shortage has been responsible for an underlying prospect of deterioration. Comparable dynamics are evident elsewhere. Macroenvironmental dislocations also arise as acid rain and air pollution, carried far from the original sources of activity, produce great damage to water supplies and fish.

The state, as such, is helpless to protect its territory and resources from many adverse environmental effects, whose transnational origins may be difficult even to locate. The state system has not seemed able to produce effective collective mechanisms of environmental protection— although neither has it yet failed. Efforts to prevent further depletion of the ozone have resulted in an impressive treaty framework which, if implemented, could lend some credibility to statist claims of capacity in the context of environmental protection. But activist groups, operating with small budgets, are often better able to raise awareness and alter behavior than are governments. The effectiveness of Greenpeace in saving certain endangered species of whales from extinction suggests what can be achieved by dedicated activists relying upon imaginative and militant tactics.

On a crowded earth facing problems of conservation of water and land resources, confronting an array of global pollution problems, and beset by uncertain risks to global climate arising out of a variety of human activities, the case for some sort of global mechanism to identify and uphold the planetary and species interest seems powerful. To defer this adjustment until the evidence is incontrovertible is likely to mean waiting until environmental catastrophe occurs and the underlying situation is beyond remedial action. These concerns underscore the incompetence of the statist world view to encompass human interests. Their relevance here is partly a matter of establishing the inadequacy of the state and partly a matter of emphasizing the possibility of greater coordination across state boundaries. A global mechanism might be able to take good advantage of computer technology to shape policy at regional and subregional levels through interaction among unofficial environmental groups around the world.

Compared with the necessity of cultural revitalization and the efforts toward it suggested above, the relevance of religious revitalization to global reform is largely unexplored. At the same time, the perspective seems important. The state, in part, has appropriated to itself many of the attitudes and roles previously associated with the religious sensibility. Without overstating, it may be said that the "worship" of technology and the willingness to destroy civilization on behalf of the survival of governmental regimes represents a displacement of the reverence and commitment more properly expressed by way of a religious disposition. The passive acquiescence of ecclesiastical authorities to such developments has contributed to the dominance of civil society by statist outlooks, especially in an atmosphere of political liberalism. In political settings controlled by Marxist-Leninist perspectives ecclesiastic authorities were severely constrained, if not repressed, and religious activities discouraged and sometimes punished.

Challenging the militarized state requires, in many settings, a kind of conviction and organization that can be provided only by religious organizations. The importance of religion as a mobilizing social force in Eastern Europe (especially Poland), in Latin America (in the diverse forms of "liberation theology"), and in the Islamic world is beyond serious doubt.[22] In liberal societies as well there are signs that ecclesiastical leaders are becoming prepared to confront the state on basic issues of societal policy: reliance on nuclear weaponry; responsibility for poverty; attitudes toward "life" and "death." The programmatic content and ideological lineage of these encounters varies, but there is a shared realization that the quality of life in civil society depends on challenging and transforming the state on the basis of some avowed normative goals. Whether the challenge is a matter more of imposing a fundamentalist creed upon a pluralist civilization or of demilitarizing liberation varies from case to case.

Amid this ferment may be the elements of new religious formations more responsive to the visions of justice associated with the cultural revisionings already discussed in this section, with what has been called "the postmodern possibility" in earlier chapters. More explicitly, we may be witnessing the preliminary stages in the formation of a religion centered on feminine symbolism and resting on a humanist and ecological tablet of commandments. It may be that various citizen-pilgrims will begin to formulate the outlines of their sense of a promised land and to plan an exodus from the oppressive structures of statism. As I have suggested, this journey may require not traveling through space but only acting upon the mandate to reconstitute political community for the sake of "the small" and "the large," reconciling individualism, localism, pluralism, and universalism.

IMAGING THE FUTURE

Marx regarded the attempt to describe the promised land as an indulgence, a species of moralizing; the real work of revolutionary thought was to mobilize social forces against the oppressive existing order. True, mere utopian musing, as associated in his day with "utopian socialists," was not clear about the need to transform power structures of the old order by means of struggle. Without struggle nothing happens, except provisionally; at most, in isolated pockets of civil society harmless social experiments may be tolerated.

But the Marxist bias against normative futurism has harmed the project of societal reconstruction. Insistence on a violent negation of the dominant class and uncritical confidence that the oppressed class can provide a vehicle of liberation have established the dismal destiny of radical politics in our time. Orthodox Marxist orientations tend to reproduce, if not accentuate, the patterns of oppression they set out to struggle against. They rest in the state, as a cynosure of liberated energies, unconditional authority and unlimited power to interpret, defend, and extend revolutionary gains. In the process, most forms of societal friction are extinguished as counterrevolutionary, including those intermediate associations arising from economic activity and religious belief. Nowhere have workers' associations been weaker than in Communist states. When the state is presumed to be the vehicle of value realization, all forms of opposition becomes "criminal" by ideological definition. In Eastern Europe, those who worked through independent groups against the nuclear arms race or the bloc system were treated in official circles as outcasts, as enemies of the people. Party bureaucrats insisted that there was no need for independent peace activities, since a state constituted on behalf of the masses is itself necessarily a peace movement.

We have learned, I think, that mere imaging of the future makes nothing happen, but that dedication to the acquisition of power may make too much happen. At this stage, following upon despair about existing arrangements and disillusionment with radical traditions, a particularly important challenge exists: to depict the emerging struggle and yet to restore confidence that it is possible to improve in dramatic ways upon current realities.

As might be expected, the imaging of the future by those oriented toward the persistence of statism is unimaginative and unrealistic. It rests largely on releasing the positive potential of the existing instruments of change, especially technology. It is a future replete with artificial organ implants, star wars–style protection, computerized substitutions for labor and thought, new agricultures of synthetic foods, and even space colonies. It posits a dehumanized landscape of automation, manipulation, and pleasureless leisure. Many technocratic futurists are infatuated with this kind of imaging, taking for granted the persistence of political forms and structures, at least short of collapse through catastrophe.

In contrast, those whose consciousness is to some degree drawn toward the outlook of the citizen-pilgrim are engaged, wittingly or not, in the work of nontechnocratic imaging. Explicit undertakings along these lines have not been sustained for very long, nor have they been able to engage the direct experiences of those victimized by the existing order. Such undertakings as, for instance, the World Order Models Project are gropings by way of intellectual effort in traditions of thought associated with rational and humanistic analysis. If one considers the antecedents of WOMP (world federalism) and its legacy (an emphasis on societal struggle, social movements, the interplay of local concerns and global aspirations), one finds evidence of an unfolding theory and orientation toward practice by its adherents and implicit acceptance, as well, of the need to educate the young to become citizens-pilgrims. Its discourse remains inadequately adept at considering either the foundations of human action in civilizational and anthropological forms, or the dynamics by which unlikely but desirable social movements can grow potent. Nevertheless, this sort of intellectual activity, seen as a correlate to social action, can make important contributions both by interpreting countervailing tendencies and by animating society with a hopeful vision of a future rooted in normative potential rather than technological prowess (although no rejection of technology is implicit).

Imaging the future has to do with working out the implications of demilitarization (internal and international) at different stages, in different settings. Understanding the contradictory forces at work suggests a dialectical view of history. When the leaders of New Zealand or Greece challenge the militarist policies of the superpowers, they both generate wide societal support and unleash a statist backlash by way of diplomatic and economic pressures.

One of the most illuminating ways of imaging of the future is studying the lives of exemplary citizen-pilgrims who are at work among us. Their lives embody a refusal to be bound by either deference or acquiescence to statism. Nor do they wage struggle by reliance on violence or even coercion. They relate fulfillment to the joy of community, not materialist acquisition. Their voices are often filled with prophetic warnings and anger; their call is best understood as a plea for religious renewal and a spiritual quest. Among those whose lives express such orientations are Bishop Desmond Tutu, Paolo Friere, Mother Teresa, Lech Walesea, Kim Dae Jung, Petra Kelly, and countless other women and men whose names we will never know.

A FINAL NOTE

This chapter has explored some aspects of the interplay between social movements and statism in our epoch. This interplay remains obscure and very context-dependent, varying through time and space, but despite the lack of specificity some general trends and possibilities are discernible. A broad framework has been tentatively set forth. The essence of what seems to be happening is an array of seemingly distinct quests to overcome the oppressions associated with the exercise of state power. The torments and energies of an awakening civil society are pushing individuals toward the extremes of terrorism and spiritualism. Given the normative identity of this undertaking, the emphasis here is upon the political potential of spiritual discovery and journey.

The present situation is confusing. The state and the state system exhibit a declining functional capacity and legitimacy, despite a certain show of adaptability on environmental issues; this decline tends to be hidden behind an intensifying reliance on internal violence and international war-making by statists with modernist outlooks. Considered in one way, statism is on the way out; in another, it is stronger than ever. More and more, various civil societies are becoming disillusioned with facets of the old ways but have yet to comprehend the feasibility of full-fledged alternatives. A primary task of political visionaries at this time is to join in the work of converting societal disillusion into creative social action to overcome the menace and begin to fulfill the promises contained in our situation, especially the visible contours of an emergent global civil society dedicated to human survival in an atmosphere of equity and happiness—a celebration as well as a necessity.

CHAPTER V

Transition to Peace and Justice:
The Challenge of Transcendence
without Utopia

IDENTIFYING THE CHALLENGE

CRUSADING IDEOLOGIES, whether secular or religious, have over the centuries offered humanity an array of visions that promised deliverance from the torments of historical existence. Some of these visions masked schemes for exploitation or pacification. Others connected liberation with the access to power of a class or a world view, but their proponents revealed themselves as betrayers of the vision, consumed by the struggle to attain control over societal structures of authority. The modern experience with national revolutions consuming their own comrades and even their own visions is freshly etched on political consciousness.

Also etched is the sterile aspirings of well-wishers who project images of desirability without convincingly relating those images to the domains of action. Utopian professions of the conviction that only world government can heal the wounds of a fragmented world society are typical, especially when the call is accompanied by a blueprint of structure and function, as if bureaucracy were self-generating and provided any assurance whatsoever of liberating effects. Equally irrelevant, at this stage, are meditative, inward shifts of attention and energy that mystically promise deliverance for the world as a whole. The guru Maharishi's claim that world peace will be securely established as soon as 1 percent of the world's population adopt meditation as a discipline is typical of this fusion of spiritualism and romanticism. Not much more helpful are the many forms of Aquarian conspiracy set loose in California, which adopt the anodyne view that the destructive features of modern civilization can be transformed by the widespread adoption of life-affirming life-styles.

Though one must acknowledge realist critiques of efforts to reform international society at a bold stroke, it remains at this juncture essential to repudiate with equal vigor the insufficiency of all well-intentioned tinkering, moderating gestures, and alleged slowdowns of the dynamics of conflict. The evolutionary model of gradual amelioration has been discredited as firmly as have more grandiose conceptions of reform. Gradualism has not significantly eroded the role of war, of arms racing, of exploitative relationships, of repressive governance, of ecological decay. To be sure, it is possible to find some isolated, if provisional and ambiguous, solid gains—an arms control arrangement to banish a particular weapons system; a variety of functional arrangements to facilitate international commerce and navigation—and these may improve normative prospects at a given stage or provide a plug for visible leaks in the dike of the human condition. But incremental achievements have shown no capacity to overcome basic patterns of danger and abuse. The cumulative trends and embedded structures of the global political system persist; they continue to extend their menace in new directions (population growth, toxic wastes, acid rain, militarization of space) and manifest ever additional distortions of the human situation.

These structures and distortions constitute an affront to human dignity and a multidimensional threat to survival and prospects for positive societal development. The evidence of oppressive practices lies in the degree of suffering and waste that could be avoided by more constructive use of resources and technological innovation, revised societal arrangements at all levels of governance, and improved approaches to the resolution of conflict between groups. There is no reason whatsoever to doubt that human nature is capable of developing and relying upon a far better set of practices with respect to the organization of life on the planet than those that now are dominant. Such an affirmation implies a solemn responsibility to seek the liberation of these positive possibilities. It does not imply optimism, nor is it predictive. Still less does it deny the demonic possibilities that could increase still further the current quotient of suffering and waste in the world. In effect, from what we know of human nature and societal experience, there is an enormous plasticity present with respect to levels of normative attainment.[1] This range of performance is certainly influenced by the character of institutional and technological setting, by the scale of the social unit, and by the attitudes toward violence, strangers, and fulfillment emphasized in the myths and sacred history of a particular community. The challenge of political emancipation is to find *plausible pathways* that might lead from *a menaced here* to *a valued there* and thereby orient thought and action in fruitful directions that realize some of the potential for a better, more satisfying world. This chapter argues that such pathways are, at best, hazardous and as yet largely unknown, that pointing the way at this time needs to be tentative despite the urgencies of the overall world situation, and that breakthroughs must be "discovered" rather than "posited." On this basis, structures of state power are disfavored as path-clearing agents of change; constructive tactical steps can be discerned and should, of course, be encouraged, but they are not the focus of this inquiry.

Yet the presupposition here is that in order for us to address the underlying dangers and threats, a new surge of democratization of political life must occur, although not in familiar forms. Finding the forms that shape destiny lies at the basis of this effort to recast the problem of political reform, and it is here that social movements for renewal and transformation seem to provide the only ground of action capable of nurturing hope. Conceptualization is partly a matter of discernment, partly a matter of showing connections and sharing experiences that will enable sparks of creative initiative to fuel larger and larger fires.

German theologian Dorothee Sölle provides a leitmotif for this voyage of normative discovery: "Submission kills. And if you think you wre born too late into too old a world which can no longer be changed then you lack faith." The opposite of submission is resistance; the unwillingness to resist implies civilizational death. In Sölle's words: "There is resistance to nuclear holocaust, there are signs of hope in communal living, there are groups who are prepared as Abraham was to leave the straightjacket of the system and to opt for life, regardless of the sacrifice." [2] At this stage, nothing is more important in a variety of settings than to encourage these dispositions of mind and body. Grassroots activism can create arenas for social creativity subject to democratic control and also religious arenas that enjoy status and support within the modern setting. When a Polish government under Communist control murders or beats a Catholic priest for his role in oppositional politics, it underscores the depravity of its ethos with particular vividness. As with the plasticity of human nature, the normative character of antistatist religious resistance cannot be presumed to be either beneficial or detrimental. A wide range of possibilities exists, many of which have become manifest in history. The normative challenge is to strengthen the more constructive potentialities associated with the religious orientation and not to embrace or reject religious pathways on an uncritical basis.

To set foot in the future is risky business. The Chinese say that "nothing is harder to predict" than the future.

It seems especially problematic to be bold in the imagination at this time. The global space of political life is more complicated than it has ever been, more interrelated for better or worse, more capable of taking transcending technological leaps beyond apparent obstacles but more vulnerable than ever to a variety of crippling catastrophes on the scale of a whole society or civilization or region or possibly of the world as a whole. The "nuclear winter" scenario validates for the imagination, if not to the contentment of skeptical specialists, that any extensive use of nuclear weaponry can easily produce a climate change of such magnitude as to disrupt civilization as we know it and to destroy most agriculture, even if the fire, blast, and radiation effects of a nuclear war do not necessarily imperil human survival.

Nevertheless, to succumb to dark forebodings tends toward their self-confirmation. It represents submission, passivity; it relinquishes altogether the responsibilities and possibilities implicit in human creativity and freedom. Besides, there exists within the human experience a disposition toward struggle, perseverance, and reproduction, especially in the face of danger—a kind of biological politics that by its very existence generates hope.

And yet it seems more important than ever to be as precise as possible. We have been disappointed so often in this century by large promises. Either nothing happens (internationalism) or too much (revolutionary nationalism). But the opposite of large expectations is not necessarily, or exclusively, the substitution of modest expectations and an adoration of what is small. Small may be beautiful yet may also be ugly, as large may be worthy of awe, whether expanses of sky or prairie, or great herds of feeding, roaming animals, or the liberation of portions of society from regressive social practices embedded in hallowed local tradition.

To work toward a better world is to grope in the dark, but not aimlessly. It is to rely on navigational clues and to build on our experience without losing sight of the degree to which a journey is always preoccupied with destinations, and their uncertainties. To extend the metaphor, to promote the safety of the journey in every possible way, while realizing fully the unsafe, unknown, unknowable terrains of passage is the moral and political objective of critical reflection. Our more specific goal is to ground confidence on the interplay of conviction and knowledge. Because this is an outlook we associate more with a spiritual journey than with energetic participation in a secular state, such a redirection of effort commends the perspective of the citizen-pilgrim who is embarked on a spiritual journey to a valued future ("another country"), primarily an orientation toward time and value.[3] In contrast, being a citizen of a state is primarily a relationship rooted in space, tested by unwavering loyalty to the here and now.

SURVIVAL, SOLIDARITY, ENGAGEMENT

Marguerite Yourcenar appends to her brilliant historical fantasy *The Memoirs of Hadrian* some "reflections on the composition" in which she notes: "It is only out of pride or gross ignorance, or cowardice, that we refuse to see in the present the lineaments of times to come. Those sages of the ancient world, unbound by dogma of any kind, thought as we do in terms of physics, or rather, of physiology, as applied to the whole universe: they envisaged the end of man and the dying out of this sphere. Both Plutarch and Marcus Aurelius knew full well that gods, and civilizations, pass and die. We are not the first to look upon an inexorable future."[4] This process of degeneration and regeneration is the largest understanding we can derive from the past and extend to the future. To avoid the maelstroms of degeneration and to discover the pathways to regeneration is to open up possibilities in any given historical setting, but such an undertaking cannot overlook the underlying contingencies of acting-in-the-world.

Increasingly, those seeking generative pathways are looking down at their own feet and at the earth that surrounds them. Dhirubhai Sheth writes perceptively of the proliferation of innovative political constellations in India that share a skepticism toward conventional vehicles for exerting influence (such as political parties and mainstream media) and toward large-scale governmental operations in general. The poor and oppressed are growing tired of waiting for the state to rescue them and assure their deliverance, and yet they are no longer disposed to resign themselves to their fate or karma, or to defer to the afterlife the satisfaction of their needs and even the pursuit of their aspirations. One of the extraordinary stirrings in our time is the spread of innovative initiatives at the grassroots and margins of human existence. Sheth writes of "micromovements which go beyond conventional national identities, and which, led usually by politically oriented social activists, function outside the frame of conventional party politics." Further, he notes the emergence of "fairly large-scale movements, spontaneous and popular and firmly rooted to the ground but breaking out of the narrow confines of chauvinism. They do not allow political parties or groups to acquire control over them. They can be said to represent the political promise . . . of the people, in that they carry the spirits of the conception of new politics."[5]

Note that such a politics is democratic in its core spirit. It is not easily indulged where conventional party or state structures are so strong and extensive as to impose their will upon virtually the entire political space. Yet as the 1989 upheavals in Eastern Europe displayed, even where the state seeks to close society down, powerful civic energies are available to ward off such absorption. The new promise, then, relies on the emancipatory potential of the people, especially those groups who are most conscious of their oppression and also animated by the spirit of self-reliance that includes envisaging some kind of alternative future, and who then organize accordingly. In essence, such an emphasis involves an inquiry into the diverse dynamics of empowerment, a disclosure of possibilities that alter our perception of the relation of forces in the world and the nature of power. To extend this envisaging in response to concrete circumstances to wider patterns of understanding is one contribution that intellectuals can make, provided they are prepared to get their hands dirty!

Such a politics is built most easily around opposition to the concrete intrusion of alien forces onto traditional lands and waterways. In general, the most severely threatened are often those indigenous peoples who stand concretely astride the path of the modernizing state—as do the tribal peoples in the Amazon River region—and whose survival as a civilizational reality is at risk. The poor are also keenly aware of policies and practices that affect their livelihoods, including the removal of resources and loss of jobs resulting from reliance on elaborate projects that involve outside technology and financing. Critical to popular resistance is the belief, even if it is only implicit, that preferable alternatives do exist, that dominant forms are not omnipotent, and that every person can participate in the work of defining acceptable forms of social reality.

More elusive as yet are patterns of self-reliance on the part of those whose oppressive prospect is seemingly remote and virtually invisible. Among such people, especially if they are otherwise quite affluent, there is a strong tendency toward complacency and denial that is powerfully reinforced by a materialist ethos and seeks refuge in an art of cynicism and hedonism bearing the name "realism." Those who have over the decades instructed us on the need "to live with nuclear weapons" as a matter of destiny are emblematic of such resignation, which can surface only in cultural moods of despair and denial.[6]

In the face of this civilizational aridity, it may be exemplary cultural and religious "performers" who acknowledge most fully and provide the most vivid definition of these monstrous yet invisible hazards. For instance, consider the words of Jim Schey in his preface to an anthology titled *Writing in the Nuclear Age*: "What all of these writers share is a devotion to language, and a sense of imperative: a willingness or compulsion to struggle with literature's bearing on survival. Theirs is a very basic consolation, that any effort to foster compassion and sustain alertness is brave, and necessary; that while no single act is enough, we are not, in fact, alone." But that engagement is inevitably political in its implications, establishing part of the groundwork for a community of believers. Schey continues: "Our determination to prevent a war must be as intense as our dread of the nuclear blast. We need all of the moral clarity and political influence we can summon, and all of us must learn to resist, individually and together: to resist death, to resist pretenses of justice and security. Ours is a civilization at a decisive juncture."[7]

The theme of resistance links these reflections on nuclearism to the more embodied, far less self-conscious varieties of new populism discerned, especially in India, by Sheth. In practice, to resist means inevitably to oppose the state and its encompassing manifestations and alliances (which include sexism). At the very least, it looks eventually toward reconstructing the state to enable effective and satisfying participation by the people, as well as to find security for societies without retaining the option of the bomb or other weaponry of mass destruction as some kind of suicidal trump for possible use in geopolitical games. The autonomy of the state in relation to societal will operates as a structural denial of democratic control.[8]

Resistance and hope are also the foundation of a new religious consciousness that can be connected with the outlook and circumstance of the early centuries of Christian experience, when the church and its faithful were persecuted by the reigning Romans. It draws inspiration, at least in the United States, from the nonviolent militant practice evolved in India by Gandhians and in the United States by the civil rights movement of the 1960s. A typical enactment proceeding from such premises was the entry by seven persons to Griffiss Air Force Base near another Rome, a small city in New York, in the early morning hours of Thanksgiving 1983. These activists, whose drama of resistance was the product of months of training, planning, rehearsal, and prayer, proceeded to Building 101, where a B-52 bomber was being retrofitted to carry cruise missiles. They perceived such delivery vehicles and missiles as first-strike weaponry, being too slow to penetrate an activated defense system. Elizabeth McAlister, one of the participants, describes their experience: "We hammered on the bomb bay doors of the B-52; poured our own blood on the fuselage of the plane; spray painted the phrases '320 Hiroshimas' and 'Thou Shalt Not Kill' and 'If I Had a Hammer' on the plane; taped to it photos of our children and children with whom we work, as well as a 'people's indictment' of Griffiss Air Force Base that we had drawn up."[9] The group on the base was apprehended and indicted for sabotage, for destruction of government property, and for conspiracy, crimes that together could produce jail terms of up to twenty-five years. "That much reality can be frightening," McAlister writes, "especially when the one facing it has three young children (aged 9, 8, and 2) whom she loves deeply."[10] Indeed, the participants did receive prison sentences, ranging from three to five years.

This was the sixth such "plowshares action," each performed by a distinct yet connected cohort of militants, all of whom were both religiously motivated and fully convinced that reliance on nuclear weaponry involved the continuing commission of the most severe category of crime of state. On December 4, 1983, a seventh comparable action took place, this time in Germany, suggesting a transnational field of visionary politics.

The resolve to resist in these ways is very much conditioned by a mixture of biblical reflection (what it means to take seriously the injunction to beat swords into plowshares) and by reference to the responsibility of parents to give their own children a decent world to grow into, "to ask how I can best love my children and to answer by working to provide for them and the millions like them, a hope for a future. And I cannot say that I hope for a future for them, without, at the same time, being willing to do something to make that hope become a reality." [11]

Statements in this spirit are characteristic of the special religious orientation of such antinuclear activists. The essence of their action is to bear personal witness to the degree to which the military policies of the state fly in the face of elementary religious, moral, and legal scruples and, in so doing, knowingly and willingly to accept the consequence and pain of prolonged imprisonment. There is also here the belief that over time their demonstrations and exposures of reality will awaken others to the necessity of protest and resistance, building at the very least a counterculture on the most fundamental issues of life and death.

The trial that follows upon such an act of resistance is integral to the emergent practice. The court, challenged to do justice, is exposed as "illegitimate" to the extent that it upholds directly or through legal maneuver the militarist practices of the state, especially the manifestations of the nuclear national security state. Expert witnesses are called upon to validate the consequences of nuclear war and to confirm allegations about the objectionable features of a particular weapons system—characteristically, that it is designed for first-strike rather than defensive missions. Other witnesses are called before the court to establish the gap between nuclear national security policy and the rules and standards of international law, as well as to discuss the extent to which violations of international law are crimes of state and, as such, occasions for legitimate resistance by individuals with reasonable beliefs, knowledge, and in the ability to act. This mandate is derived from an application of the precedent and an extension of the principles embodied in the Nuremberg Judgment of 1946, which concerned leaders of Nazi Germany, to the circumstances of ordinary citizens acting even within the confines of constitutional democracy. According to this line of reasoning—which remains controversial in several aspects and antagonistic to the claims of the state to monopolize the processes of legal interpretation—any individual positioned to act has a legal responsibility to uphold the international law of war and peace by action appropriate to the context.

Note that the encounter in court between opposed conceptions of law and justice has also the future of civilizations in contention. There is an important difference. Because of certain normative contradictions that have been introduced into the practice of states (principally, the discretion of sovereign power in relation to the subject matter of national security and the accountability of statesmen for their failure to uphold principles of international law in the area of war and peace, even if restricted to "victors' justice"), the resisters are able to invoke a counter-tradition within the authority system of the state itself to validate their own acts. Put differently, the adoption of the Nuremberg Principles as a general framework for international relations, not just as a historically constrained validation of the moral connotation of World War II, is a Trojan Horse in the edifice of statism. Not unexpectedly, statists responsible for the adoption of the principles in those special circumstance did not foresee the more subversive implications and, to the extent that these implications cannot be denied, have done their best either to ignore them or to repudiate their abiding relevance. On the other hand, those with revolutionary consciousness on the relations of state and society, have invoked these principles with growing conviction, both to validate their own claims of radical defiance of state authority by reference to the norms of the prevailing order and to manifest their commitment to an alternative order.

There is here a form of legitimated resistance that seeks to reestablish dialogue between the state and the civil society in a variety of settings. The societal insistence is that the state acknowledge its accountability in relation to allegations of illegality and criminality arising from national security policies. The acknowledgment implies not necessarily a confession of guilt by representatives of the state but initially no more than a willingness to have the legality of state actions assessed according to norms generated by the law-making process of the state system. But because courts generally operate as institutions of the state, they are rarely willing to entertain positions that question the official policy of coordinate branches of government, especially in the broad area of foreign affairs. That is, statism is hostile to the Nuremberg Principles, and despite constitutional pretensions and sanctimonious insistence on extending criminal responsibility to defeated enemy leaders, there is no willingness by political leaders to be judged by such restraints.

In reaction, agents of social change whose identity is based on resistance have begun to fashion their own institutional arrangements, not constrained by subservience to any state. That is, these counterinstitutions are receptive to the countertraditions within statism that formal actors are disposed to confine narrowly or to suppress in practice. Of course, the siting of such arrangements depends on the degree of tolerance of the territorial sovereign but not necessarily of the state whose activities are being scrutinized. Again the transnational aspects of democratic initiatives that seek to foster governmental accountability are prominent. At present, no part of the planet is exempt from state-administered law, except those in circumstances of anarchy or insurrectionary autonomy, as when a revolutionary group administers territory under its control. At least in societies that proclaim themselves to be political democracies, there remains a broad tolerance of voluntary associations, even those that adopt a consistently critical stance. The Permanent People's Tribunal based in Italy, whose work is described in the preceding chapter, is illustrative.

That action-in-resistance continues to be based on norms sanctioned by the state structure bears significantly on the identity and practices of the citizen-pilgrim. Unlike anarchism or revolutionary activism, the countertradition is *within* the political culture, even if its role is subordinated and, in operational terms, ignored by power-wielders and the media mainstream. As a consequence, the struggle is waged on *behalf* of the culture and its own confirmed aspiration, rather than from a position of hostility and alienation. Furthermore, the countertradition draws on the symbols, heroes, and texts that are hallowed by the culture, seeking, in part, the kind of radical renewal associated with the voice of prophets in the Old Testament.

LEARNING FROM THE POLITICAL CULTURE

The forms and possibilities for resistance will vary greatly with the particular features of a given situation. Even if we focus on the larger implications of local activism and of issue-oriented social movements, certain general considerations influence prospects at all stages. Some positive dimensions connected with the broader setting of action provided by "political culture" can be identified.

SEIZING THE NORMATIVE INITIATIVE

One of the liabilities of oppositional violence of a random, disruptive character is that it generally cedes the normative and tactical ground to the governing process, almost no matter how unjust and repressive. Terrorist tactics, besides being nearly always morally unsupportable, create a political climate supportive of state violence, an orientation toward encounter that is generally favorable to the state.

In contrast, oppositional tactics that premise resistance upon norms endorsed though not upheld by the state tend to give nonviolent resisters the upper hand in normative debate. Such a moral advantage can be particularly pronounced in relation to crimes of state pertaining to the prevention of nuclear war, for reasons already discussed. It must also be noted that public enthusiasm for victory in war—depending on the relative popularity and success of a war (for the West, World War II was popular, Vietnam unpopular), the political culture at home, the perception and tactics of the enemy, and so forth—often negates altogether the applicability of norms of self-restraint. To avoid the implications of subsequent allegations of criminality may require institutions of government, especially courts, to interpret "law" in an arbitrary and formalistic manner. For instance, U.S. courts attempted to avoid addressing substantive allegations about the Vietnam War and nuclear policy by treating the issues as not legally relevant, as nonjusticiable, as "political questions"— technical doctrines used to deny a defendant his or her day in court by withholding the question from a jury or refusing to allow evidence to be presented.

The effects are diverse: to discredit the concern with justice, or even law, of courts and legal arenas; to build a case for establishing "spontaneous" tribunals to fill the normative vacuum; to advance the wider attack on the state and its procedures for refusing to abide by even those normative guidelines that had been previously adopted and applied to others and that seem essential for purposes of survival and civilizational decency. By thus seizing the normative initiative, opponents of official practices and policies challenge the authority of governing institutions, often inducing increased dependence by the state on propaganda and coercion. At what point such a normative relationship alters the terms of political encounter varies from situation to situation. The breathtaking transition of activists in several Eastern European countries during 1989 from the status of criminal and persecuted opponents of the state to holders of state power illustrates how dramatically the scales of legitimacy can shift their balance.

In contrast, demonstrators in the United States during the Vietnam period were never successful in weakening the official allegiance of police and the military on the home front, despite the unpopularity of the war. This was partly a reaction to the wider agenda of the peace movement, which appeared to challenge traditional values in almost every fundamental respect and was presented by the media as aligned with those "enemy" forces in Vietnam then killing Americans sent there to fight. The media inflamed domestic sensibilities by focusing on the more extreme elements in peace demonstrations: those intent on exhibiting freakish life-styles and those who, to be provocative, carried Viet Cong flags or placards praising Ho Chi Minh. In effect, the normative high ground was relinquished by the most militant demonstrators, and the American public

overwhelmingly supported repressive police tactics, whatever its growing reservations about the viability and desirability of the war. A further
factor may have been the class elements that arose from the association of
the demonstrators with college campuses and privilege. The government
had little difficulty portraying such antiwar forces as un-American and
thus helped generate a working-class backlash. Richard Nixon was particularly successful in his efforts to rally support for his failing Indochina
policies by seeking to mobilize "the silent majority" against the agitators
at home, who were depicted as out to destroy the best of America.

Gaining the normative advantage is a complicated matter but central
to the prospects of grassroots initiatives. The state possesses the capability of punishing and destroying threats to its primacy. Tolerance either
expresses political confidence or arises out of a prudential concern that
disaffection will spread if repression ensues. Responses by central governments to ethnic and regional movements for autonomy are often illuminating; for instance, the relationship of Delhi to the Sikh movement for
autonomy and human rights in India's Punjab disclosed a shifting of posture during the 1980s from outright repression (the attack on the Golden
Temple) to one of seeming accommodation.

Often, religious leaders and church auspices can provide limited
protection to oppositional movements with quite radical potential. One
major shift in Latin American state-and-society relations, especially in Brazil, has occurred as a result of the organization of "base communities"
linked to the Catholic Church and engaged in active efforts to reconstitute
society from the ground up. In this context, a religious network evolved
over centuries can help to connect various local initiatives as well as to
expand the concerns of participants beyond their immediate situations.
Under the more authoritarian conditions that existed in Chile between
1973 and the late 1980s, the protection of churches was more defensive
in character, allowing groups of citizens some relatively safe space for
political discussion and oppositional analysis.

Because the major religious faiths have an institutional presence at the
local level, transnational mechanisms for coordination, a global interpretation of the human situation, and a normative and spiritual conception
of human fulfillment, they provide the most obvious alternative source
of authority to that of the dominant state and militarist structures. Yet
their ability to play this positive role depends on finding a consensus
that both refuses subservience to the reactionary content of prevailing
arrangements and avoids reversion to a fundamentalist interpretation of
the normative tradition. Whether religious traditions, if revitalized, are
indispensable bridges between experience at the grassroots and larger
nonstate social movements with radical programs of reform is an open

question, probably with variable answers depending on place and time. Certainly in many settings the activation of the religious sphere seems the only way to challenge the encroachments of statism. Without such wider links, local and grassroots initiatives are easy to constrain and demoralize.

Under many conditions of political ferment, religious elements have guided and influenced an apparently secular social movement. If the state perceives the oppositional movement as revolutionary in character, then it may even risk the further erosion of its legitimacy by attacking directly, perhaps brutally, prominent religious leaders who have interpreted their spiritual mission to involve support for the drastic reform of the socio-political order. The murder in El Salvador of Archbishop Oscar Romero by death squads linked directly to the state was a particularly notorious example, the more blatant because this revered leader was actually performing a Mass in the cathedral when shot dead.

The relevance of the normative dimension of struggle is suggested by government efforts to discredit such movements by placing *agents provocateurs* in their midst. The assignment of these infiltrators is generally to incite movement adherents to escalate their tactics and cross certain normative boundaries of restraint, thereby weakening public bonds of sympathy and fostering a climate in which repression is widely perceived by the confused citizenry as the lesser of evils.

The implications here can be summarized: Normative dimensions of struggle are often critical elements; an oppositional stance can be strengthened by building its case within the wider tradition of the culture; movements of opposition need to be vigilant in relation to deliberate efforts to penetrate their ranks and incite alienating tactics; this vigilance can be best exercised if leaders understand the normative terrain of the struggle and convey it effectively to the movement as a whole.

EMBRACING UTOPIA

If official structures are unable to deal with social problems successfully and seek to retain an image of decency, they may adopt wildly implausible schemes in seeking to provide justification for their persistence in a discredited mode. President Reagan's wildly enthusiastic embrace of the Strategic Defense Initiative in the early 1980s had this character. SDI offered a dark utopia that blunted the normative impact of the peace movement, which had aroused acute anxieties about the devastating consequences of nuclear war. Religious critiques of deterrence had then opened a gap between the official policies of the state and the normative consensus of the culture with regard to weaponry of mass annihilation. SDI appeared responsive to these critiques by insisting on the moral necessity of transcending deterrence and transforming that insistence into a gigantic project costing hundreds of billions of dollars, perhaps more than a trillion, thereby further concentrating research and development efforts in the military sector of society.

Never before has a major government in the West seemingly abandoned the realist paradigm in promoting its policies. Even Woodrow Wilson's alleged idealism with respect to the League of Nations was, in essence, a practical scheme to sustain United States global leadership in peacetime, an approach that might have worked to counter European appeasement tendencies in the 1930s had it been endowed with more commitment and capabilities. SDI initially was presented as a futurist fantasy of perfection, a defensive shield so impenetrable that a deterrent threat would no longer be needed to ward off enemy reliance on nuclear weapons. There were from the outset numerous reasons for skepticism about the undertaking, especially with regard to its consequences fifty years later had it been allowed to develop along the lines so effectively endorsed by Reagan's advocacy.

SDI was a dark utopia because its ostensibly normative appeal disguised its quite opposite practical effects. Besides making more difficult the reduction of superpower tensions and negotiation of an end to the nuclear arms race, SDI diverted scarce resources and talents to the military. The opportunity costs were enormous: an avoidance of economic reconstruction, and neglect of severe social problems. As well, SDI was promoted at a time when international developments had created an apparently serious disposition in Moscow to take ambitious steps to end the nuclear arms race by ending all testing of weaponry and by cutting existing stockpiles. More than this, the SDI path was destabilizing in many respects; for example, by its encouragement of strategies based on future reliance on defensive capabilities, it could increase the willingness of the United States to rely more freely on nuclear threats in crises.

Other dimensions of SDI are relevant. For one thing, it demonstrated the political culture's capacity under some circumstances to adopt a utopian approach to problem-solving. Receptivity to such an approach is greatly enhanced if the promoter possesses a charismatic capacity to persuade, as Reagan did. It also seems evident that *this* utopia was successfully presented because it reinforced prevailing political structures and social forces; even Reagan could not have adopted just *any* utopia, as was demonstrated by the backlash against what was later perceived as his brief embrace of a diplomatic vision of total nuclear disarmament. SDI was acceptable also because it reinforced the infatuation of the dominant tradition with high technology as the path to prosperity, progress, and military ascendancy.

Yet again, it is important to understand that not every high-tech uto-pian project could have been sold. New technologies of surveillance and sensing, if fully exploited, could provide the basis for disarming in an atmosphere of distrust. An assured verification capability would remove all pretext for proceeding with the arms race. Yet news of such a "trans-parency revolution" have been virtually lost in the noise. Demilitarizing high technology has little political appeal. SDI was an ingenious project that represented militarizing high tech par excellence. Not only did it confront an anxious adversary with security problems, but it rationalized and disguised an array of militarizing innovations. In this regard, it recov-ered for government some of its lost normative terrain, though it did so by misrepresentation and deception. In retrospect, the utopian side of SDI has been displaced by the orthodox realist undertaking of mobiliz-ing resources and support for the militarization of space. The idea of SDI as a defensive shield has been substantially abandoned, but many of its constituent programs have been retained, as emphasis has progressively shifted to the enhancement of existing strategic systems by utilizing space for military purposes.

The temporary embrace of this dark utopia does have a bright side. The official abandonment of "realism" (including its implicit ideology of gradualism) as an adequate foundation for governmental legitimacy opens the way to transcendence of deterrence in other drastic but more accept-able directions. In effect, the promotion of SDI stood on much common ground with the peace movement because it rejects deterrence on a nor-mative basis. Significantly, in this regard SDI attracted a measure of support from such drastic critics of deterrence as Jonathan Schell and Freeman Dyson. The lure of a dark utopia in a troubled time, then, should not be underestimated.

But neither should "the opening" associated with cracking the realist consensus. Until SDI there had been no significant mainstream move toward the elimination of the nuclear weapons threat since the 1946 pro-posals of Bernard Baruch and David Lilienthal to internationalize control over all aspects of nuclear technology, an initiative rejected by the Soviet Union, allegedly on security grounds. Those proposals, to the extent that they were seriously put forward at the time and could have been imple-mented, represented a more traditional approach to the threat of nuclear war than does SDI. They were, however, not utopian, as they depended on a disarmament bargain to refrain from certain action and on verification-of-compliance procedures. Proposals by both superpowers in the 1960s to accept general and complete disarmament seemed to fall short of seri-ous intention; they were designed mainly to achieve propaganda advan-tages with the public on the peace issue—to gain the normative initiative in the East-West struggle for hearts and minds on this most momentous question. Again, significantly, in the nuclear age to be seen as dedicated to war prevention makes a government more politically potent with its own population than to be in some measurable sense militarily superior.

Transcendence without utopia implies drastic yet attainable goals. The utopian impulse is constructive to the extent that it liberates the imagination from despair, fatalism. It also helps to extend the horizons of local and grassroots explorations beyond conventional boundaries.

INVOKING LATENT DISCONTENT

Movements that succeed often do so unexpectedly. Seemingly isolated incidents spark wider reactions; a repressive response occurs; a still more intense reaction occurs, and so on. The depth and intensity of discontent, which is often masked on a day-to-day basis, is catalyzed by events that cannot be planned. Like a match in a dry forest, a small cause occasionally has a huge effect. The explosive situation in South Africa is illustrative. At some stage, a few years ago, blacks in their townships shifted from a posture of sullen acquiescence and periodic eruption against the system of apartheid to one of outright sustained defiance and mass movement. The obscurity of the anti-apartheid movement—or for that matter of the anti-Marcos struggle in the Philippines—was largely a consequence of its decentralization. Its vitality is at the grassroots, and though the goals of activism require a reconstituted center, the wider organization and ideology are not easy to discern or to specify. Keeping the centrality difficult to discern is partly tactical, to avoid giving the repressive opponent an easy target to strike against.

The psychopolitical issue here bears on our main theme. Conventional wisdom and social science techniques cannot assess the possibilities for change inherent in a given situation because they have no way to gain insight into the level of latent discontent and the conditions under which it can become manifest. Grievances are often tolerated over a long period, but at some stage an explosion of discontent takes place, perhaps intensified by a leader with a talent for mass mobilization. Such dark geniuses as Hitler and Khomeini and such brighter geniuses as Gandhi, King, and the founders of the great religions are all able to tap into the explosive power contained in the unconscious strivings and frustrations of a people.

It is quite possible that latent discontent establishes the basis for a more positive series of adjustments to the world crisis than now seems evident. An unconscious learning process, proceeding in subterranean fashion, may be establishing the lower foundations for a dramatic shift from various fragmentary identities to an overarching global identity.

There is no reason whatsoever to suppose either that fragmentary identities will weaken incrementally or that evidence of global identity will grow in a simple linear fashion or at some logarithmic rate. What seems more plausible is a surge of identities associated with earlier normative orientations (nation, state), coupled with repressive efforts to hide or diminish the emergence of the new forces that threaten to supersede what has previously dominated. As the globalizing pressure grows, it will at some stage overwhelm the containment capacities of the old order— which, exhausted by its efforts, may tend to disintegrate rapidly and unexpectedly, or to refashion itself by adapting to the new globalizing imperatives under the aegis of conservative, market-oriented forces of corporate and financial power.

PREPARING FOR THE OPPORTUNE MOMENT

Christian thought, with its special sense of spirit incarnate at a given historical moment (the word becomes flesh) in the person of Jesus, later the Christ, is especially alert to the actuality of special contexts containing unexpected potential for sudden transformation. The Greek word *kairos* has been used by theologian Paul Tillich to focus this special Christian sense of the shattering of time in given historical situations. In secular domains, the breakdown of order and legitimacy associated with major wars has been the occasion for dramatic openings to reconstructive energies. New possibilities are disclosed, and higher risks may be accepted by those challenging the status quo. The old order may be vulnerable because it has lost authority—citizens feel less respect, or maybe less fear. While the government is preoccupied elsewhere, the volcano erupts at home. The Bolshevik Revolution illustrated this dynamic, as did the sequence of wars of independence unleashed after World War II.

Maybe we are entering a different historical space in which crises and premonitions of disaster will at some juncture provide an opportune moment. At such a point a creative, determined minority can act far beyond its apparent capabilities and find itself riding the crest of a historical tidal wave. The Bolshevik elite rose to the occasion in 1917 and forever altered the course of Russian and world history.

In the effort to forge a more hopeful future for humanity, attentiveness to the possibility of an opportune moment is of great importance. The authors of the Pastoral Letter of U.S. Catholic Bishops, written in response to an acute societal concern about the nuclear arms race in the 1980s, expressed confidence by declaring in 1983 that there existed "a new moment."[12] An occasion when the entrenched leaders blinked revealed doubts about their chosen course, a shudder not lost on the populace. At such a point, other ways of perceiving can emerge with unexpected strength to alter patterns of discourse, behavior, and policy. But their durability may be brief, challenged by the capacities of old orthodoxies to fashion responses of their own.

Keeping one eye cocked on the wider canvas of action may be the best way for grassroots movements to prepare for the opportune moment. And such an attentiveness may itself be subversive, generating by its very existence an unintentional but deeply rooted globalism as the flip side of localism, and as a defensive posture toward the prospects of repressive globalism being facilitated by technological capabilities and considerations of economic efficiency.

THE GREEN AGENDA

The experiences of the Green party in Germany and elsewhere are suggestive. The German Greens, formed as an anti-party, adopted the party format as a vehicle for normative influence, political participation, and financial support. An antiauthoritarian and anti-bureaucratic rationale makes it even more difficult than normally for the group to sustain unity, to develop leaders with wider mobilizing appeal, and to use access to governmental procedures in an effective way. Yet its members' resolve to work together at the local level and in larger arenas to resist militarism, abuse of state power, and industrial crimes against nature has been inspirational for people concerned with transformation throughout the world.[13] Behind the antagonisms that have anguished many Greens in their relations with one another and caused their movement great difficulties in its country of origin, there is a widely shared sense that the Greens are reaching toward a new post-Marxist, postindustrial politics that has significance, to varying degrees, for peoples struggling for humane survival and sustainable development in many settings.[14]

In this regard, the Green mind-set, more than any specific program, seems to provide the beginnings, at least, of a new political striving of global consequence. In this transitional setting the relationship between the local and specific, the global and universal, the human and the environmental is prefigured. The Green party does not quite fit the role of one more minority party, nor does it easily confine the range of its concerns to the territorial interests of even a reunified Germany. It is both local and nonterritorial in its most fundamental animating spirit.

Some of the shared features of the Green agenda can be noted without interpretive comment:

- a posture of nonviolent militancy, which includes a strong tactical endorsement of and participation in political activity beyond the fringes of positive law: that is, civil disobedience as a moral and political imperative;

- an ambivalent attitude toward formal institutions and procedures of the state, which can be associated neither with anarchistic traditions of the rejection of governing processes nor with liberal acceptance of the unconditional legitimacy of constitutionalism;
- a substantive concern with human rights and participatory democracy as the foundation of acceptable societal arrangements, and a related ambivalence about mainstream preoccupations with the policy issues of the moment, except to the extent that occasions for resistance are generated;
- a search for new emancipatory constituencies outside Marxist categories of class conflict, and a related doubt that workers provide the social base for societal transformation;
- a realization that relations between society and nature are as much part of core politics as are relations between state and society and between state and state, and a healing attitude toward the body politic that finds therapeutic guidance in the domains of nature and culture;
- an almost instinctive rejection of any definition of national interest that relies on geopolitical criteria, and a disposition to apprehend the character of national interest on the basis of a wider, human identity;
- a related transnational involvement in the political struggles of others as an expression of this identity, thereby opposing state-to-state interventionism and insisting upon people-to-people interventionism, a politics of peace and justice that is without boundaries.
- a response to human suffering and political oppression that eludes ideological classification and is as likely to support self-determination and human rights for Tibetans as for Palestinians.

The influence of the Green movement is difficult to measure and even more difficult to assess, but it has been considerable. One arena of influence involves party competition, and not only have Green parties sprung up in many countries and captured a significant fraction of the vote, but they have caused centrist parties to strengthen their environmental commitments to avoid losing adherents. Further, the Greens' stress on the environment, reinforced by many indications of environmental decay, has led to a dramatic heightening of public awareness about environmental issues and to a willingness by the citizenry in many political constituencies to give environmental programs higher priority than either national security or economic development. Whether the Green challenge has peaked or is still at an early stage of growth is impossible to determine at this time, especially if—as is likely in the 1990s—society attaches renewed urgency to energy concerns and to sustaining economic stability.

A GLOBALIST NECESSITY AT A TIME OF MODERATION

The 1980s closed on a mainly optimistic note. After more than four decades the Cold War seemed to be slipping gently into history, a consequence of Soviet "new thinking" in foreign policy as defined by Gorbachev's energetic and imaginative leadership. What is more, except in Nicolae Ceausecu's Romania, the oppressive circumstances in Eastern Europe were overcome without violence. These developments understandably generated an exultant mood, especially as they came about so abruptly. As of 1990, the dangers of East-West war seemed happily remote, and the prospect of general war (World War III) and large-scale use of nuclear weaponry highly unlikely.

Of course, the picture was not altogether bright. A billion Chinese were tantalized by the hope of democracy in 1989, only to have their dreams shattered by a vicious backlash of repressive state power. The economic and environmental shambles of the East European countries suggested that freedom and independence will not lift their populations easily from their legacy of hardship. The Cold War left behind, also, new uncertainties for the Third World, a fear of neglect in some places and of the intensification of regional conflict elsewhere. The plight of Africa and, especially, the complex significance of the 1991 Gulf War, are illustrative.

Newly evident for the first time since the anti-Fascist consensus that prevailed during World War II, however, is a willingness of leading states to cooperate on the main issues of the day in a framework set forth by the United Nations charter. Such a willingness is encouraging, as well, in relation to the growing urgency of the various dimensions of the global environmental challenge—a challenge that cannot be met, it is now widely agreed, without unprecedented cooperation among states, implying a considerable expansion in the role played by law and institutions. Indeed, it seems plausible to believe that the goals of environmental balance will require a network of institutions and procedures for monitoring compliance and overall conditions which, eventually and in its cumulative effect, will constitute a type of "world government."

Such a course of international relations is likely to be reinforced by parallel developments in the world economy. Institutions for mutual benefit in relation to trade, money, financial markets seem indispensable ingredients of a reasonably stable economic atmosphere. Similarly, functional arrangements to handle communications, polar regions, space travel, and ocean mining seem almost certain to take shape in coming decades, cumulatively contributing to a governance structure at the global level.

What seems equally important is that the modernist thrust toward globalism-from-above be complemented by and ultimately accountable to globalism-from-below. Globalism-from-below refers to the many facets of transnational democratic initiatives, often given expression by social movements, voluntary associations, and nongovernmental organizations and linked in a new configuration identified in this book as the glimmerings of global civil society.[15] It is within this setting of innovation, trends, and aspiration that we discover a realistic possibility for transcendence (of statism)—without utopia, but with a normative core of value commitments premised on the human interest.[16]

CHAPTER VI

The Global Promise of Social Movements: Explorations at the Edge of Time

$\mathbf{A}$ FOCUS on social movements with restructuring agendas itself incorporates a political judgment about how best to achieve drastic global reform at this stage of history. Implicit in this judgment is the view that conventional party politics, even in functioning democracies, has lost its restructuring capabilities and, further, that violent forms of revolutionary politics are not likely to enhance the overall realization of world order values. In this regard, the new social movements seem at present to embody our best hopes for challenging established and oppressive political, economic, and cultural arrangements at levels of social complexity, from the interpersonal to the international.[1]

One feature of these social movements is to connect practices in everyday life with the most general aspirations of politics, including global restructuring. Thus, when Solidarity or Charter 77 leaders call for trust and integrity as operative principles for relations among citizens confronted by authoritarian government, their call if heeded has itself transformative reverberations at all levels of political life. Or when inquiry is directed toward overcoming abuse in interpersonal settings (male-female; parent-child; teacher-student), the resulting political engagement alters the perception of the character of abuse in the public sphere of politics. The new social movements, and the theorizing that accompanies their emergence and evolution, reconstitute our understanding of "the political" and "the global." By bringing "peace and justice" into intimate social relations, we cause a distinct revolutionary challenge to arise that threatens to subvert all modes of oppression. And contrariwise, by refraining from addressing the oppressive element within ourselves, we cast grave doubt upon claims that ideas can play liberating historical roles on behalf of political movements purportedly dedicated to emancipation in one form or another. Both by enlarging our sense of "the political" and by

125

insisting that everyday practices contain an element of "the global," new social movements are dramatically altering our understanding of what the pursuit of a just world order entails in a variety of concrete situations.

NOTES ON PERSPECTIVE

Assessing the global political potential of various social movements requires taking account of their overall yet not unconditional rejection of *violence* as a means and *state power* as the principal end. These movements are also skeptical about the procedures of *normal* politics even in societies that possess an operative liberal democratic framework of rights, political parties, and elections. (Such generalizations are risky, however; temporary accomplishment of the peace movement in Western Europe was to restructure and radicalize the leadership of social democratic parties in several countries, including West Germany and Great Britain, especially in relation to defense and environmental policy.) As well, these movements and their adherents exhibit skepticism about the animating creeds of the pre-1960s: socialism and nationalism. Furthermore, they do not have confidence in the capacity of the trade union movement or the welfare state to address the contemporary urgencies of societal distress.

The social movements at the core of the new politics (democracy, human rights, feminism, ecology, and peace) have taken hold mainly in the constitutional democracies of the West, although important parallel developments especially in Eastern Europe, India, and Latin America started to exert influence in the 1980s. The overall outlook reflects, of course, the specific setting, especially the presence or absence of a high-tech economy. In general, nationalism (as a counter to colonial memories and interventionary policies) is a more positive ideology for social movements in the South—especially if it upholds the political, economic, and cultural autonomy of a country—than it is in the North, where it is associated with imperial projection, the arms race, and war-making. The South, as later discussion of context suggests, remains less concerned with strategic trends and nuclearism than with development, peace, order, and security within continental, regional, and local settings.

The relation to religion is also uncertain and contradictory. In general, the holistic emphasis of the new movements unfolds in organic connection with spiritual interpretations of the human situation, interpretations that often stress the liberation potential of established religious tradition. In this regard, solidarity between rich and poor, between antiinterventionists in the North and nationalists in the South, between ecologists and peace people is often most militantly expressed by those who devoutly profess a religious faith. At the same time, those who are threatened by the transforming demands of the new politics and the uncertainties of the world situation may invoke fundamentalist validations of traditional values, including notions of separatism ("chosen people") and moral absolutism (holy war against various categories of infidels). These polar manifestations of religious consciousness are both relevant to the new struggle to shape the cultural setting, the values, beliefs, and myths that condition politics.[2]

Further, emphasizing social movements as political actors limits concern to those movements that possess a liberating orientation. This orientation can be established in diverse forms, but generally it renounces violence as means, and it subordinates the control of state power to other goals. What, then, is the relationship to such struggles as the quest for democracy in South Korea or Chile and the anti-apartheid movement in South Africa? In these settings, violence enters as a tactic of challenge, although the political encounter arises mainly out of mass upheaval; but state power is definitely a principal and immediate goal, although subordinated to more attainable objectives involving social, economic, political, and even cultural reform and reconstruction. In this regard, state power is a tactical necessity (to realize programmatic ends) rather than an end in itself, but if unexamined in that role, the dangers of statism remain immense. The new order will expect too much from state power, and a new leadership can be easily tempted by repressive options as popular disappointment sets in and enemies are identified to explain the failures of "the revolution." The struggles to dislodge dictators and corrupt leaders do bear centrally, however, on the process of achieving humane governance and equitable development, and somewhat upon the character of "security" (especially, if state-centered militarist repression is at stake).

As the very different Sandinista and Aquino movements showed, elements of tactics and outlook connect these Third World political movements significantly with the normative priorities of the new social movements that have emerged in the North. The situational factors require a broad encompassing framework to disclose links with global-scale tendencies that are supportive of people-centered security and transformation.

At the same time, without a formal democratic framework the constraints on social movements seem far greater, although the ability of Solidarity to prevail in Poland is a heroic demonstration of what can be done in a political setting that treats nonviolent oppositional politics as criminal activity. The wider significance of social movements with transformative agendas is definitely associated with the existence and quality of the democratic process. Indeed, one shared ingredient of these movements is their anti-state, antibureaucratic character, which is a negative way of expressing their confidence in "the people" as progressive agents of history and in "civil society" as the crucible of change. The essence of democratizing is to increase the political space to mount pressure for change from "below."

Political militants have few illusions left about violence and armed struggle, but their confidence in the will of the people often remains romanticized. Evidence suggests that vengeful and authoritarian sentiments are often embedded in a political culture as its dominant, democratic motif. The Iranian masses evidently endorsed Islamic terror, at least before the long war with Iraq, and celebrated the antidemocratic style of leadership associated with Ayatollah Khomeini's rule. Harry Eckstein's study of "civic inclusion" (extending democratic participation, especially education, to the poorest sectors of American society) confirms in a modern, supposedly enlightened setting the prevalence of antidemocratic orientations.[3] To grant power to the people provides no assured beneficial normative consequences. Everything depends on conditions, the experience and outlook of those who have endured exploitation and suffering, the quality of their leadership, and the flexibility of the opposition. In South Africa, for instance, the anti-apartheid movement may yet proceed either in a vengeful, violent direction or in the far more reconciling direction emphasized by Desmond Tutu and Nelson Mandela, as well as on the government side by Frederik W. De Klerk; tactical and normative support for both inclinations continues to exist at present. No single pattern of beliefs can be described as fully expressive of human nature; rather, there are many potential configurations, depending on circumstances.

The militancy of a given movement may also be a reflection of existing oppressive structures, a feedback effect of the sense that established self-corrective and evolutionary mechanisms are futile, too feeble, or not available. If women were to be liberated, they themselves had to boldly act on behalf of a liberating process. Similarly, if future generations are to inherit a resource base and biosphere of comparable quality to what now exists, then environmentalists must protect endangered aspects of nature with more radical methods than those provided by lawful approaches, arguably even with their own bodies if necessary. Within the broad framework of environmentalism, the several radical orientations that have emerged are clustered around two sets of ideas: governmental and economic institutions cannot be made responsive enough to the depth of the environmental challenge, and priorities associated with restoring ecological balance should no longer be subordinated to social concerns of human society such as maintaining economic growth and overcoming poverty. That is, the originality of these strong-willed initiatives is, in part, evidence of the conviction that conventional political options are not viable in many contexts of social change, and that extralegal radical action is indispensable and could even prove effective, despite the advantages enjoyed by the established structures of power and wealth.

Given their character, the influence of such societal initiatives, especially those on the fringes of legality, is almost impossible to assess.[4] To begin with, existing leaders are unwilling to admit the degree to which shifts in official attitudes and policies have been caused by populist challenges, and the mainstream media help support the view that public protest is ineffectual. As a result, the activities of movements and initiatives are generally perceived as entirely local and their existence seems fragmentary at the level of interpretation. Or they are polemicized, as was the case in East-West discourse, in order to attribute weakness and indecency to the adversary, and their wider relevance is discredited. Yet perhaps this assessment is too superficial. The rise of the new social movements may be part of a process of mobilizing latent discontent with the prevailing forms of order and authority in a given civilization. In the end, it is this latent energy that offers the best hope for a realistic challenge directed at existing oppressive structures. With it, anything is possible; without it, nothing is.

There are problems also of cohesion and communication. The new movements are exploratory and include quite a wide range of outlooks among their adherents. Perhaps it is questionable to group disparate initiatives within an issue area (say, environment or human rights) in an aggregate of the sort implied by the seeming coherence and solidity of the term "movement." Internal coherence is very difficult to sustain except in a crisis atmosphere. Coalitions made for tactical purposes easily fracture under the pressures of either success or failure. These fractures are "news" and give an often exaggerated impression of disunity, an impression that itself may be self-fulfilling, promoting still further disunity and demoralization. To overcome fracturing, especially by loss of contact or demoralization, requires contact and communication, which depend upon adequate resources. Many social movements operate on tiny budgets and cannot possibly afford to create and sustain integrated transnational networks of like-minded groups and individuals. These organizational obstacles are made even more formidable by hostile institutional responses, including efforts to manipulate such movements by insinuating informers or *provocateurs,* and to obstruct them by questioning travel credentials and the like.

Perhaps the greatest perplexity of all is associated with the great weight of the various distinct contexts deriving from cultural setting, political system, historical circumstances, and stage of development. For societies preoccupied with problem-solving at the level of a given state or region, or even at the level of a specific local political and economic community, wider preoccupations seem virtually irrelevant. In the Middle East, for instance, the political struggles between Arabs and Israelis, between modernizers and fundamentalists, and between Egypt and its Mesapotamian rivals take up virtually the entire political space. There is little disposition to question more widespread patterns of reliance on violence or to give up the traditional political goal of control over state power as an end in itself. Africa, too, seems beset by immediacy: famines, masses of refugees and displaced persons, racial and tribal war, acute indebtedness, and an array of demoralizing secular problems arising out of corruption and incompetence. The eschatological concerns of nuclear war or ecological collapse may remain, by comparison, remote and abstract in such settings—although even in areas of the planet removed from modernism, there is a growing concern about the future.

The situation in China seems similar but for quite different reasons. China seeks a balance between population, resources, and technique in working out a sustainable developmental approach. There is an evident tension between a general willingness to let leaders work out practical and reasonable solutions and the emergence of mass discontent over economic and social policy, periodically tied to strong expressions of democratic resistance. Similarly, the peoples of Latin America seem overwhelmingly concerned with issues of democratization, poverty, and indebtedness. In short, the pressures of context constrain the political imagination somewhat rigidly yet concentrate the available resources of activists on work that needs to be done.

It remains correct to insist that shared vulnerabilities are now of a global character, that we cannot as a species escape a shared destiny, given degrees of interdependence and the assured effects of nuclear war or ecocatastrophe. Because many social movements operating within specific settings tend to be preoccupied with their immediate challenge, it is particularly notable when Bishop Tutu journeys to Hiroshima for the forty-first anniversary observances or when Petra Kelly, E. P. Thompson, or Noam Chomsky speaks and writes on behalf of forgotten victims of oppression and neglected dissidents. But these gestures of commitment do not go to the essence of what motivates most activists on a day-to-day basis. In fact, leaders with a more cosmopolitan outlook may lose influence unless they are immersed in the daily routines of struggle, being regarded as more interested in their own wider image than in the concrete issues back home.

Furthermore, where political systems and cultural settings do not regard social movements as natural modes of popular participation, then their existence tends to be nominal, if at all. Such a characterization applies to much of the nondemocratic portion of the world political system; until the revolutionary events of 1989, it was especially true for the Soviet bloc, and it remains descriptive of China, North Korea, Iraq, and many other states. To claim an exclusive role for social movements in relation to the larger world order issues is to ignore the potential contribution of states acting through their governments. A more sensitive account of the various roles of actors in promoting positive change under varying circumstances needs to take account of contributions being made by people and by governments, including governments of societies that apparently exclude or marginalize the role of social movements.

An emphasis on global implications tends to derive from those portions of the planet that harbor imperial dreams. This does not mean that the globalism of social movements has a secret imperial agenda but rather that the less burdensome context of the immediate reality, together with the globalist undertakings of corporations, governments, and media, infuse the imagination of reformist First Worlders with a global-scale conception of problems and solutions, and a correspondingly reduced feeling for the overwhelming intensities of local and regional preoccupations. In effect, an ideological unevenness on matters of perception restricts communication and effectiveness. Such restrictions cannot be eliminated, but better mutual understanding can help establish the foundation for more useful kinds of dialogue and social action.

There is one final element present. The guided transition to the future promoted by postindustrial statists, modernizers, antimodernizing fundamentalists, and groups prone to disruptive violence ("terrorists") can produce only two responses, both unsatisfactory: the first is breakdown and chaos as consequences of conflict, technology, and failure to adhere to limits; the second is a managed order that excludes the poor and marginal from participation and, over time, widens and hardens the gaps separating those who are saved from those who are damned. Whether these dismal prospects come about gradually or rapidly, they cannot be eliminated by either evolutionary reform of existing state and market structures or revolutionary reversal through violent risings from below. Whether we overcome this dark destiny depends on what takes place on the commanding cultural heights of values, beliefs, and policy orientations in the years ahead, and the degree to which the cumulative impact generates a positive experience of global civil society. Only fundamental shifts in world view can produce a flow of adjustments with sufficient magnitude and coherence. Social movements are *one* important source of exploration and enactment relating to world views associated with the whole planet, with spiritual and ethical solidarity, with reverence for nature, with an outlook of stewardship toward the future, and with new modes of humane governance.

But not the *only* source. Others include certain cultural and technological activities; crises, accidents, and education; "silent revolutions" in life-style and ambition; enlightened behavior by governments and their leaders to solve problems and provide models; cultural artifacts in the form of music, painting, literature; the transnationalizing character of international institutions and professional associations, especially if operating under democratizing value circumstances.

The optimistic view is that this process of cultural revisioning is more basic than the variations of context, and that it is helping establish almost invisibly a series of new political possibilities at *all* levels of social organization. An aspect of the message of the new movements is that "politics" concerns human relations, including especially those within the family and between women and men, and that state control over these domains by coercive apparatus is bound to be resisted. The state is not as domineering as many have supposed, even in highly authoritarian political arrangements. More space exists for "political" resistance and informative politics than has been understood. In this regard, the cumulative impact of social movements may remain largely "underground" until it erupts at a moment of societal crisis and reshapes the relation of forces in an astounding fashion that was not at all evident in the earlier consideration of trends or views of experts. Revolutionary openings, as in 1989, disclose the magnitude of hidden forces for change. To be hidden is not at all the same as to be uncaused or even spontaneous. The events of 1989, although rapidly overtaken by subsequent developments, are impossible to imagine even in retrospect without a decade or more of prior creative struggle by resistance forces.

Similarly, social movements seem attached to hidden political possibilities as yet not seriously acknowledged by the culture. To be ready requires, among other resources for change, conceptions of process (means), visions of end states (alternatives), and an overall image of human nature and freedom that affirms self-transcending energies. To imagine how we can survive and develop with dignity as a species, given the capabilities and technologies at our disposal and the risks and dangers we confront, is the essence of the speculative challenge. To acknowledge limits while recognizing opportunities in the continuous multifaceted struggle is to fashion a future that engenders hope and spontaneous support from as many sources as possible. To name this process in the spirit of democratic transnationalism is to be committed to the seriousness of the project of renewal, and that is why it helps to speak, somewhat in advance of history, of the advent of global civil society.

A FIVE-DIMENSIONAL GUIDE TO PRACTICE:
AN AGENDA FOR THE 1990S

It is pretentious, and even arrogant, for intellectuals to prescribe from the safety and isolation of their ivory tower. Besides, such prescriptions are often sterile, falling on deaf ears.

Yet to relate and interpret ongoing patterns of social struggle is the essence of any engaged political life. In this section the main attempt is to be responsive to and learn from the social movements that are at the front lines of political exploration. Coherence derives from the many varieties of quest to improve the quality of life throughout the planet at all levels of social organization. Since to participate politically is to seek an understanding of hopeful paths to the future, the next section touches upon "the promised land," the outcome of the present journey, which itself is little more than a resting place for a further voyage. In this crucial respect, our conception of human nature and social fulfillment is associated with freedom expressed through a continuous process of self-transcendence.

Such provisional perfectionism may be deceptive at a historical moment when the most obvious imperatives are "defensive"—to save our world, our society, our cities and countryside, our families and personal lives from further decay, from falling apart altogether. Yet the distinction between defensive and creative or restorative social action is artificial. The message from the fields of battle is that no defensive strategy will work unless it rests upon dedication to an affirmative, socially comprehensive vision of human relations. It is not useful for the body politic to recover slightly; the social movements of renewal draw their energy from restorative imagery, an experience of genuine health, and a conviction that such health is normal and attainable. These movements also realize that getting the opportunity to administer the state on behalf of a radical vision is no longer the answer, if it ever was—at least not prior to a dramatic and pervasive reconstruction of practice with respect to relations between women and men, industry and nature, politics and violence, and rich and poor. In this sense, the "politics" of the movements is to constitute a new order woven from within the work of culture, summoning its most profound levels of thought, feeling, and action and by such exertions to provide new contexts and directions for individual and group behavior.

Yet such radical and personal modes of exploration risk becoming precious indulgences, if cut off from more traditional and explicit responses to human suffering. If workers strike or persecuted minorities demonstrate, their privations properly solicit responses from all who identify with the aggrieved, including the new social movements. When the Green

party adopts the cause of Turkish workers in Germany, it is expressing its
conception of human solidarity in a tangible form; for Greens to ignore
such concrete circumstances of distress would impair the clarity of their
symbolic communication and reduce their normative stature. A characteristic feature of modernist projects for political renewal—say, the World
Federalists or the Bahai religion—is their failure to exhibit compassion
by joining in the specific resistance activities of victims of persecution
occasioned by concrete abuses of state or communal power.

In this transitional decade of reaction against the dying, obsolescent,
yet remarkably resilient order evolved in the West by way of state power,
technological innovation, consumerism, and the prevalence of military
and paramilitary modes of conflict resolution, it may help give substance
to normative strivings to propose a five-dimensional agenda (D-5) of interrelated *public sector* concerns.[5]

- *denuclearization:* steps to lessen the risk of nuclear war and to repudiate
  reliance upon nuclear weapons as instruments of interstate conflict, as well
  as challenges directed toward reliance on the civilian use of nuclear power.
  This weaponry has been perceived as "immoral" and "illegal" by influential
  sectors of society, and the Chernobyl tragedy disclosed that the difference
  between civilian nuclear accidents and the military use of nuclear weapons
  is, at best, a matter of degree,[6] the ending of the Cold War amid dangers
  of further proliferation of weapons of mass destruction and serious risks of
  regional warfare strengthen incentives to reduce, if not eliminate, nuclear
  weapons.
- *demilitarization:* steps to reduce the role of military personnel and military methods in governance structures, particularly at the level of the state.
  Such an emphasis stresses civilianization and greater dependence on persuasion and consent in relations between the state and civil society; also,
  shifting allocations of budgetary resources, and a fiscal policy not tied to
  military Keynesianism.
- *depolarization:* steps to moderate the ideological and geopolitical rivalry
  between antagonistic centers of power at global and regional levels and,
  above all, to end moralistic and fatalistic views of conflict as struggles between good ("we") and evil ("they") and of the inevitability of violent
  conflict to such struggles. The 1990s began with the virtual disappearance of East-West polarization but with considerable danger of North-South
  or worse, Islamic/Arabic/fundamentalist versus Christian/West/modernist)
  varieties of polarization and of those of regional scope (India versus Pakistan on the future of Kashmir; the PLO versus Israel on the future of Israel
  and Palestine).
- *development:* steps to assure positive use of renewable and nonrenewable
  resources to satisfy human needs in various countries and regions, as well
  as to diminish damage to the natural environment and risks associated with
  ultrahazardous technologies. Sustainable development, to borrow the catch

phrase of the Brundtland Commission on Environment and Development, means more than reconciling growth with environmental protection; it also implies according a priority to poverty in the development agenda and a bias against the more wasteful forms of consumerism and civic life-style.[7]

- *democratization:* steps to end governmental abuses and to give greater voice and influence to the preferences and attitudes of civil society than to those associated with the special economic and bureaucratic interests that now dominate the structures of state power. The specific shape of democratization varies with the character of current state-society relations, as well as with the situation of a given country in relation to global conflict. It also reflects the specific configurations of political ferment in different situations, but above all it strives to strike a better balance between control from above and demands from below, and to do so within a framework of supervening human rights that imposes limits on both governmental policy and democratic preference.[8]

Action plans, the effectiveness of social movements, and overall patterns of political behavior can be assessed in relation to these five dimensions of world order process. This normative framework suggests a practical and realistic orientation toward action; it is not intended to identify the outer limits of normative potential (a topic briefly considered in the following section).

It is possible to identify strategic arenas of encounter in which the outlook of the new social movements is becoming manifest during this transition period.

RESISTANCE

The strength of existing structures and the threats posed by their main lines of policy continue to generate exemplary actions of resistance by individuals and groups, varying through space and time. The purpose of such resistance is symbolic communication beyond the framework of lawful activity. Resistance implies negation, and it expresses both the urgency of the challenge and the impotence of mainstream responses.

In the settings of human rights, peace, ecology, and feminism, the more severe challenges help generate a culture of resistance. Resistance may be intended to mobilize mass sentiments (as in movements for formal democratization), to block deployment of nuclear weapons systems (antinuclear resistance has taken numerous forms in the United States, Europe, and Pacific Region); and to challenge foreign policy initiatives. The main objective of resistance may be to heighten public consciousness, to challenge the complacency of adherents to the status quo, and to give those who act for the dominant, militarized structures an opportunity to behave differently.

In this transition period, the characteristic tendency of resistance activity is to work from a radical overall orientation to what is being opposed, to insist now upon the social forms of a promised land whose constitutionalism embodies world order values. Connected with this tendency is an oppositional style that converts resistance into an appeal to "the other," seeking conversions rather than casualties in the course of struggle. It reveals a great faith in the normative potential of human nature and organized society, as well as patience to let it unfold slowly over time. When activists from Ground Zero block the tracks of trains carrying components of Trident missiles, they are manifesting not only opposition to nuclear warfare, especially in its first-strike mode, but an overall rejection of violence, an acceptance of nonconsumerist life-styles, a refusal to rely upon patterns of hierarchical organization, an insistence on feminized and spiritualized politics, a depth of commitment that sustains and builds energy without depending on the lure of "victory." This joining of issues and perspectives suggests that "action" includes the construction of cultural foundations for a politics of the future that will live up to the full range of normative pretension, grounded on an implicit sense that the peoples of the world must assume direct responsibility for the overall stewardship of the planet. Also implicit is a transcendence of intra-human boundaries between generations, genders, races, and nationalities; human solidarity is so deeply accepted by this resistance ethos that it seems to be taken for granted.

It is exhilarating to notice how universalistic these forms of resistance, spontaneously enacted in grassroots settings, have become in tone and symbolic content, despite the unevenness of existing situations in various countries and regions. The theme song of the Great Peace Journey, a transnational peace initiative originated in the mid-1980s by a group of Swedish women, announces "we are gentle, angry people," expressing the paradoxical attitudes that underlie a decisive rejection of what is and an equally decisive refusal to fight fire with fire. Of course, in many critical parts of the world there is no space, as yet, for public forms of resistance—or, more accurately, popular forces have yet to discover the "hidden" spaces that even authoritarian politics cannot control. If "politics" is extended to encompass the "personal" and "private," resistance can never be altogether precluded, no matter how totalitarian the intention of rulers.

DELEGITIMATION

Closely connected with resistance activities is a wide array of movement undertakings that cast doubt directly or indirectly on the legitimacy of existing governmental procedures and institutions for assessing guilt and innocence. The most tangible expression of this doubt takes the form of challenges to the right of the existing government to govern; a more limited expression is the organization of "tribunals," on the authority of citizen initiative, by which to judge official policies.

The democratization movements of the late 1980s, both those that succeeded and those that failed, emerged out of the sinews of civil society in reaction to oppressive patterns of governance perceived as "illegitimate." In such a setting, especially given the tactical and principled refusal of these movements to challenge illegitimate governments by recourse to violence, the main purpose of political action was to express censure and to demoralize the leadership itself. Aided by Gorbachev's acceptance of the critique mounted by these movements, the leadership in a series of East European countries collapsed beneath the weight of its own illegitimacy. Even repressive leaders normally depend on a semblance of consent by the citizenry—or a mandate of heaven—to legitimate their political rule. If illegitimacy can be effectively established, it can become an overwhelmingly powerful weapon in the hands of those who seek a new, more democratic political order.

The pioneer exploration of the tribunal mode of judicial scrutiny was undertaken in the late 1960s under the aegis of Bertrand Russell to inquire into the legality of the policies being then pursued by the United States in Vietnam.[9] The rationale for the Russell Tribunal was a self-proclaimed finding that the failure of both governments and international institutions to protect the sovereign rights of Vietnam created a normative vacuum that could be appropriately filled by individuals of high moral standing. At the time, the substance of the allegations against U.S. war policies was what made the tribunal controversial, but in a more profound sense its radical quality was bound up with the implicit rejection of a statist monopoly of the forms of governance. Individuals and groups who set up a tribunal to consider issues of public policy represent an effort to wrest control over the wellsprings of legitimacy from the state, and it is true that their motivation is not open-minded but results from a condemnation of the policies that preceded the existence of the inquiry. Liberal sensibilities may therefore be offended by the one-sidedness of the proceedings, but their distress varies with the political context; the same Western liberals who were outraged by the partisan character of the Russell Tribunal applauded the parallel initiatives associated with Soviet dissidents in the West who constituted tribunals in the early 1980s to pass judgment upon Soviet practices in relation to international standards for human rights.

What is suggestive here is the dynamic of this process. Since the Vietnam War, dozens of tribunals have been established in Europe to reach decisions about controversial issues of policy. The League for the Rights of Peoples with headquarters in Rome, which set up the Permanent People's

Tribunal in 1976, provides various resistance groups with an institutional avenue by which to develop their case against the legitimacy of the existing order, whether the matter at stake is intervention, environmental policies, or human rights.

Operating along similar lines are the commissions of inquiry constituted by private initiative. There have been a large number of such commissions in the area of human rights. The MacBride Commission, established by a group of prominent citizens in England, investigated and issued a report on the international law aspects of the 1982 Israeli invasion of Lebanon.[10] Again, the commissions do not exert much influence but do disclose frustration with the capacities of governments to uphold or comply with international law and morality and a refusal to accept governmental authority as final.

ACCOUNTABILITY

The fragmented political organization of the planet may not coincide with the locale of harmful effects associated with the activities of sovereign states. As a consequence, issues of environmental protection and conservation, of ultrahazardous technologies, of antimilitarist peace initiatives may involve the response of social movements in civil society to the activities of foreign governments.

The July 1985 explosion of the Greenpeace vessel the *Rainbow Warrior*, as the result of a French intelligence operation carried out while the ship was moored in Auckland with approval at the highest level of government, is emblematic of the link between resistance and accountability.[11] The efforts by the New Zealand government to hold France accountable were rather feeble, especially given the blatancy of the encroachment on sovereign rights and the resulting loss of life. But France possessed considerable economic leverage as a major importer of some specialty exports (lamb brains, for example) that were perceived as important sources of foreign exchange for New Zealand's struggling economy. As well, New Zealand's government, was ambivalent about the Greenpeace militancy on the nuclear testing issue, despite its own opposition to the French nuclear testing program in the Pacific region.

This instance of state-sponsored terrorism illustrates the accountability gap, especially where the principal culprits are safely situated in a distant capital city and, as here, only intelligence operatives were temporarily detained. Through a mediation effort by the United Nations Secretary General, New Zealand did at least receive a monetary award and the assurance that the particular agents would be confined by French authorities on a remote Pacific island for several years—a duty quietly abridged without eliciting further protest from New Zealand officials. It is worth pondering the difference in treatment accorded "private" and "public" acts of political violence that cause civilian death. During the Vietnam War, an antiwar group of militants exploded a bomb in a military research laboratory at the University of Wisconsin, killing a graduate student who was unexpectedly working in the building late at night. The chief defendant, Karl Armstrong, was sentenced to a long prison term and served more than eight years. The contrast with the treatment of those French agents who, in the course of their duties, exploded two bombs without any concern about loss of life illuminates the differences in reaction to state violence and civic violence.

The wider Greenpeace provocation was to monitor, protest, and resist French nuclear testing in the region of the Pacific islands. Here again, the statist refusal to desist from testing that was harmful to health, the environment, and resources indicates the weakness of the established legal procedures of international society to challenge official behavior. Only a private transnational actor was able to mount a challenge. It operated with a framework of militant nonviolence but generated a violent style of statist reaction. Without a political system that makes governments accountable, issues of this sort can often be addressed only by action undertaken without official sanction.

World War II created among the victorious powers a momentary flourish of commitment to an ethos of accountability on the part of political, military, and societal leadership. This flourish produced the famous war crimes trials, especially of defeated leaders of Germany and Japan, held in Nuremberg and Tokyo, and the resulting body of law generalized as the Nuremberg Principles, which affirmed the importance of holding *all* governmental leaders internationally responsible for *future* crimes of states. Yet the impulse to establish a permanent framework of accountability remains suspect, as it was always intertwined with the immediate setting, which included a grand display of victors' justice and an interest in educating the world about the losing side's policies of genocide and cruelty. There was never a willingness to consider the behavior of the leaders of the winning side from the perspective of international law; hence, the experiment in accountability was flawed from the outset. Subsequently, these governments resisted most efforts to institutionalize the Nuremberg framework and acted in conflict situations in a manner that would have produced criminal indictments had the Nuremberg Principles been implemented by the establishment of procedures and institutions in the years after 1945. Nevertheless, with these gestures of imposed accountability a seed was planted, however unintentionally.

Revival and Appropriation of Nuremberg. Social movements have been recently drawn to the symbolism and rootedness of the unfulfilled Nuremberg promise and have sought to gain control over its symbolic appeal to conscience. A Nuremberg Pledge, prepared in December 1985 and circulated among lawyers' groups throughout the world, commits individuals within the sphere of their lives as citizens and professionals to uphold the Nuremberg Principles and to extend their application to new areas.

More significant is the use of Nuremberg in the setting of citizen efforts to question the legality of foreign policy initiatives that rely either on illegal weaponry or on overall patterns of military action. In Europe and the United States, many peace activists have engaged in "civil disobedience" under a claim of right: namely, that international law binds governments and that individual citizens have a duty to secure compliance. Although courts and judges have generally repudiated these challenges to governmental supremacy in the war/peace and human rights areas, the movement to extend the domain of constitutionalism to encompass foreign policy has begun to have some success. This reliance on law against government is a definite reversal of outlook for political radicals, contrasting with Marxist-Leninist dismissals of legal institutions and procedures as inevitably tainted by class origins and affinities.

Dealing with Deposed Dictators. Ever since the Shah fled Iran in early 1979, there have been calls for some kind of legal process to punish the perpetrators of alleged crimes of state, as well as to recover national wealth wrongfully converted to private use. "The ghosts of Nuremberg" underlay the resolve of the initial postmilitary government of Raul Alfonsin in Argentina to proceed against those military and political officials responsible for atrocities (torture and disappearances) during the period of harsh military rule. Efforts to attach accountability, however, were resisted by those sectors of the bureaucracy associated with the policies of the prior regime, especially by the armed forces and the internal security establishment. This kind of resistance in Argentina and also in Uruguay, Brazil, and Chile threatened the viability of the new democratic order, leading to a variety of compromises and retreats in relation to the commitment to hold accountable those responsible for crimes of state. Indeed, a reverse practice and doctrine of "impunity" developed in the late 1980s, shielding offenders from indictment and judicial process.

In 1990 there were calls to try Saddam Hussein as a war criminal by application of Nuremberg standards. Even former U.S. Secretary of State George Shultz endorsed such an objective, and may represent the first time since World War II that a prominent person associated with government has proposed a specific prosecution based on Nuremberg, a suspect endorsement given its self-serving North-South implications.

Protecting Peoples and Resources from Technological Breakdown.

Bhopal and Chernobyl suggest the complex phenomena at issue here. Distant perpetrators of harm to individuals can withdraw behind the safety of national boundaries, and government at different levels of political organization is either implicated in the event or fails to respond adequately. As a consequence, civil society is challenged to fashion effective humanitarian and political responses, to question whether governments and corporations can be entrusted with full authority to deploy and regulate the ultrahazardous technologies that are increasingly relied upon in modern productive enterprises. This sort of concern gives way, in turn, to issues of life-style, values, and the meaning of life. It also stimulates "volunteers" and organizing from below. Young people in India spontaneously set up a series of paramedical programs in Bhopal to help victims do physical therapy over prolonged periods to recover use of their lungs; the Soviet rivals competing for the world chess championship in 1986 both donated all their winnings to disaster relief on behalf of Chernobyl victims.

Of course, it is better to prevent an accident than to assure a constructive reaction, but once there is a breakdown, existing modes even of extra-statal response seem weak and ineffectual. There is a need to reach the various layers of authority that shared responsibility in a complex net of relations involving local, intermediate, and central governmental participation and complex linkages with the corporate operation, itself complex and diffuse. The political sense that governmental and corporate actors should be made accountable is becoming a strong mobilizing issue, but it may be a difficult and controversial matter to agree upon the nature of the harm and, even more, to allocate responsibility.

The Soviet government responded to the Chernobyl event by depriving some of those charged with negligence of their Communist party status, which entailed a loss of privileges and was undoubtedly intended as a kind of social ostracism as well. Whatever the merits of such "sanctions," this response involved the imposition of accountability by an extralegal mechanism available to the state; holding responsible the individuals who act on behalf of bureaucracies is partly intended to reassure the citizenry that the state is concerned with societal well-being. There is, of course, also a real possibility that in the aftermath of Chernobyl the Moscow leadership wanted to shift as much responsibility as possible to the level of the Ukraine, a constituent republic. Such a move would seem associated with the new awareness by all governments—even those who reject liberal democratic forms of accountability via elections, checks and balances, and the like—that their legitimacy and maturity are being drawn into question by their inability to protect society from the ghoulish dangers of technological breakdown (whether by negligence, accident, or subversion).[12]

Other approaches to accountability are being developed in various substantive and geographic settings. The United States Congress has in the last decade started to legislate "sanctions" to implement international standards on whaling activities and to discourage fishing methods that imperil protected species (for example, indiscriminate tuna fishing that results in the capture and death of many dolphins). The basic technique is to require the executive branch of government to certify the existence of prohibited activities and then, after due notice and a period of time, to attach policy consequences, such as imposing prohibitions on imports related to the violations. A similar approach has been evolved to relate the extension of foreign assistance to the maintenance of democracy (or, at least, civilian government) and the protection of human rights.

RELIGIOUS POLITICS

Not all forms of religiously oriented activism are relevant here.[13] Excluded are those that rely on violence, seek to transform the state into a theocracy, and fail to incorporate the whole of humanity into their professed imagery of salvation. Obviously, fundamentalisms are excluded, but so are liberating struggles that employ violence in a systematic fashion, except possibly in circumstances where violent resistance is the only alternative to acute oppression. It is complicated to assess reliance on violence by the Sikh movement for autonomy in the Punjab, by the Sandinistas during their struggle against Somoza's forces, or by the African National Congress in the course of the anti-apartheid movement. It is necessary to determine the degree of oppression and oppressive violence, and the capacity of the dominated political culture to fashion effective nonviolent alternatives. One side of the complexity of holding commitments to both nonviolence and liberation was captured by the decision of the Colombian revolutionary priest Camilo Torres back in the 1960s to take part in guerrilla combat situations but to carry an unloaded gun.

What seems to be arising out of the efforts by social movements to reshape the cultural grounds of politics is a new combination of challenge and opportunity for churches and religious traditions. It is a challenge in that it certainly jeopardizes the protected status of church and clergy and may involve severe retributive violence; it is an opportunity in that it invites churches and clergy to join the people in their resistance and quest for renewal and to put religion on the side of justice and of the victims of injustice. Throughout the 1980s, churches and clergy provided resources, facilities, and crucial encouragement to the social movements themselves, offering an invaluable kind of reassurance that the new militancy was not alien to widely felt mainstream values and traditions. A religious element also is congenial with the antimaterialist, antisecular character of the new movements, as well as with their universalistic sense of human identity.

Even secular movements with an antiecclesiastical outlook have come to welcome the spiritual awakening of adherents of formal religion, and to alter their own style and program so as to build coalitions between revolution and religion.

Sacramental Politics. The renewed effort to follow this very old and hallowed path seeking to gain secular goals by spiritual means, is largely nonviolent. It is illustrated most vividly by the words and acts of Miguel d'Escoto, the Nicaraguan minister of foreign affairs during the decade of Sandinista governance and one of four priests in the Sandinista cabinet. As Father d'Escoto describes his own urge toward creativity in high governmental office: "We Christians have our own special arms that we must use—prayer, fasting, processions with hymns, vigils." [14] Such a perspective led to what he called *la insurrección evangélica* (evangelical insurrection) and produced his celebrated *el ayuno por la paz* (fast for peace) for thirty days in July 1985, initiated as a protest against U.S. aid to the contras and an effort to gain the upper hand in the "spiritual war" with the upper echelons of the Catholic clergy in Nicaragua, especially Cardinal Miguel Obando y Bravo. D'Escoto succeeded in endowing his fast with symbolic content and political significance. For any close observer, such a sacramental approach to power completely contradicted the propaganda of the Reagan administration and the anti-Sandinistas that the leaders in Managua were hardened Marxist-Leninists with an ingrained totalitarian mind-set. The fast attracted attention in many places, especially in church circles throughout Latin America. There were displays of "prophetic solidarity," including many endorsements by Catholic bishops and other Christian leaders.

Subsequently, Miguel d'Escoto initiated *el Viacrucis por la paz* (the Way of the Cross for peace), adapting a traditional expression of popular piety in Nicaragua that draws on the symbolic resonance of Jesus' suffering and vindication during the last days of his life. This *Viacrucis* started on the first Friday of Lent, February 14, 1986, in Jalapa, near the Honduran border, and progressed to Managua, some 300 kilometers away, over the next two weeks. The procession of pilgrims, including the foreign minister, stayed at peasant homes and took part in religious gatherings at churches en route. At Esteli the local bishop embraced and blessed d'Escoto before 20,000 people. The entire procession was an effort to sanctify the Sandinista cause, to win popular support, and to express a distinctive revolutionary identity.

In a larger setting, d'Escoto's approach represented an overall Sandinista search for political survival, given the pressure and hostility of the United States, and a mobilization of support within and beyond Nicaragua. It complemented Nicaragua's recourse to the World Court, an appeal to international law as a way of resisting U.S. efforts to destroy the Sandinistas. Both sacramental politics and recourse to international law rest partly on the assumption that it matters to have the moral and legal advantage in a struggle between adversaries of unequal wealth and destructive capacity. Such an assumption arises out of the same sources of normative strength invoked by new social movements, seeking to prevail by their numbers and resolve but without reliance on destructive force. A distinct concept of struggle is implicit, one that depends for its outcome on an inner dynamic: how strong the will and capacity to resist and endure pain on the "weak" side, and how strong the will and capacity to inflict pain on the "powerful" side.

Closely connected are other undertakings with religious backing that involve witnessing and vigiling. Witness for Peace, organized by U.S. churches, sent several thousand ordinary Americans to dangerous war zones in Nicaragua during the 1980s to report the real character of combat, thereby challenging official Washington's propagandistic presentation of the contra war. As well as an expression of conscience, such witnessing becomes a personal commitment to discover "the truth" at a time when even in constitutional democracies, reality is filtered to the citizenry by way of state-organized disinformation and propaganda campaigns and a subservient media.

In this period the images and forms of religious traditions can be summoned on behalf of peace and justice, to challenge a purely military conception of political struggle. To the extent that spiritual and moral energies are thus mobilized, the cultural setting of politics shifts. This potentiality is not the only one, however; religion can, as easily, serve the interests of those in control of oppressive structures. The issue is in part one of relating religious influence to the weight of conflicting pressures in a variety of contexts.

Feminizing Religion. The spiritual resources of religious tradition have been deformed by patriarchal features and structures. A commitment to the full emancipation of women implies a new cultural striving not only to embody sexual equality but, more than this, to overcome the patriarchal bias of texts, rituals, and institutions. A new language of the spirit is required, and being sought, as well as practices that accentuate nurturing, mothering, feminist relationality and specify the sacred as a reflection of the feminine.[15]

EMPOWERING TRANSNATIONAL ARENAS

The global scale of some basic trends, especially in relation to economic and environmental policy, have induced governments to seek global frameworks for assessment and prescription. As a consequence, starting at Stockholm in 1972 with environmental issues (followed by questions of population, food, and human settlements), using the organizing capabilities and formal auspices of the United Nations, intergovernmental conferences were held to clarify substantive challenges. These occasions aroused media interest, generated a considerable body of specialist literature, and revealed vividly the enfeebling constraints on action if it is conceived in conventional state-to-state terms. Such meetings confined the severity of the global-scale problems emergent in international life but also displayed the insufficiency of capabilities on the international level, creating an overall impression of empty rhetoric and impotence, which deepened cynicism about prospects for collective responses at the global level.

Whatever vitality did emerge was often associated with the so-called counterconferences, various assemblages of activists and groups concerned about the subject matter, drawn to the place by the glamour of the formal event, but expressing a more radical conception of what was needed. The counterconference outlook instinctively manifested an ethos of human solidarity, as well as an understanding that the new political reality described in earlier chapters as global civil society was present in nascent form.

The most recent event of this character was the United Nations World Conference on Women held in Nairobi in July 1985. It brought together women from all over the world, gathered in the form of official delegations of governments, to discern the actualities of gender discrimination and to work out a declaration of response and a call to action. Apparently, according to accounts by participants, feminist energy dissolved the characteristic formalism of international governmental events. Even more exciting for participants were the informal, often spontaneous counterconference happenings.

One planned nonofficial dimension of the conference was provided by the Peace Tent, a large blue-and-white striped tent set up at the University of Nairobi by Feminists International for Peace and Food "to provide the women of the world with a space for frank, informal discussions, sharing, singing and dancing; the rules stated that, when anyone addressed a group, there was to be no clapping or cheering, no booing or hissing; each woman was to be accorded equal respect." A statement prepared by the organizers expressed the spirit of this undertaking: "The Peace Tent is the international feminist alternative to men's conflict and war. It is the place where finding peaceful solutions to conflicts, both in personal lives and in the public arena, is the priority. . . . In the Peace Tent, women can substitute women's truths for patriarchal lies through dialogue, films and exhibits, women's joy for patriarchal pessimism through song, dance and art. The aim of the Peace Tent is to bring women's peacemaking will and consciousness to the world which so desperately needs it." [16] Evident here, is the reliance on cultural forms to attain political results and the expansion of the political to include what was hitherto regarded as personal, private. On this occasion, feminism endorsed a holistic view of action that defined its positive energy by contrast with masculine reliance on violence, war, and hierarchy.

The delegates to the Nairobi conference reported back the sense of excitement and empowerment that arose directly from the discovery by women from diverse cultural and class backgrounds of the powerful affinities associated with their shared experience of both the feminine predicament and the feminine transforming possibility.

In general, these global occasions create transnational networks of individuals and groups across existing boundaries and substantiate the reality claimed for global civil society. Additionally, they make evident the impotence of governments in the face of global-scale problems and suffering, thus contributing to the process of statist delegitimation. Indeed, negative reactions have become so prevalent that governments have grown reluctant to sponsor such events, realizing that the good effects of displaying concern about the shortcomings of the world are more than offset by the bad effects of exhibiting their collective inadequacy. As a result, future networks and global arenas may have to be created by the new movements themselves—not an easy task, especially for groups beset by funding problems.

ENVISIONING THE LONG REVOLUTION

> Once the inevitabilities are challenged, we begin gathering our resources for a journey of hope.
>
> Raymond Williams, *The Year 2000*

Whether the goals and processes of transformation can become self-sustaining for large numbers of adherents is a matter of controversy. Does it deepen motivation of activists to clarify the contours of the promised land? Or is it dispiriting because it lacks a definite enemy to struggle against, defines evil as an abstraction, and can never be specified with enough plausibility, consensus, and vibrancy? The evidence is conflicting, yet it seems worth drawing out some shared normative expectations about the character of a transformed world, if only to improve communication among the many different social actors and to strengthen the overall sense of a unified direction for radical reformist efforts. Such reflections are conditioned by the caveats earlier set forth, especially the limits on specific context in a world of uneven experience and the provincial and historically constrained character of the perspective of any particular observer.

The new social movements of the West have lost some of their particularity by expressing a certain overall commitment to the future that draws on common elements: a central preoccupation with "sustainable development" implying restraints on market forces and skepticism about quantitative yardsticks of productive excellence; repudiation of war and political violence as inevitable and acceptable instruments of social conflict; adoption of transnational identity patterns and affinities that arise from shared commitments; support for the claims of oppressed peoples and a commitment to greater equality of life-style across societies and regions; imagery of wholeness as expressive of the liberation process and as compatible with nationalist goals of self-determination; skeptical and selective attitudes toward technology and modernizing forms of development; a refusal to regard access to state power as the prime stake of political activity, even if formal procedures of democracy are established; emphasis on local, personal, grassroots mobilization and engagement as the crucial test of political potency; protection of and communion with nature as part of the new political space; promotion of democracy and human rights at the state level to assure minimum decency and to provide political space for exploration, reconstruction, and alternative forms of relationship, production, management, and organization; an emergent awareness that the decisive political battleground for the remainder of this century is associated with an activation of cultural energies for reshaping prevailing attitudes, myths, beliefs, virtues, vices, world views, and underlying assumptions about the character of human nature.

The presentation of the more visionary content implicit in the new politics is not meant to remove it from present relevance. This material informs present activity by being latent in the consciousness of most participants, despite the realization that the prevailing order is antagonistic and may remain so for a long time. The visionary perspective is intended to prefigure (without prescribing) the content of the promised land and to facilitate clarifying dialogue between those in various rooted circumstances in the world. The preceding section identified a five-dimensional field of normative progress during a transitional period of involvement that is ongoing and of indefinite duration. This section is removed from history in the limited sense that it describes a desirable future that can unfold out of an altered cultural setting.

Envisioning a future implies a coherent claim to regard alternative ways of organizing and conceiving of basic life structures as possible within history. The importance of coherence encourages a mutually re-inforcing set of predominant features. Several aspects of the interrelated societal whole are discussed here: security; development; environment; governance; world view. Such a classificatory scheme seeks only to high-light critical features, not to exhaust or reduce the overall social reality.

SECURITY

The ideal of protecting individuals and groups with minimum reliance on violence implies substantially disarmed military establishments and weaponless police force. Protection has a subjective side (feeling secure) and an objective side (being secure). Hostile propaganda can create gaps in the connection between feeling secure and being secure. A secure social order feels secure and is secure.

The current focus on security in international relations as specified by governments is built up around what has come to be called "national security." Such a focus emphasizes the security of elites and regimes, not necessarily of society and people. By contrast, the visionary imagery of security emphasizes people, society as a whole; it does not confine the scope of protected persons to a specific group. Desirable forms of secu-rity emphasize interdependence and a cooperative set of relations based on mutual benefit: We cannot be secure unless others are secure, includ-ing being satisfied with their economic and political situation. Such an understanding of security is almost diametrically opposed to current stra-tegic forms of security associated with structures of hierarchy and the logic of deterrence. According to this logic, we deter better if we in-timidate others, making them feel and be insecure in the sense of being maximally vulnerable. Since both sides in international (or other) con-flict relations subscribe to such thinking, an arms race almost inevitably ensues, especially if resources are being devoted to military research and development with the objective of gaining the upper hand or, at least, not being relatively disadvantaged. When a conflict formation dissolves, as has been the case with recent East-West relations, the arms race men-tality may also dissolve—or it may persist in altered form by generating a new focus of antagonism, as has occurred in North-South relations.

In a revised security atmosphere, reassurance about intentions and capabilities would be a major undertaking. To avoid having others be or feel threatened by violent behavior presupposes equitable structures in the world economy, procedures for resolving disputes, and "legislative" adjustments in relations between political communities. Implicit in the new social movements is a double premise: violence does not protect in an acceptable manner, especially at an international level; in an altered cultural setting it is practical to achieve security nonviolently.

Of course, there are many intermediate stages, varying with the character of local, national, and regional circumstances. Of great importance is the demilitarization of state-society relations within given countries, and a shift toward nonprovocative defense postures, doctrines, capabilities in state-to-state settings, especially in those strategic settings where nuclear weapons are now deployed and relied upon.

The attainment of people's security as outlined above cannot be separated from other transformations that undercut the character of current patterns and modalities of conflict. What makes people secure in a happy family is dependent, above all, on an atmosphere of love and gentleness. Whether a deepening experience of human solidarity, the adoption of an ecological ethos, and the establishment of a global welfare system and social safety net can enlarge the social unit that experiences happiness is, of course, unknown—but there is no solid reason to doubt the possibility.

RESOURCE USE

The ideal is to encourage the efficient and sustainable use of resources to assure production flows that will satisfy basic human needs and will not cause large gaps between classes, regions, and societies. Development can be shaped in many satisfying, acceptable directions, but the constructive use of resources for positive and sustainable human ends is a unifying theme.

This ideal contrasts with current actualities: wasteful use of resources; environmentally destructive patterns of production; dedication of abundant resources to military and paramilitary purposes and to luxuries, despite large sectors of acute poverty and many urgent needs for collective goods within existing states and in certain regions. The prevailing forms of social accounting and operating procedures for market mechanisms allocates resources in a manner that frustrates efforts to use them for human betterment in an ecologically sustainable manner. At the same time, economies organized under the direct control of the state have been totally discredited.

A major obstacle on the path of the ideal has been acquiescence by organized labor to the dynamics of market capitalism. Capitalist societies must develop greater sensitivity to ethical and ecological factors. If such sensitivity emerges in the next few decades, it need not result in an austere life-style that reduces the world to a common subsistence standard, an ordeal of grayness. As with security, this visionary kind of resource use and planning cannot become established within materialist, acquisitive cultures, especially as deformed by demand creation through advertising.

The oil crises of recent decades disclose the close connection between the hierarchial structures of international political and economic life and the war system; hierarchy of control over resources implies reliance on war. Resource equity is associated with the phasing out of war in human relations. Given the unequal and uneven distribution of vital resources for energy and food, more globally constituted arrangements for price, distribution, and allocation will be required. Such arrangements entail a cooperative restructuring of governance for the planet, visionary yet attainable, and indispensable if modern industrialism is to be superseded in a nontragic manner.

It seems possible to conceive of the emergence of developmental pluralism with respect to appropriate resource use, and planning that is constrained by a shared cultural notion of human need and ecological balance. Without sentimentalizing the distant past, we can recognize that indigenous peoples seemed often to achieve and maintain for centuries an equilibrium between society and nature in a variety of tribal settings, informed by reverence for nature and by an underlying ethos of stewardship and conservation.[17] Whether postmodern society and societies at various stages of industrialization can reconstitute such a cultural grounding for positive development is uncertain. At the very least, social movements seem alive to this crucial reorientation based on values and no longer believe that lifting encumbrances from the operations of the market or assuring that production processes are nominally controlled by the working class will provide the basis for a positive human future.

ENVIRONMENT

Closely associated with security and resource policy are relations between production and consumption processes and the maintenance of environmental quality. The modern industrial era—spurred on by the illusions of limitless growth, an ascending curve of profits and productivity, and ever higher standards of living for all classes—paid virtually no attention to harmful environmental effects until the early 1970s. Then a variety of forms of pollution, especially of basic resources previously taken for granted (air, water, land), caused a momentary cultural tremor. This surge of concern was climaxed by the appearance of the Club of Rome's study *The Limits to Growth* in 1972.

Unfortunately, early attention to the environment was linked to an apocalyptic view of history and emerged without benefit of either a politics of positive adjustment or an ethics of empathy. As a result, environmental warnings tended to be assimilated into the noise of the culture and were treated as largely exhortatory. Public pressure did cause some governmental efforts at the regulation of toxic effects, disaster response, and energy conservation, but no fundamental changes of the humanity-nature equation were initiated in critical areas of transportation, ultrahazardous technology, petro-chemicals in agriculture, waste disposal, and city planning.

Because of the absence of any explicit normative outlook, many who identified with the poor in the North or with the South, dismissed environmental concerns at first, even regarding such concerns as a sinister means by which to perpetuate hierarchy and exploitation in the post-colonial era. As detrimental environmental impacts began to be felt around the world, however, this attitude has shifted dramatically, and in the 1980s those who most closely represented the grassroots poor in the Third World became convinced that the control and protection of local resources against removal and degradation was at the core of political action. India, for instance, has emerged as a hotbed of grassroots environmentalism with hundreds of separate, independent groups as well as more generally concerned organizations. The growth of respect for the cultural perspectives of indigenous peoples has also grounded environmental issues in a variety of interpretations about right livelihood for individuals and groups.

The ideal of environmental policy is to preserve and even enhance the resource base of the planet as a whole and of distinct communities. This ideal is more than a matter of preserving the material conditions for life on the planet. It also expresses an important feature of the new religious consciousness that endows nature with a sacred and spiritual quality, closely associated with human fulfillment; to destroy nature, or poison it, is to manifest an acute form of alienation. The entry into space exploration, despite its diversion of scarce resources, has beneficially reinforced this kind of awe in the face of the vastness and splendor of nature. Rediscovered in space is a sense of human limits less anguishing than that revealed by such high-technology frontiers as suggested by the chilling metaphor "nuclear winter."

The visionary revitalization of the environment also emphasizes the intimate connection between local action and general dispositions of mind and spirit. To view resources, including human labor, as a valued end, not just as a means to more abundant production, is of the essence of achieving a social order based on freedom, mutual respect, and self-esteem.

GOVERNANCE

Not necessarily government but governance seems an ingredient of an envisioned promised land. The quest is for the gentlest forms of authority, forms that do not intrude on freedoms, do not create a huge gap between citizens and institutions established for their benefit and yet facilitate security, resource use, and environmental quality. Obviously, core concerns arising out of oppressive governmental structures have to do with bureaucracy, violence, and technology. In the present world political setup, the most general forms of authority are closely associated with the war system, the arms race, and an anti-democratic style of upholding "national security," even in political atmospheres that otherwise possess the forms of constitutional governance.

The minimal elements of humane governance include responsiveness to citizenry; unconditional respect for human rights; reliance on education and persuasion to achieve societal order; mechanisms for alleviating grievances at the pre-crisis stage; acceptable ethical standards involving welfare for those who are deprived and the absence of discrimination among diverse ethnic, religious, and racial groupings. Also essential yet more difficult to envision is the weakening of existing political boundaries, many of which have been established by conquest and sustained by violence and intimidation—and at the same time, the strengthening of boundaries surrounding what Christian Bay usefully identified as "natural political communities": those held spontaneously together by bonds of affection, feelings of affinity, and tradition. To enjoy this sort of political participation is not at all incompatible with a simultaneous acknowledgment of species identity, an acknowledgment spurred by both practical and normative considerations. The possibilities for governance of this type depends on a substantially transformed cultural setting along the lines specified.[18]

Because of our emphasis on new social movements and global-scale problems, governance patterns must be receptive both to planetary requirements and to those of a local and personal character. Space cooperation, as a metaphor of the obsolescence of action that is the exclusive product of the political will and technological prowess of a given territorial fragment, can be treated as a metaphor of an emergent holism. At the same time, issues of sexual deviance and child abuse suggest the obsolescence of a political domain that excludes the private and personal. Such an enlargement of politics should not be confused with the advocacy of intrusiveness. On the contrary, the essence of governance would include strengthening respect for privacy and the encouragement of practices of tolerance.

Ideal governance ultimately implies self-governance and spontaneous governance. As in the earlier phases of Marxist visionary thought, it implies a withering away of the state, especially of crude forms of governance (in the mask of "government"). Unlike the Marxist tradition, however, societal preparation for humane governance involves transforming the cultural grounding of politics rather than awaiting the ascent of the pro-letariat, as the last and most inclusive liberating class, by way of violent revolutionary victory. The flaw at the root of state socialist disappoint-ment is to suppose that self-dissolving power structures embodied in insti-tutional bureaucracies can be established within the current framework of materialist civilization and a geopolitical order built around hierarchy and exploitation and resting upon capabilities for violent self-help (that is, war).

This view of humane governance is tied to cultural preparation, a process by which the legitimacy and resolve associated with current structures of government and hegemony are eroded as other modes of governance gain prominence. The exploratory domains of the new social movements provide learning experiences—not always easy—in less hier-archal and more cooperative social, political, and economic structures.

ETHOS

By ethos is meant values, world view, and the ground upon which normative positions stand. Some kind of reinforcing metaphysics is nec-essary to clarify why particular values are preferred and their realization so fervently desired. This grounding also helps deepen an affirmation of human solidarity and explains why species identity is a source of both pride and hope, not just a sentimental wish at this time of evolving human consciousness. The cosmopolitan direction of new identity patterns is taken for granted by many social movements with particularly strong attachments to local identities.

In a sense, the ethos of a promised land is the consciousness, mani-festing itself in all domains of existence, that includes expectations about security, well-being, and fulfillment for individuals and groups. This ethos is necessarily deferential to the local and diverse, as positive elements in the vitality of cultural interaction, and at the same time sensitive to the historical occasion for broader frameworks of cooperation, interaction, and shared exploration based on mutual benefit. An important dimension of this ethos is a genuine attitude of stewardship, not only to preserve the prospects of generations to come but also to enact through policy and behavior respectful attitudes toward the ecological limits of human endeavor, including a conservatism about risking the long-term effects of ultrahazardous technologies.

This ethos implies a reorientation of citizenship in order to go be-yond loyal and diligent participation in the collective life of a territorially delimited society that qualifies as a sovereign state. The citizen sensitive to the claims of this emergent ethos needs to extend his or her notions of participation in dimensions of both space (beyond the territory of any particular state) and time (beyond the present, reclaiming past wisdom and safeguarding future generations). Citizenship so conceived is not meant as an affirmation of a nonexistent global community; to become "a world citizen" by self-proclamation is both too easy and ineffectual. Rather, implicit in the ethos is the outlook described earlier as that of the citizen-pilgrim, one who is embarked on a journey of deliverance that is centered on the continuing struggle to create a future approaching normative horizons that now seem mere aspirations; one who inhabits as an informing context a rudimentary stage of global civil society.

This envisioned ethos is also an aspect of the emergent "realism" that awaits transition from government to governance.

CONCLUDING OBSERVATIONS

A big uncertainty is whether the new social movements will be able to adapt, evolve, and grow or possibly reemerge, borne by the same current of normative energy but wearing different masks. Another is whether their techniques of transnational political action will challenge established, oppressive structures or will coexist by occupying space at the margins that is accepted as a safety valve or as a supplement to processes of co-option. In an assessment of prospects, it is important to resist the trap of determining relative capabilities by measurable strengths. The potency of the new movements is normative, without tangible substance, but capable of effecting sudden conversions that acknowledge symbolic leaders and change the composition of cultural soil. This potency may also be disguised, being borne invisibly or latently by the culture, until it erupts as an unexpectedly powerful tendency. The political possibilities are connected with the gradual establishment of a new foundational ethos, a kind of "continental drift" associated with the unknown geology of cultural transformation.[19] With such an ethos, confidence grows that radical change is plausible, that global civil society has already started to provide a nurturing set of possibilities for the future.

There is another distinguishing trait here. Positive expectations about the future no longer depend on staying with what Raymond Williams called "Plan X": that is, guided management at the state level that proceeds on the basis of the given to seek calculated advantages for the self.[20] Such commitments do not depend on the mystical liberation of violent challenge, whether by terrorist or social revolution. Nor do they suppose a *satori* of practical wisdom resulting from trauma at the brink, the apocalyptic view either of responding or succumbing. Nor do they place much confidence in the fear-driven imagery of "the four horseman" grimly galloping across the planet spreading disease, famine, war, and misery.

Social movements are confident because of their inner faith in cultural creativity and the power of a new ethos to transform the old order. In the drama unfolding in our time these new movements need reinforcement from a reconstituted movement of less advantaged workers which relocates its understanding of both the means and goals of struggle, and from a resurgent religious activism which finds its spiritual significance in adherence to an envisioned ethos of cultural transformation. As citizen-pilgrims carry forward these struggles in various spheres, it is likely that new images of political community will take shape in the imagination of participants, reestablishing our sense of what is possible and desirable. From such a perspective, the sharply demarcated managerial style of politics will seem an increasingly archaic, yet still dangerous and destructive, approach to organizing collective life for the future of the planet.

PART THREE

Rooted Utopianism as Political Option

The choice of rooted utopianism has been evident in earlier chapters. These final chapters seek to deepen the implications of this choice in a number of more specific settings. The settings are not entirely arbitrary, but they do reflect concerns that have been given priority by world orderists during recent decades.

Chapter VII offers a proposal for building an accountability to international law into the foreign policy of constitutional democracies. Its discussion is set in the particularities of debate in the United States but has wider structural and policy implications. The relevance of international law is in its adaptation to the inner connections between state and society and its assimilation into the rights of citizens to be protected against governmental abuse. In this regard, the extension of law to foreign policy is part of the enterprise of constructing the foundations of world order in the earth.

Chapter VIII picks up the earlier concern with culture to challenge the modernist embrace of nuclearism: that is, the most evolved technology of destruction although no longer the latest or most sophisticated. Yet nuclearism, even after the Cold War, remains a cultural and geopolitical menace. Weaponry of mass destruction is retained for threat and conceivable use, a disposition at odds with religious, moral, and legal traditions of restraint. Also, such weaponry might be used in some context and thereby cause unspeakable injury to innocent peoples and possibly to economic and environmental stability as well. The chapter invokes cultural resources as potential and actual sources of resistance to nuclearism.

The next chapter resumes earlier discussions in Chapters V and VI about the path to global reform. The specificity of Chapter IX is its preoccupation with sovereignty and ways to evade it, a preoccupation that also inquires whether "sovereignty" cannot be democratized and transnationalized, made to do service on behalf of the politics of transition to postmodernism.

Finally, Chapter X looks backward at this enterprise through modernist eyes, considering the claim of realist thinkers in international relations to give students and leaders the sort of policy guidance required by the realities *of the international situation. The discussion is put in the context of the United States experience since World War II, and a distinction is drawn between realism as a reaction to pre-1945 American idealism and realism as a basis for thought and action in a setting increasingly beset by globalizing forces from above and below. As might be expected, the underlying critique of realism offered here is that it takes for granted the persistence of modernist forms and capabilities at a period of history when these forms and capabilities are not able to address crucial dimensions of international life associated with globalizing environmental, economic, and ideational tendencies.*

CHAPTER VII

The Extension of Law to Foreign Policy: The Next Constitutional Challenge

IN THE *FEDERALIST* No. 1, Alexander Hamilton raises the foundational question as to "whether societies of men [*sic*] are really capable or not, of establishing good government from reflection and choice, or whether they are forever destined to depend, for their political constitutions, on accident and force." The adoption of the Constitution and the generally favorable experience of the United States over the course of two subsequent centuries have created an overall conviction that the framework adopted for the governance of the country has worked remarkably well. The Constitution has served as an inspiration to numerous other peoples who have more recently achieved independence, despite the controversial role played by the United States as a political actor in the course of the anticolonial movement.

Granting this unprecedented success in state-building, the *Federalist* viewpoint needs to be tested these days in a context of calls for reassessment and renewal. A group of individuals, no matter how prophetic or how careful to preserve room for maneuver on the part of succeeding generations, cannot do away with the continual need to reassess in view of fundamental shifts in circumstance and outlook. In the face of such a challenge the question posited is whether the society of men and women that constitutes America is capable of renewing its social contract on behalf of the safety, well-being, and public good of the citizenry conceived of both as a whole and individually.

The premise of this chapter is that the constitutional treatment of foreign policy—its execution and restraint—was contoured around a specific set of eighteenth-century concerns of the postrevolutionary colonists—mainly, how to achieve republican control over war-making without losing entirely the efficiency associated with royalist or monarchical concentrations of authority in the crown or creating too great a vulnerability to populist passions. Ever since the earliest days of the republic, it has been commonly supposed that a weakness of the constitutional arrangement was this commitment to distribute war-making authority, and foreign policy more generally, between Congress and the executive branches: that is, to apply the principle of separation of powers (and the complementary friction of checks and balances) to the external conduct of public affairs.

The main positive and practical rationale for the constitutional arrangement is the desirability of making recourse to war as deliberative as possible, even semipopulist, by relying heavily on the legislative branch, acting in its representational role, to restrain an impulsive presidency. At the same time, the conduct of war once properly declared should be primarily entrusted to the unified control of the president in his (or her) role as commander-in-chief. A serious legislative check on presidential powers was introduced in the form of continuing congressional control over appropriations needed to carry on and expand the war.

In this century such a solution for issues of war and peace seems increasingly unworkable, given changes in the world, in the character of war, in the position of the United States as a global superpower, and in the resultant formation of a powerful segment of government that has a definite vocational and ideological stake in a hostile world and in a permanent military buildup based on perpetuating international tensions. The problem of "the imperial presidency" is one dimension of what has emerged to unbalance the original constitutional arrangement. But this might be rectified by pursuing the largely unexplored option of reinterpretation, leading to an expanded role for courts *within* the four corners of the constitution as enacted. Such an option suggests that the existing style of judicial deference on foreign policy issues was never unconditionally mandated by either authoritative text or unambiguous intentions of the Founders, and that there is interpretive space to reassess the appropriate judicial role in light of the policy imperatives of today and the long-term well-being of the citizenry, conceived as "the public good."

But beyond this effort to provide through reinterpretation a new constitutional equilibrium in the form of counterweights to the growth of the executive branch there lies a more fundamental, largely substantive problem. A basic assumption embodied in the Constitution is that the government as a sovereign entity has discretion to use force whenever the appropriate institutional mechanisms and political leadership determine it to be beneficial in light of national interests. True, American presidents, even Ronald Reagan, have invariably claimed a foundation in international law for their most contested uses of force. Reagan alleged that inter-American collective security arrangements authorized the invasion of Grenada in 1983 and that the self-defense provisions of the United Nations Charter were an adequate legal basis for the air attack on Libya in April 1986. George Bush rather feebly declared that Noriega's "declaration of war" on the United States and harassment of U.S. military personnel justified the invasion of Panama and the removal of Noriega as head of state in late 1989. Most spectacular of all was the rush to large-scale war in the Persian Gulf crisis of 1990–91.

The practice of providing legal cover, however, is not the same as acknowledging a constraining framework of international law as applicable to foreign policy. Such a framework would involve some form of review process to enable challenged policies to be assessed impartially. At minimum, an international law framework would mean the possibility of judicial review of executive policy decisions in domestic courts and, as well, a show of respect for adverse rulings of competent international bodies, especially the International Court of Justice (ICJ).

The guiding assumption of this chapter is that increasingly, the failure to abide by disinterested interpretations of international law badly serves the national interest and the well-being of the citizenry.[1] This legalist critique of constitutionalism in foreign policy can be regarded as an argument on behalf of two types of reform: reinterpretation of the separation of powers in the setting of foreign policy to upgrade the role of courts; and a possible structural adjustment, though not necessarily by formal amendment, to assure disinterested judicial review of contested foreign policy decisions under international law. These goals are part of a larger plan for greater responsiveness by governments to disinterested assessments of international law, including the evolving interest of citizens in establishing constraints on governmental choices in foreign policy.

The constitutional process has, of course, exhibited remarkable flexibility in accommodating normative sea changes during the life of the Republic. Assuring individual liberties, extending the franchise to women, offering increasing protection of law to racial minorities, and providing welfare benefits to the poor have all been achieved in accordance with changing mores, popular pressures, militant social movements, and shifting images of the appropriate role of government. True, the emancipation of blacks depended mainly on successful recourse to extraordinary means outside the constitutional process: a long, bloody civil war. And in one crucial instance, the oppression of native American peoples, the Constitution has never offered adequate protection for basic rights.

The subject matter of foreign affairs has been generally perceived not as presenting a structural challenge of accommodation so much as presenting recurrent crises of mediation in the relations between the presidency and the Congress as to the proper distribution of function. Most debate continues to concentrate on the appropriate contours of respec-

tive roles for the distinct branches of government, a shifting set of boundaries reflecting changes in public mood, the impact of particular leaders,
the success or failure of a given initiative especially in the area of war and
peace, the ebb and flow of power between coordinate branches of government, and the degree of activism of the United States in controversial
matters beyond its borders. During these two centuries of practice there
has also been a spiral, cumulative trend toward concentration of power in
the executive branch, creating a growing sense that Congress is grasping
awkwardly and ambiguously after power but lacks the will or capacity to
perform successfully if it extends its prerogative in foreign policy matters
beyond a distinctly subordinate and essentially passive role. On the one
side, the executive claims virtual supremacy over the execution of foreign policy initiatives, even if these are at variance with congressional will
and public preference; on the other, Congress is continually criticized for
trying to micromanage foreign policy. Congress itself is ambivalent, not
wanting the responsibility often associated with questioning fundamental
premises of foreign policy in the national security area (should the United
States engage in covert operations? rely on nuclear weapons? intervene
on behalf of democracy?) and yet seeking the prominence of meaningful participation.[2] Generally, then, there has been a tug-of-war over the
quality of participation in the procedural realm of policy-making, rather
than resolution by reference to matters of substance.

True, if a presidential policy backfires or breaks down, Congress can—
especially through its hearing process in an age of television—briefly
occupy center stage and in this way expose, challenge, discredit those
who carry out foreign policy, including even the president. But it can also
be humbled and thrown back on the defensive by an effective witness,
as Oliver North brilliantly demonstrated during the Iran-Contra hearings.
It was Colonel North who emerged as the hero, despite his display of
scorn for the general understanding of what the Constitution required
from the executive branch, at least on the question of faithfully executing
validly enacted legislation. Both the long ordeal of the Vietnam War and
the extraordinary departures from normalcy disclosed by the Iran-Contra
scandal are suggestive not only of this potential congressional role but
of its severe limits. The performance of the role is generally dominated
but also consumed by considerations of domestic politics, media dynamics, and retrospective appraisal; it only tangentially touches on matters
of substance or on the excesses of foreign policy per se. To build an impeachment consensus against Nixon in the aftermath of Watergate, it was
necessary at the last to drop charges pertaining to combat operations in
Cambodia, despite clear evidence of presidential deceit in the execution
of a policy that cost many lives, American and Cambodian.[3]

The main effort of Congress during the last twenty years has been to resist erosion of its constitutional mandate, in an era of expanding executive claims and capabilities, to act in foreign affairs. Congress wants to be in on the action, to participate, to know state secrets, and to share war-making prerogatives; but by and large it is not eager to share real responsibility for controversial foreign policy initiatives and remains content to be subordinate on substance so long as it is consulted, its dignity is respected, and the policy in question seems to be succeeding. The Iran-Contra disclosures suggest a special instance of aggravated assault on constitutional expectations because even responsible members of the Departments of State and Defense were shut out by White House action through particular individuals on the National Security Council, who in turn relied on a private network of shadowy operatives to carry out foreign policy initiatives that enjoyed neither public backing nor congressional approval and, indeed, defied legislative intention—although they did seem to reflect the overall preferences of the president.[4]

The Problem of Limits

My focus here is on the underlying structural problems that have emerged over the course of decades both from the limitations in the constitutional arrangement itself and from a pattern of understandable yet arbitrarily narrow lines of interpretive practice in the courts. The consequent interpretations are arbitrary in the sense that a far more expansive view of judicial function could have evolved quite legitimately, given the openness of the constitutional language and the inability of the framers to foresee the sorts of issues that have emerged in the last half-century or so.[5] As matters now stand, a serious constitutional inadequacy that involves a great risk to public safety and to the well-being of the national political community has resulted from the self-denying definition of function that has been generally offered by the courts.

Here is the crux of the problem: The Constitution was drafted at a time when recourse to war and force as instruments of state was a matter of national discretion *under international law* and when the influence of the United States was largely hemispheric because it deliberately opted (via Washington's Farewell Address and subsequent policy) to avoid the maelstrom of geopolitics historically associated with Eurocentric conflict. As a result, the prospects of war were closely connected with the territorial defense of the country and its citizens, plus brief assertions of military power to uphold hemispheric interests against European encroachment and, as time went by, an expanding Pacific naval presence.

The change of circumstance came in this century—or, arguably, just prior, in the Spanish America War—especially with the two world wars, and an expanding U.S. involvement with geopolitics since 1945. In each of the world wars the United States was drawn out of its isolationist stance to intervene (decisively, as it turned out), to alter the course of conflict in Europe, and to take part in the shaping of peace. After World War II the United States emerged as the dominant world power, not only militarily but economically and diplomatically as well. It also developed a national leadership convinced that interwar isolationism was no longer viable, that the United States needed to remain a presence in Europe during peace-time to avoid yet another breakdown of international order at its center. Such an outlook complemented and reinforced the view of the Soviet Union and the ideology of Communism as expansive and hostile, the collapse of the colonial hold over the Third World, and the availability of weaponry of mass destruction on a scale that made the outbreak of warfare between strategic rivals a manifestly self-destructive if not a suicidal venture; hence, it shifted the emphasis of security policy to containment by deterrence.

In brief, the post-1945 activity of the United States in the world has underscored the inadequacy of the constitutional framework as it has evolved either to secure the national interest or to enable the kind of mediation between coordinate branches of government that was originally envisioned. Indeed, the preoccupation of the Constitution-makers was tilted toward checks upon executive prerogative. The American Revolution brought to power and influence a group of citizens who risked their lives to detach the United States from a royalist system in which the citizenry and their representatives had no effective check on the ruler. One thing the framers were agreed upon was that they did not want a king in charge when it came to initiating war—even though the Hamiltonian wing, arguably, wanted something functionally equivalent to kingship, especially in the conduct of foreign affairs. But it was the basic consensus at Philadelphia to vest the power to declare war in the Congress, and to limit the president in foreign affairs to designated roles as commander-in-chief and principal negotiator.

Yet there was a degree of incoherence, perhaps inevitably, from the outset. The Hamiltonian perspective was powerfully asserted in early patterns of state practice and quickly became ascendant as the United States became ever more expansionist: to be successful, the country needed a unified foreign policy that could provide the stability required for the growth of commerce and trade, the key to influence and prosperity for a republic. Even Jefferson, the arch-foe of Hamilton, largely capitulated during his presidency, a capitulation expressed in foreign affairs by sending American naval units far away to engage the Barbary pirates off the shores of North Africa. In the nineteenth century, Congress generally supported the executive in a course of foreign policy, although some controversy on goals and means arose in relation to the War of 1812, the Mexican War, and, most of all, the aftermath of the Spanish-American War.

More important for our purposes, there were no legal criteria to provide limits on the extension of presidential power or, more generally, on governmental power. International law did not purport to regulate recourse to force beyond the vague directives of the "just war" doctrine, directed at the heads of sovereign states and appealing to a Christian conscience supposedly held in common and written out in legal language by influential jurists such as Hugo Grotius and Emmerich von Vattel. In such a context, courts naturally were led to perceive and treat foreign policy controversies as matters of judgment within the domain of leadership, matters properly regarded as "political questions" not susceptible to judicial assessment. Individual citizens were to be protected by representative institutions and generally lacked a legally defined right to challenge foreign policy. The perverse result was that only in the property area did individuals discover some basis in international law to challenge foreign policy initiatives.

In the famous "Steel Seizure" case a majority in the U.S. Supreme Court held that President Harry S Truman could not send federal troops into the steel mills to assure the flow of war equipment needed by soldiers fighting in Korea.[6] In *Flast v. Cohen* it held that a taxpayer with a general grievance could make a claim even if lacking a specific interest arising from some severe loss.[7] On the other side, especially in a series of cases involving citizens objecting to the call to serve in Vietnam, courts found that the objections were "political" or that the litigants lacked "standing." Similarly, in more recent years, a series of antinuclear cases have generally but not invariably denied citizens any opportunity to present their legal grievances to a court and have imposed prison sentences on individuals who, on the basis of their conscience and their understanding of international law, believed it their duty to obstruct the deployment or operation of weapons systems.[8]

In the background is the development of international law and its reinforcement within the political culture, especially by religious organizations. Beginning with the Hague Conventions of 1899 and 1907, agreed limits were placed on the *conduct* of warfare, especially a variety of rules designed to prohibit tactics that did not distinguish military from civilian targets. Later came the Pact of Paris or Kellogg-Briand Pact of 1928, which limited *recourse* to force as an instrument of foreign policy to situations of self-defense. This conception became the cornerstone of modern international law governing the use of force and is embodied in Articles 2

(4) and 51 of the United Nations Charter. A further twentieth-century development has been the creation of international political and judicial institutions with the competence to pass on contested claims for the use of force in international relations. This development enables but does not prescribe an escape from the subjectivity of allowing each government to decide for itself that *its* uses of force were defensive and those of its opponent aggressive.

On another front, the governments of the world and especially the United States agreed in the wake of World War II that policy-makers, including heads of state, were individually liable for crimes of state committed in relation to war. The Nuremberg and Tokyo experiences were landmark developments that planted seeds of a new understanding about the political obligations of citizens. The Nuremberg concept was extended down the ladder of responsibility from the level of primary leaders and applied to doctors, judges, and business executives who were associated with implementing one or another facet of officially sanctioned Nazi and imperial Japanese policies.[9] The logic of Nuremberg is even wider, suggesting that anyone with knowledge of crimes of state has a responsibility to act to prevent their continuation, and that no superior order or sense of patriotism arising out of national identity should inhibit this primary duty.[10]

These broad legal developments have been reinforced by some crucial bureaucratic and technological changes in the character of state power. Since 1945 the United States has assumed a peacetime role as guardian of the status quo in large portions of the non-Communist world. This has produced the need for a continually rising military budget and capability, as well as a major intelligence network to provide information about developments everywhere.[11] The world political system framed by notions of territorial sovereignty, rights of self-determination, and the renunciation of force is contrary to the drift of an interventionary diplomacy, no matter what the character of the moral and strategic claims of the intervening side. There is no persuasive way to reconcile respect for international law with foreign policy priorities that include the mission to resist political movements in foreign countries whose program and outlook are deemed hostile to U.S. national interests.

Two effects ensue. The first is pressure to keep the interventionary policies as secret as possible. The United States government has often attempted by way of "covert operations" to uphold its geopolitical role without acting in a manner that directly flouted the UN Charter or inflamed public opinion at home and elsewhere. The interventions in Iran (1953) to restore the Shah and in Guatemala (1954) to overthrow a leftist government were typical of this new approach to foreign policy. To the extent that containment was challenged directly in Korea (1950–53) secrecy was not needed; when the North attacked the South, the U.S. intervention was generally deemed appropriate and "legal," being a response to a prior military initiative across an internationally recognized boundary and thus an instance of collective self-defense, an interpretation upheld by the United Nations and a consensus of governments.

The second effect of the pressure to intervene is regression in relation to the rule of law, especially when international institutions do not give their blessings to the more controversial undertakings of American foreign policy. This loss of U.S. diplomatic leverage correlated especially with the decolonization process, the postwar recovery of Europe and Japan, and the persisting rivalry with the Soviet Union and with left-oriented politics. From the mid-1960s onward, the United Nations could no longer be counted on to rubber-stamp United States foreign policy and indeed began to give voice to harsh criticism. The Vietnam War was a watershed in this process of legalist disenchantment with the U.S. government. The attempts by government lawyers and civilian apologists to reconcile American war policies in Indochina with international law seemed empty rationalizations outside the United States and have been virtually disregarded in non-Anglo-American scholarship. In the Reagan-Bush years, the process of disenchantment has become explicit, even shrill; the invasion of Grenada (1983), the air attack on Libya (1986), the interventionary policy of support for anti-Sandinista forces, and the invasion of Panama (1989) are exceedingly difficult to reconcile with prevailing understandings of international law. The World Court, in a carefully reasoned judgment whose main findings were supported by twelve of the fifteen participating judges, held that U.S. intervention in Central America during the early 1980s was a serious and multiple violation of international law. Even more significantly, however, the adverse judgment was repudiated by the United States government without occasioning any serious backlash even among mainstream opponents of Reagan policies—political forces from the opposition party in Congress and elsewhere that have been critical of support for the contras intended to overthrow the Sandinista government in Nicaragua. It is almost as if there exists a national consensus that the policy should be debated on "its merits" without permitting the merits to include the legal status of the policy itself.[12]

The evolving technology of war, especially its nuclear dimension, has undermined the constitutional idea of war-making in fundamental yet largely unacknowledged respects. Even without nuclear weaponry, "enemy" missiles and rockets used in conjunction with modern guidance and delivery systems can produce a situation in which neither time nor space could give the United States any secure period between "peace" and "war." These developments were underscored by the lesson of Pearl Harbor, which persuaded the postwar generation of American leaders that the country would be vulnerable to surprise attack, despite its oceanic buffers, if it did not maintain military readiness.

Nuclear weapons in a bipolar world emphasized this new reality. Wartime, or at least the prewar posture of constantly rehearsing an imaginary war, became the norm.[13] The new reality meant a large enduring and unavoidable influence for the military, a recurrent argument about the extent to which the government should be able to take special action beneath the banner of national security, and an unbalancing of the governmental arrangement of checks and balances envisaged at the outset of the republic.

Arising out of this situation have been associated developments pertaining to nuclear arms. Because these weapons are so gruesomely destructive, there has been a special inhibition on discussing their strategic role in foreign policy, including occasions of actual threats and potential use. Given the nature of modern conflict, there would likely be no opportunity for wider consultation and participation during an international crisis, and certainly not once such weapons were used. The secret, decisive character of the prerogative to shape nuclear weapons policy that has been lodged in the presidency without prior discussion, guidelines for use, or notions of accountability is an unprecedented erosion of both popular sovereignty and separation of powers; it draws into question the reality of constitutional democracy on the most vital question of public policy.[14]

In sum, the Constitution arose at a time when the country was weak and modest in capacity, when it was insulated from war by oceans, and when the status of war could be sharply differentiated from a normally prevailing condition of peace, enabling a clear possibility under most circumstances of making a reflective decision to resort to war. In the nuclear age and in the setting of the United States as a global power with an ambitious overt and covert interventionary agenda (reaffirmed and extended in the form of the Reagan Doctrine), the loose structure of the Constitution no longer serves our citizenry well. This assessment is confirmed by the growth and development of legal rules and international institutions that withdraw discretion from governments, but also provides national policy-makers and judges with legal criteria and procedures by which to assess objectively the propriety of foreign policy. In light of all this, it is time for courts to reinterpret the judicial function in relation to foreign policy. A strong argument now supports advocates of a creative judicial role, for an approach, in this setting that rejects Alexander Bickel's affirmation of the call in the *Federalist* No. 79 to develop "the passive virtues."

The time is now ripe for judicial expansion, for the dramatic endorsement of the active virtues that is occurring despite the dogmatically passive mode coming to dominate the U.S. Supreme Court.

The Problem of Judicial Passivity

Louis Henkin's influential writing on the Constitution and foreign policy rests on an essential confirmation of the viability of existing arrangements and the absence of either political will or normative necessity to make major changes.[15] Henkin discounts the view that the Vietnam War provoked "a constitutional crisis," arguing instead that the Constitution envisaged the push-and-pull of congressional-executive relations, weighted in favor of the presidency, should a foreign policy initiative come under heavy fire. He is scornful also of judicial efforts to resolve such tensions by passing judgment on the relative merits of contested institutional positions.[16] In effect, his general assessment allows the play of governmental forces to shape the direction of United States foreign policy, which effectively leaves the locus of authority to initiate and sustain war-making in the executive bureaucracy.

This conclusion is bolstered by Henkin's view that the overall system "cannot be effectively improved by constitutional amendment," an attitude that expresses both a confidence in muddling through and "a perhaps tired conclusion that that is the best one can hope for in human government."[17] Such a disposition leaves the governmental control of foreign policy about where Justice Sutherland left it in 1936 in his famous majority opinion in *United States v. Curtiss-Wright,* a rationalization of presidential hegemony that has been extended far beyond the holding of the case. An oft-quoted dictum captures the spirit of Sutherland's attitude: "Not only, as we have shown, is the federal power over external affairs in origin and essential character different from that over internal affairs, but participation in the exercise of the power is significantly different. In this vast external realm, with its important, complicated, delicate and manifold problems, the President alone has the power to speak or listen as a representative of the nation."[18] The reach and pernicious influence of *Curtiss-Wright* was exhibited by Oliver North's reliance on its authority to justify his various undertakings disclosed in the course of the televised Iran-Contra hearings. The scholarly views of *Curtiss-Wright* are more critical and circumscribed, providing a basis for either narrowing its influence to its holding (bearing on the constitutionality of a delegation of authority that gave the president discretion to restrict export licenses for arms sales to a war zone in South America) or disregarding its dicta on the broad theory of external relations.[19]

It seems correct to conclude that it is not currently feasible to contemplate a formal revision of the Constitution by resort to the amendment process, nor even to suppose that Congress is likely to do more than assert its prerogatives vis-à-vis the executive. Such assertions, likely to be resisted at every stage, are essentially defensive and formalistic in character, especially if the nearly two decades of experience with the War Powers Act is representative. The president routinely restates the view that the War Powers Act is unconstitutional, and Congress overlooks the most significant instances of noncompliance, apparently seeking only ritualistic conformity to the legislative guidelines on reporting and authorization. The cumulative tendency is assuredly to reinforce ever more strongly the actuality of presidential hegemony—by way of secrecy, the national security doctrine, the manipulation of information and the media, the projection of bureaucratic influence, patterns of deference, and the undermining of congressional independence by special attention to lobbies and through new patterns of political financing. After policy failures and revelations of presidential excess, brief periods of reaction occur, as has happened in the aftermaths of Vietnam, Watergate, and Iran-Contra, enabling Congress to extend its role—but the main effect is to alter the *form* of interaction without touching on its substance. The War Powers Act of 1973 and the legislative effort to constrain covert action by the CIA are illustrative of both the assertiveness and the impotence of Congress. The executive objects to congressional interference but in fact is not challenged at all and, at most, alters patterns of consultation and reporting. That is, the political consensus within government and among contending political parties is content with existing arrangements applicable to foreign affairs, including the ebb and flow of congressional and executive assertiveness and the overall tendency to concentrate control of foreign policy in the presidency.

For reasons suggested in Part One, this set of arrangements is unsatisfactory: the growing gap between functional and normative imperatives calls for fundamental constitutional reforms and a break in the political stasis that precludes reform. Because the statist, realist response is to accept the political constraints evident in Washington and confine attention to small adjustments at the margins, my argument is that the energy for constitutional reform will not emerge independently in Washington on the basis of rational analysis but will arise, if at all, in response to citizen initiatives and political mobilization at the grassroots level. Whether this mobilization process will culminate in a political climate that would make practical projects of constitutional reform a realistic prospect is impossible to assess at present. At the same time, it is misleading to discount altogether the grassroots ferment that exists, or to assume that only what seems realistic to policy-makers operating at the governmental center of state power establishes political limits. Especially in a democratic society, it is the exercise of popular sovereignty that ultimately provides the basis for both governmental legitimacy and social change. Such a perspective seems appropriate where the old framework of rights and duties is rigidly confined to the old patterns of practice, despite the pressures mounted by a more interdependent and fragile world.

Without entering into detailed argument here, we may conclude that the reshaping of our world view has to do with both the *globalization of the common good* and, consequently, *the necessity for placing limits on governmental discretion in the area of war and peace.* Such a process of reshaping challenges the political culture of modernism. Modernism continues to dominate bureaucratic and institutional politics with its notions of unconditional statism, as well as its confidence that reason, science, and technology can preserve the common good, despite the acknowledged reality that political leaders act out of circumscribed laissez-faire assessments of national interest.[20]

To prepare the political ground for a Magna Carta of the nuclear age requires a continuous process of reflection on activity at the grassroots as well as analysis of the formal outcomes of the operation of the institutions of government. The resistance of institutions to new claims by the citizenry is not the last word. The process of political renewal at every crucial stage of the normative development of democratic practice has depended on a push-and-pull interplay between the state and civil society, carried on beyond the limits of routine electoral politics. The civil rights movement is a recent instance of such a process in the setting of race relations. The quest by women and gay people for an economic and political order that is more receptive to their needs and life-styles is being partly played out in the streets as an aspect of the quest for formal legislative acknowledgment and reform. Such a dynamic is also visible in the area of war and peace; societal pressures for normative constraint (both legal and moral) are being mounted on a largely extralegal basis with a declining show of concern about the workings of the apparatus of government, including party rivalry for control of elective office.

The national security consensus flowing from Washington—especially from its bureaucratic recesses of power—during the Cold War has successfully disciplined the formal political process, including elections and representative institutions. As a result, shifts in the degree of discretion to use force in foreign policy are not even on the agenda of mainstream politics. Two illustrations may help clarify this assertion.

First, despite the recurrent discrediting of covert action, its unconditional repudiation by government is never seriously discussed even by those most critical of a particular instance of excess. In the Iran-Contra hearings, for instance, the sole focus was on the degree of presidential knowledge and on the consequence of circumventing CIA management of covert action. At no time was the issue raised as to the long-term damage done to the United States reputation as a result of covert action, nor was any assessment made of particular instances as contributing or not to the realization of U.S. foreign policy goals. And never was the substantial question raised as to whether covert action could be reconciled with law, morality, and U.S. reciprocal expectations of the appropriate behavior of foreign governments.

A second illustration relates to the use of nuclear weapons. Apparently, most Americans think that the policy of the United States is to use nuclear weapons only in retaliation against a nuclear attack; in actuality, the official doctrine in Europe and elsewhere is to retain a first-use option and to transmit such a threat. Such a crucial matter as the legitimacy of nuclear weapons as instruments of foreign policy has never been challenged in the course of presidential debate or congressional discussion. Again this absence of challenge flies in the face of prudential considerations (ways to reduce the risk of nuclear war) as well as normative ones.

Yet there are citizens raising these and related questions, acting out of moral conviction and, increasingly, from a sense of legal right and duty. These actions are fairly widespread but generally reported only locally or by shoestring operations in the form of poorly distributed newsletters.[21]

The reason that these barely visible developments at the edges of the political process deserve attention is twofold: the moral and legal coherence of their claims, and the practical implications of redefining security in a more normative, less militarist fashion. In other words, current boundaries on political discourse as a result of the national security consensus require us to examine the claims for reform being mounted at the margin, remembering that "the margin" is inhabited by concerned citizens, and that the boundaries between the marginal and the mainstream can become quickly fluid in periods of crisis and controversy.

It is not feasible to examine here the numerous legal cases that have been decided over the past decade or so, or even to assess whether there is a gradual trend toward endowing these claims with an increased legitimacy. Suffice it to say that these cases cluster into several categories of resistance to official policy: first, resistance to various dimensions of nuclear weapons policy, especially the development and deployment of allegedly first-strike weapons systems;[22] second, resistance to covert action and forcible intervention in Third World countries; and third, resistance to policies associated with severe abuse of human rights, especially those connected with "constructive engagement" in South Africa or the return of "illegals" to Central America, where they face a prospect of destitution or even persecution. What is relevant to this argument for constitutional reform is the underlying rationale, which bears upon the nature of citizenship, patriotism, and the rule of law as expressed in the legal defenses mounted by defendants and their counsel.

Two closely interconnected lines of argument in these cases are fundamental to the central theme of bringing law to bear on foreign policy. The first asserts that any citizen has the authority to oppose *on constitutional grounds* a policy that is *reasonably believed* to violate applicable treaties and customary rules of international law. In effect, each citizen has a judicially enforceable claim to a lawful foreign policy. This claim is not a *substantive* innovation, because treaty rules of international law are already "the supreme law of the land" by virtue of Article VI (2) of the Constitution, and customary rules are binding as a result of consistent Supreme Court authority. Bringing law to bear on foreign policy requires a procedural innovation, however, to the extent that it depends on reversing a line of judicial decisions that affirm presidential supremacy in the area of foreign affairs. Either by denial of the citizen's standing or by acceptance of the view that the policy in question is a "political" matter, the governmental obligation to uphold international law is relegated to the status of nonjusticiable issue. In effect, the presidency is given discretion to interpret the implications of applicable international law, including an option of flagrant violation. This treatment is reinforced by an implicit taboo across the whole political spectrum upon criticism of government policy as violation of international law.

The second strand of argument arises from the authority of the Nuremberg Principles as applied to domestic legal controversy. The post–World War II prosecution of German and Japanese leaders and policy-makers for their failures to uphold international law was a strong step in the direction of individual accountability. Although it has not been reinforced by internationalization (such as an international criminal court with independent financing and enforcement) or in practice (for example, formal calls by the organs of the United Nations for application of the precedent), the Nuremberg Judgment and its holdings have been received into the body of international law in an authoritative manner.[23] The Nuremberg Principles set limits on governmental actors, but they also provide a criterion for law that is outside the state and give citizens an objective basis on which to validate claims of resistance and disobedience as "legal."

Although this kind of refusal to respect domestic law is often considered to be "civil disobedience," its rationale relies on another logic. Ever since Thoreau, the essence of civil disobedience has been to accord moral claims priority over legal claims, assuming that the moral claims are asserted nonviolently. Civil disobedience calls upon citizens to honor their conscience if it conflicts with enacted law. The Nuremberg logic goes a step further. It establishes the priority of international legal claims over symbolic domestic legal claims. The citizen should be able, as a matter of right, to question whether governmental conduct is in violation of international law. Such a procedural opening would compensate to a certain extent for the absence of international mechanisms of implementation. It would also reconcile the obligation to uphold international law with the statist character of world order, allowing the application of the Nuremberg Principles to be a matter of sovereign duty. Finally, the validation of the Nuremberg Principles would be a structured way of acknowledging the long-term interest possessed by all peoples in the establishment of public policies that require adherence to international law on matters of war and peace, thereby neutralizing the tendencies of politicians to be preoccupied by considerations of short-term expediency and to be neglectful of the public good.

A citizen initiative by way of nonviolent and symbolic action— whether trespass on official facilities to assure termination of aid to the contras, or blocking a train carrying Trident warheads—is intended to trigger an encounter with the state that stands behind contested policies. It is meant to be a moral and legal challenge that provokes public discussion and legal assessment in the course of judicial proceedings. The citizen-activist contends that his or her action was prompted by objection to an unlawful foreign policy and normally accompanies that contention with offers of proof, including expert testimony to establish a reasonable basis for the belief in illegality.

The government response tends to be one of procedural preemption: namely, that the citizen has no standing to invoke international law in relation to foreign policy and, beyond this, that the court has neither the competence nor the constitutional mandate to pass legal judgment. The disallowance of the international law argument is often reinforced in a highly contrived way by disallowing expert testimony, especially with a jury present (most judges are quite adept at listening without hearing when the occasion warrants), and by delivering jury instructions that seek to limit their assessment to the uncontested facts of the (symbolic) violation of domestic law, giving the jury no space within which to return an acquittal based on the contested facts of a violation of international law. In such circumstances, defendants in a criminal proceeding are effectively denied their "day in court," because the element of "intent"—upon which the international law argument rests—is never fully examined.

In actuality, there are only vague precedents to validate this complex process of judicial closure, and there have already been several breaches: that is, instances in which a citizen appeal to international law *has* been accepted as a defense in a prosecution for alleged criminal misconduct.[24] There are also indications that prosecutors have been reluctant to prosecute, juries to convict, and judges to sentence whenever the international law perspective is allowed entry. The constitutional reform needed is a legislative mandate that courts should adjudicate *substantively* whenever a defendant invokes an international law argument as an integral element in a defense against criminal charges. Such judicial scrutiny would serve to offset some of the effects of the national security consensus that keeps challenges based on international law out of the political process. It would also absorb into judicial practice those developments in international law over the past several decades which clarify limits on the use of force overseas and which establish human rights standards. Finally, allowing such challenges in courts would reempower citizens in a manner that would promote the revitalization of democracy and, simultaneously, support the accountability of officials at all levels of political organization for failures of international law. Further, the internal dynamics of adjudication would be enlivened: The courts would become arenas for principled controversy and public education on matters of war and peace, and juries would be prompted to serve as the conscience of communities in settings of severe normative tension. Giving citizens the procedural basis to assert their right to a lawful foreign policy would deepen and strengthen popular sovereignty, redressing in part the currently unbalanced relations between state and society.

The argument presented here reduces to this: Consistent judicial application of international law would introduce a needed check in the overall system of separatism of powers; such a check would contribute to the long-term well-being of one's own society and recognition of the growing practical significance of restraining uses of force overseas.[25] Pioneers in this development are the small groups of individual citizens who accept risks of indictment and imprisonment. Giving citizens standing to raise such claims would both strengthen international law in relation to national security policy and extend notions of public accountability to the domain of foreign policy, contributing thereby both to the public good and to a needed process of adjustment at the state level.

Official reluctance to proceed in such a direction remains overwhelming. It rests ultimately on an implicit willingness to associate sovereignty with unrestrained presidential discretion and national advantage with an unrestricted military option. To overcome this resistance will require social struggle and, marginally, the persuasiveness of legal argument. And yet if we look ahead to the next century there seems little doubt that a most important contribution to the evolution of constitutional democracy at this stage would be to endow citizens with an effective right to a lawful foreign policy by way of judicial protection.

This argument has been developed almost exclusively with reference to the circumstances of the United States, but its force is intended to apply elsewhere as well. Perhaps in constitutional settings where a government is less inclined to project military power, there may be greater potential for establishing a constitutional practice enabling citizens and their representatives to test the lawfulness of foreign policy by reference to international law as well as in relation to domestic law, thereby creating precedents and practice that can carry forward the basic idea of legal limits on foreign policy.

CHAPTER VIII

Can Culture Tame Nuclearism?

THIS CHAPTER is based on the conviction that attitudes embedded in cultural beliefs and practices emerge to condition behavior in significantly specific directions, often underlying the way security is pursued by organized political communities and often setting limits on acceptable patterns of action. The limits are no less influential because they remain implicit or because efforts to crystallize their content are beset with difficulty. It is my judgment that a better understanding of these cultural beliefs and practices is connected with our struggle to avoid nuclear war.

A premise of this inquiry is that the development and testing of nuclear weapons pose severe threats to the environment. The prospect of a large-scale nuclear war is active in our collective imagination, giving us a powerful scenario centering on the death of nature itself—the result, according to some scientific conjecture, of a "nuclear winter." The accuracy of such a scenario is not as significant for our purposes as are the connections drawn between nuclearism and environmental quality and survival.

The ending of the Cold War brings us relief from the bipolar conception of international society with its implicit reliance on an exchange of nuclear threats. The new world setting has made the dangers of nuclear war seem more remote, and this is, of course, desirable. But the weaponry remains and may become far more widely accessible in the decades ahead. Nuclearism has not been repudiated in the aftermath of the Cold War. It seems more plausible to contemplate a nuclear-free world in the 1990s than it did a few years earlier, yet not less urgent.

The chapter first discusses the character of cultural norms, their relevance to the structure of social behavior, and the extent to which they are embodied in patterns of reliance on nuclear weapons—especially those that have grown up around the role of violence and war in the relations among sovereign states. It then presents the network of relevant cultural norms as consisting of contradictory but not symmetrical pressures on collective behavior; those that support war and state absolutism, and provide the ground upon which nuclear weapons policy rests, are far stronger than the contrary norms that privilege nonviolence and condition the use of violence upon some proportionate and rational relation between means and ends—what is conceived of morally as "just war" and politically as "prudence." Next, an inquiry into law shows that legal efforts to condition behavior may falter if they run against the current of cultural norms and that unfortunately, this opposition exists in relation to efforts to prohibit reliance on nuclear weapons. Finally, the chapter considers cultural developments that are generating new norms and strengthening weak norms of inhibition in an overall tendency of mounting a challenge to nuclearism, in part by undermining obsessive reliance on violence to achieve security and eroding the claims by governments that the viability of the state is such an unconditional interest that it warrants risking human survival. However elusive this emerging situation, it helps us understand both the difficulties and possibilities of constraining reliance on nuclear weapons.

ORIENTATION

The connection between cultural norms and environmental protection is elusive, complex, and almost totally unexplored. There is an important body of literature that associates underlying attitudes and images of physical reality (the Hobbesian social contract, the Newtonian mechanistic framework) with the unfolding of an autonomous technology in a manner harmful to nature.[1] Indeed, the main flow of cultural energy in the West has been in the direction of the unconditional destruction of the environment. There is even reason to read the Book of Revelation, placed at the end of the New Testament, as an authoritative prophesy of the end of the world, its imagery suggesting that an apocalyptic nuclear and ecological destiny is inevitable.[2] Fundamentalist interpretations affirm such an ending of history as reflecting the will of God and, accordingly, a fate that it is futile and possibly, sinful to resist. More broadly, this underlying apocalyptic expectation helps explain the relative passivity of contemporary Western societies in relation to the prospect of nuclear catastrophe.

Nuclear weapons culminate trends initiated centuries ago, building on evolving societal capabilities, to produce more and more destructive technologies. The use of atomic bombs at the end of World War II to assure a decisive and punitive defeat for Japan confirmed grotesquely the willingness of governments to destroy in war whatever might contribute to the realization of state goals. That is, the diplomacy underlying war is unconditional; the only ethos that is generally respected is a commitment to victory at a cost that does not weaken the resource basis of the prevailing side, which may include preserving the economic base of the defeated side. This Clausewitzian view of military necessity gives the state a mandate to regard national security as an absolute; no means to protect it are rejected out of hand, from the mass destruction of unarmed civilians and social infrastructures to the total destruction of life-sustaining biospheric stability. There are no acknowledged limits on war that take precedence over perceptions of military necessity.

At the same time, the prevailing drift of technology, war, and cultural identity is not the entire story. There is also an ethics of limits and restraints operative as a counterweight to these sheer calculations of power. Law, morality, and prudence introduce some significant sources of constraint; even state absolutists claim to be rationalists operating in a framework of proportionate means-to-ends considerations. If the means of destruction are disproportionate to the end, then the culture—which includes the mind-set of the war-makers—is supposed to scream "No!" Growing public concern about atrocities, massacres, and survival risks suggest that major world cultures may be getting ready to scream so defiantly as to break the momentum of nuclearism.

This play of contrary forces is at work in relation to nuclear weaponry. The basic rhythm continues to propel nuclearism, billions of dollars being devoted to innovating weapons systems more dangerous than anything now deployed and to the continuing militarization of space, despite the moderation of East-West conflict. The initial conception of a Strategic Defense Initiative expresses the drive to extend nuclearism even beyond earlier boundaries. But SDI also embodies in its rationale an acceptance of the notion that it is not proper to threaten the use of nuclear weapons against civilians, even in the name of deterrence. Some years ago the RAND Corporation conferred its prestige as the most prominent national security think tank on the conclusion that the doctrine of Mutual Assured Destruction (MAD) was in flagrant violation of the international law of war and that such violations undermine the legitimacy of government in a political democracy.[3]

A further set of considerations informs this inquiry. The existence of cultural norms in the West is complemented by non-Western and premodern traditions. Within these traditions much support exists for the view of nature as a sacred surrounding for human activity, an ecological absolute of preeminent cultural status. Yet here, too, countertraditions exist within the cultural heritage. Ignorance, greed, local corruption, and materialism can produce an acceptance of careless technology that threatens people and the environment. The disposal of toxic wastes in the Third World and a variety of polluting circumstances—caused in part by municipal and governmental negligence, or worse—disclose the vulnerability of non-Western cultures, despite the existence of rich traditions respectful toward nature.

It is not unreasonable to believe that these non-Western cultural traditions, with their far more participatory view of the connections between human activity and nature, might mobilize resistance against reliance on nuclear weapons as legitimate instruments of conflict. Such a posture has been struck by most Third World governments over the years within the United Nations and elsewhere. It is tempting to explain such attitudes totally as tactical or opportunistic opposition to the possession of nuclear weapons by ascendant states. But there are other elements present, including a sense that domination during the colonial era was largely an expression of the capacity of the West to use its technological prowess for destructive purposes.

Different versions of cultural nationalism emerging in many non-Western societies include a critique of Western attitudes toward nature, in which nuclear weaponry is perceived as epitomizing this destructive disposition as it has developed in the West.[4] Of course, countertrends emphasize the assimilation of the full plenum of Western attitudes and beliefs as a necessary precondition for modernization and, with it, prosperity and power. But the enthusiasm for modernization across the board has dimmed or disappeared in many non-Western societies, partly as a consequence of some severe environmental disruptions arising from a failure to take precautions with respect to ultrahazardous technologies; the accidents at Bhopal and Chernobyl have made a strong impact on political and social consciousness in many countries.

Also emerging is a growing acknowledgement that all peoples have a stake in the prevention of nuclear war. The Five Continents Initiative (heads of state from Greece, Argentina, Sweden, India, Tanzania, and Mexico) of the early 1980s, seeking a nuclear test ban, expressed an overall transnational effort to turn public opinion in an antinuclear direction. Part of this motivation is the appreciation that the effects of nuclear weapons radiate far beyond the territory of belligerent powers and threaten ecological viability in many respects; therefore, reliance on these weapons, even the preparation to use them, cannot be treated as a matter of sovereign discretion entrusted to the wisdom of the particular governments that possess them.

It is also possible to interpret recent trends as giving rise to global cultural norms, including the illegitimacy of all dimensions of nuclear weaponry: preparation, possession, and participation.[5] Important antinuclear movements in nonnuclear societies are promoting policies of nuclear disengagement. The antinuclear legislation enacted by New Zealand (refusing port entry to nuclear ships despite the strenuous objection of the United States) is illustrative, especially as it is coupled with the rising influence of the premodern reverence for nature associated with the Maori people.

RESPONDING TO NUCLEARISM

Any use of nuclear weapons entails environmental disruption to some degree. Any large-scale reliance upon or exchange of nuclear weapons threatens severe environmental damage, quite probably of an irreversible or at least very long-range character. The debate as to whether nuclear exchanges above a definite threshold would, depending on the character of the targets, trigger the onset of "nuclear winter" suggests the potential magnitude of environmental disruption in the event of nuclear war. Even participation in the nuclear arms race involves continual nuclear testing, underground or in space, that produces serious environmental damage. Past atmospheric testing, especially in the Pacific region, has caused serious forms of environmental disruption. Island atolls such as Bikini have sustained long-lasting damage as a result of tests conducted more than thirty years ago.

Most research and analysis have concentrated on the consequences for humans of environmental disruption: for instance, the effects of climate changes and temperature drops on agriculture and food supply. A concern with the environment as an end in itself is relatively unusual in the nuclear war literature.

The argument of this chapter is that restraining reliance on nuclear weaponry is vitally important to environmental stability and quality. Indeed, an ethos of environmental protection presupposes stopping nuclear testing, as well as assurances against the use of nuclear weapons in the course of armed conflict. Any contribution to the delegitimation of nuclear weaponry or, more broadly, weaponry of mass destruction is a contribution to the overall protection of the environment. In this regard, of course, efforts for nuclear disarmament are appropriate, as well as those forms of control that reduce risks of nuclear war and restrict or eliminate nuclear testing. In the current world setting, a comprehensive test ban agreed to by the two superpowers would help reduce existing patterns of environmental harm associated with ongoing nuclear testing.

At the same time, there is increasing consensus among international law experts that all (or most) threats and uses of nuclear weapons violate existing international legal standards. The United Nations General Assembly in a series of resolutions going back to 1961 has declared the view of the organization that any threat or use of nuclear weapons is illegal.[6] International legal scholars have lent their expert authority to this overall conclusion.[7] But note that even these prohibitions on threat or use do not forbid possession or development of nuclear weaponry, or assert that retaliatory use in the event of a prior nuclear attack is necessarily illegal.

Nor are such conclusions universally accepted. The governments of the United States, the United Kingdom, and France maintain the minority view that these weapons are not illegal per se unless explicitly prohibited by treaty, arguing that legality must be assessed only in the particular circumstances *after* a use of nuclear weapons, by reference to normal criteria of "military necessity" and customary rules of international law forbidding indiscriminate, disproportionate, inhumane, and unnecessary weaponry and tactics.[8] Such undeclared nuclear powers as Israel and possibly India, South Africa, and Pakistan also appeared to have reserved their nuclear options. Even those nuclear powers subscribing to no-first-strike positions, such as the Soviet Union and China, retain nuclear weapons capabilities for potential retaliatory use. Yet from the perspective of environmental protection, only an absolute and fully reliable prohibition would be altogether satisfactory. Environmental impact would not, quite obviously, be altered by the presence or absence of a plausible legal justification. Any use, "legal" or not, would be damaging and could be disastrous to local, regional, and even global ecosystems, extending harmful effects across space and through long intervals of time.

This brief review of legal perspectives relative to nuclear weaponry suggests two broad conclusions: first, that the legal condemnation of nuclear weaponry is controversial and incomplete, as well as ineffectual with respect to governments that currently rely on nuclear weapons as an essential ingredient in their national security policy; second, that a legal approach to prohibition cannot assure environmental protection as long as possession and development rights exist and retaliatory options are retained.

The relevance of cultural norms can be now more precisely considered. As matters now stand, for reasons suggested above the existing patterns of cultural norms generally work against the policies of environmental protection in relation to nuclear weapons, making efforts to achieve even moral and legal prohibition somewhat problematic and subject to breakdown in the event of political crisis. Despite this pessimistic assessment, cultural norms could be made helpful, or at least less of a barrier, in improving the climate of respect for existing legal norms and in strengthening public pressure for more comprehensive and effective formal frameworks of restraint—especially if contrary cultural norms, now marginal, could be strengthened to provide support for antinuclear policies.

LAW, CULTURAL NORMS, AND NUCLEARISM

There is no clear link between positive international law and cultural norms. It is a matter of empirical investigation as to whether and in what circumstances these dual sources of normative authority are complementary or antagonistic.

An example may be clarifying. In India, it is the law to stop at traffic lights, but the practice is to ignore changes in signals even in the presence of heavy traffic and police. In Canada, not only is there great deference to traffic signals and an assured willingness of the police to apprehend and punish violators, but law consciousness is so great that pedestrians accept as binding the rules requiring them to cross busy roads only at designated crossings and when signaled to do so, and then only within the confines of pedestrian lanes. The differences between India and Canada are numerous, but one difference is a cultural attitude toward the bindingness of law, at least in the area of urban traffic control.

A similar circumstance pertains in international political life, especially given an absence of polity—institutional capabilities and other centralized means of enforcement. The existence of treaty rules may or may not point to a pattern of compliance at the level of practice and to retaliatory response in the event of a detected violation. The existence of the legal rule is not by itself very important unless it generates strong spontaneous patterns of compliance and response to noncompliance. In general, with relation to the laws of war and peace, structures of compliance are operative only where relatively strong reciprocal interests are perceived by leading participants. For instance, between belligerents that perceive themselves as equal, rules protecting prisoners of war tend to be upheld. Compliance is less common if ethnic differences exist, or if each side views the other as an "illegitimate" belligerent. For instance, some Western governments are unwilling to grant captured PLO fighters prisoner-of-war status, allegedly because doing so would confer a degree of legitimacy upon an adversary that has been heretofore treated by most of the West as a terrorist organization, a characterization that helps justify decades of anguishing refusal to negotiate or otherwise examine Palestinian grievances.

The proscription of weaponry is an especially problematic area of international law, especially where one side perceives an advantage in a given weapon, or its armed services are bureaucratically committed to a certain line of tactics. For instance, the U.S. Air Force has been able to mount decisive pressure within governmental bureaucracies and the Congress in favor of bombing tactics, despite official studies repeatedly casting grave doubts on the military effectiveness of most past bombing campaigns and evidence of widespread indiscriminate damage and large-scale civilian suffering—an attitude strongly reinforced by the critical role of air power in producing a decisive battlefield victory in the Persian Gulf.

Nuclear weapons present very formidable problems in this regard. The policies and targeting plans governing their use are closely held state secrets. There is no acknowledged procedure to guide and shape these policies even within governmental structures. The possessors of nuclear weapons do not accept the authority of those organs that have so far condemned nuclear weaponry and many facets of strategic doctrine as illegal. Strengthening the legal regime after the fact is not a satisfactory approach, given the probable magnitude of suffering and devastation following even limited nuclear use. Furthermore, the efforts to mobilize legal prohibition has not been, as yet, very specific about the need to avoid environmental destruction.

Indeed, the relevant body of international law literature is relatively insensitive to environmental concerns.[9] It is sometimes argued that a use of nuclear weapons against a naval concentration on the high seas might be a "legal" use because it would be directed against a military target and there would be no inevitable large-scale damage to civilians. Such an interpretation gives no consideration to whether marine and atmospheric ecosystems might be severely damaged, or whether environmental damage can be put forward as a sufficient "legal" objection, given the traditional emphasis of international law on differentiating military from nonmilitary targets.

Two possible changes of a mutually reinforcing character emerge. First of all, the reach of legal prohibition should be extended to forbid weaponry that is calculated to have, or cannot avoid having, a seriously disruptive environmental impact. Such an extension of international legal consciousness might alter, possibly in a decisive form, the debate about whether there are ever legal grounds for the use of these weapons, whether verification can be reliable, and whether even their possession is permissible. Such a standard of prohibition is not unknown in international law; for instance, the Biological Weapons Convention (1972) prohibits not only possession but also development of biological weaponry.

The other possibility is to accept the existence of the legal regime on nuclear weapons as comprehensive but recognize that it must be reinforced socioculturally to become effective (rather than nominal) law. Effectiveness would then become a matter of action from below, the action of popular movements that act as vehicles for the formation and development of transnational normative opinion. Yet as with cultural norms generally, there is no assurance that the overall effects of such a populist extension of authority would be positive. The embrace of apocalyptic destinies, the assurance that "the other" is evil, and the mandate to use destructive violence in the service of perceived good all work against restraint, legal or otherwise, in the event of antagonistic interaction between opposed political communities. In the setting of war, cultural norms tend to associate security with military prowess and virtue with victory. Nuclearism is so dangerous partly because it *is* generally sanctioned by the most relevant and powerful cultural norms, and this militarist mandate is difficult to overcome by moral argument or legal prohibition.

Yet there are some cultural norms which, if strengthened relative to others, could move political conflict away from nuclearism. There is above all the submission of war itself to the discipline of instrumental rationality. This discipline has produced a growing realization that nuclear weapons are never usable, that they are not, in Robert McNamara's assessment, even military weapons in a true sense.[10] The growth of nuclear skepticism has been countered by a variety of justifications for deterrence as the best adjustment to the presence of nuclear weaponry, especially given the alleged irrationality of trust in an anarchic world of antagonistic sovereign states.[11] Deterrence in whatever form, it is argued by nuclear apologists, provides the least evil scenario and becomes the realist apotheosis of rationalist attempts to adapt national security policy to the actualities of nuclearism. The *only* role of nuclear weapons, it is said, is to *threaten* unacceptable retaliatory destruction in the service of a policy designed to maximize prospects for the prevention of nuclear war. Such an approach is defended "rationally" by the claim that "peace" has been maintained among major states and in Europe since 1945 despite severe conflict; and, that conventional warfare, given the developments in nonnuclear weapons technology and deployments, would be a very horrifying experience (as became manifest during the final days of the Gulf War); and that without nuclear deterrence the outbreak of such conflict could quickly lead to the use of the nuclear weapons that remained in the possession of the opposing belligerent states.

The fracture of rationality in nuclear war settings has been largely disguised from the culture and even presented by nuclearists as "nuclear rationality."[12] Yet such an image of rationality has come under attack from several distinct directions and has been strongly challenged at times. One source of significant attack has been the tendency of mainstream religion to take a strong normative stand on the nuclear question. The 1983 Pastoral Letter of the American Catholic Bishops challenged many of the bland assumptions of nuclear deterrence from the perspective of a non-pacifist, "just war" framework, raising issues about both the character and disproportionateness of the violence.[13] However, the pastoral letter acknowledged the conditional acceptability of limited forms of retaliatory deterrence during a limited period of dedicated quest for a reliable means to move toward a world without nuclear weapons. Antinuclearists were disappointed by the failure of the bishops to intensify their condemnation of nuclearism in light of the now manifest refusal of the United States government to endorse even the goal of a world without nuclear weapons.

Another source of challenge has been the assertion of normative concerns by professional associations. During the early 1980s, lawyers and medical doctors mobilized their colleagues to oppose reliance on nuclearism. But this transnational process of opposition and resistance, culminating in an award of a Nobel Peace Prize to the International Physicians for Social Responsibility, was limited in time and intensity. To some extent, this normative pressure focused on "the freeze" as a minimal goal or first step, a proposal containing a commitment to stop the arms race but not necessarily obliging governments to abandon deterrence or even to forgo reliance on nuclear weapons in the event of a failure of deterrence.

A further challenge to nuclearism has seemed closely connected with the transnational feminist surge. Women have been at the forefront of many peace movement activities, and feminists generally argue that war and, especially, nuclearism are expressions of patriarchal structures and patterns of abuse.[14] Feminism has also given expression to the outlook of the reemergent goddess, embodied in the sacredness of the earth and resistant to those activities that would cause enduring damage to nature. Feminist peace initiatives protesting missile deployments in Europe were vivid examples of this multidimensional challenge against nuclearism; militant actions led by women were directed against fundamental structures and assumptions of militarist views of national security.[15]

Gorbachev's Kremlin also has fostered the vision of a world without nuclear weapons; the Soviet leader even enticed Ronald Reagan spontaneously to endorse such a vision during the brief summit encounter in Reykjavik, Iceland, in November 1986. But the mainstream backlash in the United States against the concept of total denuclearization and Reagan's unwillingness to stick by the Reykjavik pledge reinforced the general assessment that it remains "utopian" to consider the replacement of nuclear deterrence at this time. Nevertheless, the Soviet commitment to a process of denuclearization was a significant development of the early 1980s, although by 1990 Gorbachev's internal troubles and other foreign policy priorities had led even Moscow to put its antinuclearist proposals on hold.

Whether taken singly or cumulatively, these various normative moves seem to lack the capacity and qualities of perseverance needed to overcome nuclearism in the near future. The state structures already in place, with their militarist assumptions, have been able to dominate the debate about rationality. And even the antinuclearist orientation rests most of its case on anthropocentric consequences for human society, not on any intrinsic or separable deference to the worth or sacredness of the environment.[16] Nature remains in this critical sense incidental to the debate, despite the devastation that would certainly result from any large-scale use of nuclear weapons. The ecological effects, if discussed at all, are invoked to emphasize the intolerable character, even the impossibility, of human existence in a postapocalyptic setting. Films such as *Road Warrior* portray a postapocalyptic natural surrounding that is completely barren and ugly but do so only to stress deteriorated societal conditions and horrifying human consequences.

Cultural Norms and Environmental Disruption

For purposes of clarity, I confine the concern here as narrowly as possible. My focus is on environmental protection from nuclear weapons *use*. Threats, although troublesome from other perspectives, are not by themselves damaging to the environment, nor are possession and research. "Development" of weaponry is not itself a cause for specific concern unless testing of nuclear devices is involved; then environmental damage would be produced.

A further characteristic of this analysis is the importance placed on distinguishing various concrete effects of the nuclear arms race. This emphasis implies at least two important conclusions. First, prospects for environmental disruption must be understood in relation to a nuclear arsenal *in being* (there are claims that the dangers of actual use could increase even as the size of the arsenal decreases); therefore, one must judge what set of feasible policies most diminishes the prospects of a major war being fought with nuclear weapons. Moreover, environmental damage may result from *any* use of nuclear weapons whatsoever, whether deliberate or (given the characteristics of stockpiles, doctrines, and safety practices) inadvertent; from this standpoint, the testing of nuclear weapons can be considered a type of use.

A further problem arises from the impossibility of evaluating opposed lines of risk assessment. There are those who contend that the proliferation of nuclear weapons enhances overall stability and decreases overall prospects of use. The consensus on this issue is that more states with fingers on the nuclear trigger will be destabilizing and (its racist corollary) that non-white or Third World fingers are likely to be less restrained and reliable; that is, nuclear deterrence will be less dependable as a war prevention posture relative to its dependence on non-Western governments. But others take the view that proliferation is inevitable; that it will extend to non-governmental political groups, including those relying on terrorism; and that the maximum inhibition on the further spread of nuclear capabilities is therefore desirable. The main argument here is that we cannot validate our judgment of relative risk except by analogy and prejudice, yet the reliability of such extrapolations is controversial, and for every analogy there exists a counteranalogy.

Against this background, cultural norms operate in complicated, ambiguous ways. A central question is whether constructive intervention can strengthen cultural dispositions against environmental risks and the damage that could result from nuclearism. At this time, in my view, deference to environmental quality as a source of restraint is not separable from the overall effort to avoid nuclear war and the wider dynamics of a global arms race; hence, the topic of environmental protection in relation to nuclear weaponry needs to be conceived indirectly. Indirection implies giving attention mainly to counter-nuclearist pressures, regardless of whether they are explicitly concerned with the environmental factor or, as is more likely, concentrate on the avoidance of nuclear war to ensure human survival, with protection to the environment as a bonus if they are successful. There is, to be sure, some revulsion against nuclearism because it threatens the miracle of life and beauty on the planet, quite apart from overriding preoccupations with preserving the human species.

From the perspective of constructive intervention, then, those factors that discourage the arms race and dependence on nuclear weapons will have the secondary benefit of making environmental quality more secure. Mobilizing cultural norms to serve these goals is a neglected dimension of social policy.

NEW SOCIAL MOVEMENTS

Several transnational social movements are bearers of ecological values: the environmental movement itself, protection of indigenous peoples, the overall women's movement, the peace movement, and the struggle for human rights. These initiatives overlap to a considerable degree, but they all have the effect of questioning the war system, statist priorities, and technological momentum. Alongside the renewed appreciation of premodern heritages has emerged the contours of a postmodern possibility associated with an extension of ecological priorities to all modes of existence: that is, what has been termed "deep ecology." [17]

These developments are potentially significant for the struggle against nuclearism. This double challenge (historical and prophetic) being directed at modernism suggests an increasing influence for a cluster of cultural norms that find reliance on nuclear weapons an intolerable social practice, expressive of unacceptable attitudes toward war, state power, and technology and, most of all, toward life itself. [18]

THE SHIFTING BALANCE OF LEGITIMACY

The normative repudiation of nuclearism by doctors, lawyers, religious traditions, nonnuclear governments, artists, and, more selectively, even professional military personnel suggests the existence of a wide array of cultural reinforcements for restrictive attitudes toward the legality and moral acceptability of nuclear weaponry. The effects can be perverse: An escalation of nuclearism may be proposed in large part to deflect these normative criticisms, as has been the case with "defensive" weapons and the militarization of space.

Nevertheless, on balance there has been a strong normative turn against nuclear weapons during the last decade. This turn was given an initial impetus by Soviet initiatives, especially the unilateral moratorium on nuclear testing and far-reaching proposals for a world without nuclear weapons. It was reinforced by those with impeccable national security credentials in the West who proposed as an initial denuclearizing step a shift to "no first use" strategy and doctrine. [19] This momentum dissipated, however, and the 1990s began in a mood of nuclear complacency.

AN ETHOS OF NONCOOPERATION AND RESISTANCE

The change in normative climate also had an effect on the acceptance of governmental authority. Legal and religious traditions have reinforced resistance activities based on conscience, including a strong impulse to oppose locally the presence or deployment of nuclear weapons capabilities and nuclear tests, especially those perceived as having nonretaliatory or first-strike properties. [20] That hundreds of individuals arrested and prosecuted for protests at the nuclear test site in Nevada during the 1980s reflected a growing conviction that the United States government was locked into nuclearism in an international setting, whereas the

Soviet Union was offering responsible methods to support the dynamics of denuclearization embedded in provisions for an extensive verification mechanisms.

In some sense, such a rise of resistance activity, including serious acts of defiance by individuals of high moral standing, can be interpreted as a kind of cultural alarm bell, a warning that the societal fabric is being rent by existing patterns. If civilizations ignore such warnings, internal decay and collapse can follow. Some believe that the turningpoint in the Vietnam War came in 1962 and 1963 when several Buddhist monks burned themselves to death as a public protest against the corruption of Vietnam brought on by the war. The extremity of such symbolic protest was intended to convey the dire conditions that existed in South Vietnam at that time. Priests, nuns, and other religiously devout women and men have risked extended and repeated imprisonment and physical injury to sustain their normative challenge to nuclearism, as well as to certain other foreign policy issues, including intervention in Central America and support for apartheid South Africa. Brian Willson, run down in the mid-1980s by a U.S. Navy munitions train while protesting the shipment of arms to the contras, had to have both his legs amputated.

Conflict between conscience and respect for political authority goes back at least as far as Antigone's refusal to obey Creon's strictures on the burial of enemies in ancient Thebes. More recently, this pattern of conflict has been extended by the Nuremberg experience. The prosecution of defeated leaders after World War II generalized for the first time the notion that respect for law—in these instances the international law of war and peace—takes precedence over the duty to obey the *diktat* of the state. Disobedience *within* the state can then become a matter of law observance in a wider setting. Indeed, upholding the Nuremberg Principles becomes the first, overarching duty of citizenship.

Here the critical relevance of cultural norms should be evident. The embodiment of the Nuremberg Principles in general international law can be either an empty ritual, like the operation of traffic lights in New Delhi, or a transformative process by which the overall relationship between state and civil society is gradually reversed, especially with respect to such salient dimensions as nuclearism and environmental protection.

NUCLEAR DISENGAGEMENT

A parallel tendency can be discerned at the governmental level. For several decades members of the two great blocs went along with the nuclear implications of their relationship to a superpower. There was a

serious early effort at nuclear disengagement by Japan, but this was discounted as a special case because of Japan's "nuclear allergy," a deferred
symptom of the Hiroshima and Nagasaki experience.

More recently, however, partly as a product of a long process of
growing doubts within civil society, opposition political parties and even
elected governments have tried to pursue a policy of nuclear disengagement. New Zealand's refusal to allow harbor entry of nuclear-capable
naval vessels provoked a crisis within the ANZUS alliance. The stand of
Prime Minister David Lange attracted sympathetic global attention and
enjoyed consistent support at home, despite some adverse economic
repercussions during a period of recession. Other political parties, especially those associated with Social Democratic parties in Western Europe,
have also reflected the growing weight of antinuclear sentiments. These
sentiments, it should be stressed, embody a tilt in cultural balance against
earlier practices of deferring to the state in matters of national security
policy. Moderate tendencies can, but do not necessarily, help create the
political space for denuclearizing moves on the part of the government.
The ferment from below creates fissures and divisions among leaders and
within bureaucratic structures enabling a break from nuclear deterrence
orthodoxy.

At the same time, strong obstacles impede the emergence of the newer
cultural norms. In particular, members of the permanent bureaucracies
of all governments tend to oppose any break in transnational links with
superpower elites. These officials enjoy their access to intelligence, joint
maneuvers, and new technologies, even if their role in the alliance process
is very subordinate. Also, the bureaucracies often feel distant from the
antinuclear electoral sentiments that tend to exert pressure on elected
politicians.

Another opposing process arises from the configuration of international economic forces, making smaller states vulnerable to leverage from
geopolitical centers of nuclearist policy. Small countries that need capital,
credit, and markets can be destabilized by falling out of favor with the
main political actors in the world economy.

FAVORABLE HISTORICAL SETTING

The postwar trends following the victory over fascism and the early
onset of the Cold War mobilized the main societies of the world for
prolonged tension and confrontation. In that bipolar circumstance, blocs
were organized around the opposed alliance systems in Europe, each
dominated by a superpower. In this highly charged atmosphere the

nuclear arms race took shape, as well as the prevailing convictions that nuclear weapons were both necessary to deter catastrophic war and potentially usable as decisive instruments of warfare. The latter conviction definitely surfaced in Washington during the Dulles-Eisenhower years, being crystallized in the strategic doctrine of massive retaliation. In that period, geopolitics dominated all other considerations; the dangers of nuclearism were generally unappreciated, and issues of environmental disruption were not perceived as relevant at all.

The ending of the postwar world occurred in the 1960s and 1970s with the reemergence of Japan and Germany as major actors; the failure of the United States to prevail in Vietnam; the rising challenge of OPEC and the nonaligned movement; the domination of the United Nations General Assembly by the Third World; the attainment of strategic parity by the Soviet Union; the inability of the Soviet Union to legitimate its imposition of Communist rule in Eastern Europe; and in 1975 the acceptance of the postwar European boundaries in the Helsinki Accords. Of course, 1989 changed many prevailing attitudes, establishing a much more definitive transition to a new era of European and global history. In this multipolar setting, social forces in civil society began to consider whether their interests and values were served by nuclearism. As a result, the moral and political space expanded to enable cultural norms opposed to sovereign control to become more influential, especially in the smaller countries.

ELITE DEFECTION

Notable also in this period was the anxiety about the eventual breakdown of nuclearism by former members of policy-making elites, including those with national security credentials. Expressions of deep concern from figures such as Robert McNamara and George Kennan are indicative of deeper stirrings in the culture on these matters.

Kennan, who earlier had derided moralist and legalist influence on American foreign policy, announced his own change of heart in the form of a "confession" that appeared in a preface to a book of essays: "I am now bound to say that while the earliest possible elimination of nuclear weaponry is of no less vital importance in my eyes than it ever was, this would not be enough, in itself, to give Western civilization even an adequate chance of survival. War itself, as a means of settling differences at least between the industrial powers, will have to be in some way ruled out; and with it there will have to be dismantled (for without this the whole outlawing of war would be futile) the greater part of the vast military establishments now maintained with a view to the possibility that war might take place." [21] Such radical gropings gave a greater plausibility to those elements within the overall culture drawn to nonviolence or to more transformative solutions to the current security dilemma.

In effect, the 1980s suggested that the nuclearist consensus might be about to crack, and crack in such a way as to challenge the institution of war itself. Unfortunately, those challenges have been dissipated and the 1990s commenced with a renewed pronuclear solidity.

CONCLUSION

The connection between cultural norms and environmental protection proceeds in many directions. At present, an important shift seems to be occurring in the tectonic plates of civilizational orientation. For a variety of reasons, nuclearism appears to be on the defensive, but certain lines of weapons innovation could produce a new surge of nuclearism at the core of security policy. The American insistence on proceeding with the militarization of space is expressive both of a rising tide of criticism of the deterrence rationale for nuclearism and an effort to adapt nuclearism to a new global political order.

At this stage, it would seem useful to reinvigorate the normative repudiation of nuclearism by promoting at least two undertakings on a formal, explicit level:

- circulate a Nuremberg Pledge to citizens in all walks of life to work for accountability by leaders in and out of government to the existing international legal rules governing recourse to and conduct of war; the pledge would also remind individuals, including ordinary citizens, of their responsibility to implement international law even against their own officials and policy-makers;
- prepare a draft Ecocide Convention that would emphasize the duty of leaders and policy-makers to take account of the distinctive threat to the coherence and durability of nature which arises from the prospect of any use of nuclear weapons.

The ending of the Cold War has had the paradoxical consequence of reducing pressures on leaders to abandon reliance on nuclear weapons. With the moderation of East-West tension, a mood of nuclear complacency, even indifference, has set in. Most ominously, this mood may express a belief that nuclear weapons can now be "safely" employed in North-South confrontations. Before the ground phase of the Gulf War, for example, there was media speculation about the possible use of nuclear weapons to save lives or in retaliation for Iraqi reliance on chemical weapons. Nevertheless, it seems likely that renewed normative pressures may be generated in coming years against nuclearism, possibly arising out of anxieties associated with proliferation prospects and with the emergence of nonnuclear weapons of mass destruction: chemical, biological, and radiological.

This normative pressure may be reinforced by shifts in the attitudes and tactics of military establishments. There are some indications of a declining place for nuclear weaponry in strategic calculations, even in North-South settings, based on the view that such weaponry is too "provocative" to rely upon; further, it can be displaced not only by almost equally destructive nonnuclear weaponry but by far more sophisticated forms of weapons guidance that make reliance on indiscriminate destruction far less militarily necessary and justifiable.

Quite possibly, then, by the end of this decade normative and pragmatic factors will converge to renew with greater vigor than ever the challenge against nuclearism.

CHAPTER IX

Evasions of Sovereignty

As yet nobody has drawn a map that reflects the new order.

Lewis Lapham, "Leviathan in Trouble"

THE PROBLEM OF SOVEREIGNTY IN LIGHT OF THE COMING GLOBAL CIVILIZATION

THERE IS these days an ever more widespread belief that a world map composed of sovereign states no longer provides (if indeed it ever did) a useful conception of how the world as a whole is constituted. In the spirit of popular commentary, Lewis Lapham, editor of an influential American monthly magazine, suggests that if someone were to try depicting "the new order," it would "look more like medieval France than nineteenth century Europe."[1] Lapham's image of the feudal precursor to the modern state system implies a multitude of overlapping types of authority, arising from royal, ecclesiastical, and economic sources, which were at once more centralized and less territorially exclusive than we generally imagine of our own age. Such a deconstruction of the modern state is a suggestive image of late twenty-first-century realities, perhaps, but it is surely premature and quite misleading as a descriptive basis for recasting our understanding of present international realities. An evocation of the feudal order helps us little to grasp what lies just beyond the horizon of an unfolding future. Territorial states remain the predominant political actors in our world, although their interactions are becoming bewilderingly complex and their operational reach increasingly extraterritorial even as their capacity for autonomy is cumulatively eroded.[2]

Indeed, a strong case can be made for treating a map of states as more accurate than ever before. The global dynamics of nationalism in recent

196

decades has created greater viability for many weaker states, at least in terms of resisting the most blatant forms of military encroachment by ascendant states. The actual situation is uneven and complicated, but it is certainly easier for many militarily subordinate territorial governments to organize resistance to interventionary diplomacy and thereby to safeguard their sovereign character against imperial designs. Even the superpowers have faced increasingly formidable challenges to their respective control over so-called "blocs" or "spheres of interest." Military superiority is far more difficult to translate into political control than it was in the previous century, when mass mobilization around militant nationalist creeds was unusual. And economic penetration has become more difficult in its cruder forms, requiring elaborate arrangements to limit or disguise foreign capital. The need for indirection is a tribute to the potency of nationalism as a reigning political ideology. Governments can no longer sustain their full legitimacy—either in relation to their own society or with regard to the outer world—if they grant foreign allies special privileges within their territory. Foreign military bases are increasingly difficult to establish, and most of those that exist are under mounting political pressure from the local population. There are exceptions, either where a government lacks any autonomy (and any pretense of legitimacy) or where it is faced by a security challenge that makes a foreign military presence appear a genuinely necessary form of collective self-defense rather than a platform that serves the wider geopolitical strategy of a distant great power. Of course, whether these generalizations will hold up in the post–Cold War situation of international relations is uncertain, especially given the probability of consensus in the North and disunity in the South, as well as undisputed U.S. preeminence as the sole global actor.

Nor are all states adequate vehicles of nationalist claims. Many "nations" (self-consciously ethnic units) are "entrapped" within a sovereign space administered by a government that is controlled by a different nation. Such a state may be autonomous vis-à-vis the external world, but its internal legitimacy is constantly subject to interrogation, if not assault, by assertive and alienated national minorities. In such circumstances, crises of governability are evident. The state lacks the capability to produce either order, justice, or security against unwanted outside interference. Contemporary Lebanon is currently the most aggravated instance, but roughly analogous problems torment many societies to varying degrees, providing government with expedient justifications for abandoning democracy and human rights and exposing human populations to acute forms of daily-insecurity with respect to basic human needs.

Can we portray the current shape of world order by a conventional map of states? Or is it better to conceive of the world as a criss-cross of patterns based on different issues, regimes, and perceptions? I would argue that a sophisticated atlas is preferable to a map, that we need many different ways of looking at the planet as a whole, ranging from the photographs sent back from space satellites through geoeconomic presentations of resources, trade flows, arms trade, and military alliances, as well as space coordinated with population size and standard of living. Mapping differing expectations about the shape of the future would certainly disclose the priorities of a political vision based on world order values.

Hypotheses about a coming global civilization are put forward, partly descriptively, partly normatively, as an overlay upon this debate about the role, viability, patterning, and variety of sovereign states. The contention goes beyond either liberal formulations of interdependence or Marxist formulations of global class structure and international division of labor.[3] In effect, an emergent global ethos suggests the reality of a shared destiny for the human species and a fundamental unity across space and through time, built around the bioethical impulse of all human groups to *survive* and *flourish*. Such an ethos has implications for the assessment of problems, the provision of solutions, and the overall orientation of action and actors. For most people and leaders, this sense of shared destiny does not displace a persisting primary attachment to the state as a vehicle for aspiration and as an absolute, unconditional bastion of security. As the "nuclear winter" imagery dramatizes, leaders of nuclear powers seem prepared to threaten the overall survival of civilization and even risk partial or total extinction if such a threat seems necessary to uphold the sovereign identity of a particular state or, more narrowly, the persistence of a particular regime type and governing elite. The logic of war in the nuclear age devours the self that is the object of protection and holds hostage the entire human race, including the idea and reality of unborn generations and indeed the whole life process. From a religious perspective, it is a blasphemy to creation, the sacred work of divinity, to contemplate as a deliberate and discretionary undertaking by human agency the destruction of the world; nuclearism is indefensible both in the most fundamental philosophical sense and in its practical relationship to human well-being.[4]

There is thus at the base of our inquiry, a powerful set of paradoxical forces at work: As the territorial state becomes more vulnerable to what takes place beyond its sovereign reach, it acquires a capability that generates many varieties of extraterritorial harm as side effects of "normalcy." Such a loss of territorial moorings exposes the problem of the political organization of international life from the perspective of state sovereignty. It is difficult to avoid some degree of conceptual confusion at this point. If sovereignty inheres in the people, not the state, then a delegation of authority can be reinterpreted or even reclaimed by popular action. Sovereignty, by democratic theory, is not to be automatically identified with the state, yet in modern practice—especially in matters of international policy—the state, even the democratic state, has increasingly operated without encountering substantial challenges from "below" and generally without significant citizen participation; statist understandings of sovereignty tend to prevail.

In the discussion that follows, the inquiry into "evasions" starts from the empirical reality that "sovereignty" is perceived as concentrated in states. The recovery of sovereignty through the reinvigoration of democratic practice would work against the current tendency to identify sovereignty exclusively with the central governing process of territorial states enjoying international status. The notion of sovereignty rests on an overall congruence between authority, capability, territoriality, and loyalty. That is, at least conceptually and to varying degrees existentially, states, claim, often credibly, the authority and capacity to provide security and welfare for the people within their territory in exchange for expectations of loyalty and obedience from the population. Such a practical adjustment has also been combined with the belief that war and conflict provide both a foundation for protecting diversity (or difference) at acceptable costs and, contrariwise, a legislative process for achieving change that is incidentally assimilated into the validating processes of international law by way of "the peace treaty" (even territorial changes achieved by "aggression" have been given full legal effect). Without war, the international status quo would arguably have been frozen with respect to the size and scale of operative units.

Patterns of incongruence take on such great significance at this historical moment because of their *consequential* character. The theoretical "discovery" of incongruence is by itself interesting; incongruence could over time weaken the loyalty and legitimacy claims of the state but would probably not be effectual on its own in the face of the capacities of the state to propagandize and coerce. But today, the human subservience imposed on citizens is quite extraordinary, especially under conditions of democracy where access to damaging information tends to be greater, and thus the vulnerability of people to breakdowns of international order cannot be disguised. The consequences of nuclear winter, of global warming and ozone depletion, of rainforest destruction, of air and ocean pollution are quite literally shattering to human prospects. This mismatch between capabilities and challenges is bound to cause severe tensions between state and society in the years to come.

Yet states will endeavor to fashion responses to these challenges, and over time the state has displayed a considerable capacity for adaptation as well as resilience. State leaders have already given expression to the growing need for cooperation, including self-limiting standards. The impressive intergovernmental reaction to the prospects of harmful effects arising from ozone depletion is illustrative. With great haste and in a spirit of seriousness, once a consensus was formed as to cause and harmful effect, an international agreement was negotiated, the Montreal Protocol, whose central mandate is a commitment by treaty members, starting in 1989, to phase out by the end of the century 50 percent of those chemicals (especially chlorofluorocarbons) that deplete ozone. Subsequently, even before the treaty was in force, there were private and public acknowledgments that the plan, even if fully implemented, was woefully insufficient, and indeed, with the surprising help of Margaret Thatcher, a more stringent supplemental agreement on phasing out CFCs was accepted. Some corporate users *voluntarily* agreed to substitute more expensive components, beyond treaty requirements, and public officials called for more rigorous standards, asking that a commitment to the total elimination of CFCs be substituted for the present duty to cut down by half.[5]

This regulatory process is a test of whether, in the face of vested economic interests unevenly distributed among state actors, it is possible to move toward an effective regime of prohibition even in a situation where the evidence of severe harm arising from the prohibited activity is substantially uncontested. The Montreal Protocol lacks an enforcement capability. If other states implement it, then a failure to implement will not seem so serious; if others cheat, then additional cheating will not matter that much, and why should some ensure higher production costs if others don't? Such a *structure*, by its calculus of separate interests, is dominated by the pursuit of the well-being of the fragment or part, reinforced by the conviction that to forgo advantages merely shifts benefits to other state actors, as when a state withholds arms from warring parties. Can the aggregated interest of these separate and dissimilar perspectives be translated into policies that protect the well-being of the whole (which comprises all the parts, including itself) within *existing* structures? There is no assured answer at this point. There may never be a clear response. The conditions of each instance may shape a series of understandings not necessarily fully consistent with one another: How widely shared is the information about the probable gravity of the harm in the event of persistence? How deferred in time is the harm likely to be? How great are the economic costs of adjustment? Can they be shifted or otherwise offset? How aroused is both world public opinion and the particular climate of opinion in important countries? How easy is it to detect noncompliance with agreed standards? How likely are Third World countries to be guided by cost efficiency factors? To what extent will richer countries, especially those most responsible for the particular form of environmental harm, bear a proportional share of adjustment costs?

Ozone depletion may be an important test, both because of its own bearing on future health and well-being and because it presents an adjustment challenge that is significant in its requirements but not overwhelming. The nature of the test is severalfold: Can commitments of compliance be monitored and upheld in the absence of enforcement mechanisms? Can the depth of commitment be made responsive to the severity of the problem during an interval of time when successful adjustment is still possible? Is a regime of prohibition already too late in the sense that the process of harmful effects cannot be arrested or reversed by the time the political will is mobilized to take cooperative action? These are some of the general issues to be considered if our concern is with the adjustment capabilities of the state system by way of cooperative action.[6] There is also the question of whether the more difficult adjustment required to arrest global warming can be agreed upon and then effectively implemented in sufficient time. Such an adjustment calls for a gradual shift away from burning fossil fuels as a primary source of energy for heating and transportation. What seems involved here is the nature of modern industrial society as it has evolved in the West.

The second dimension of resilience as a feature of statism concerns the affective loyalties of peoples. Given the way state and society interact in the modern world, the state is seen, increasingly in the postcolonial era, as a necessary (and desirable) frame for advancing and safeguarding nationalist aspirations. Those nationals who have no state (Palestinians, Kurds, indigenous peoples) are exceptionally vulnerable to repressive tactics, especially as they are located within a state that is largely a vehicle for realizing the incompatible interests of a rival "nation." Since all territory belongs to existing states, and the loss of territory is generally considered an unacceptable encroachment on sovereign rights, the presence of rival nations within boundaries is regarded by established governments as an active or latent threat. The effect of nationalist energies is to fragment the world political structure to an even greater degree, but state resistance of these energies results in denial of self-determination and reliance on coercion. Increasingly, the "self" in self-determination can be manipulated to restrict its relevance to existing territorial units as acknowledged by membership in the United Nations and other criteria. Conferring "nationality" by legal decree, or by issuing a passport, does not displace or overcome existential feelings of nationalist identity, and their denial. This nationalist creed seems, if anything, to be intensifying, although unevenly. It is primarily to satisfy nationalist aspirations that many people in different state settings are voluntarily risking their lives and displaying courage and commitment to alter existing political arrangements.

The significance of nationalist potency for my argument is this: Many state structures are being challenged by nationalist movements. The states generally resist these challenges by reliance on coercion, considering such resistance itself a sovereign right if exercised within territory. Consequently, the nationalist movements often seek the protective and assertive frameworks of the sovereign state, including a reliance on human rights. Although they are usually motivated by a territorial project, their political outlook often includes a sense of solidarity with other struggling nationalisms and a dependence for support on international institutions; it can be understood as a common quest for human rights *within* the existing statist structure.[7] If our concern is with world order values—associated here with acting in response to a global ethos—then many of the various nationalisms are potentially capable of making positive contributions to an improvement of the relationship between human population groups and political institutions.

This contention can be specified to a further degree: attaining statehood would fulfill the process of self-determination of peoples for certain national movements, itself a normative accomplishment; increasing the congruence between nation and state would reduce violent conflict and presumably allow more political attention to be devoted to the global agenda.

But there are severe structural problems. By 1990 there were more than 800 nationalist movements in the world but less than 200 states. Many among these 800 claimants are small, weak, dispersed, nonviable, but not necessarily resigned to their fate. There is no prospect that all these nationalisms can be accommodated by grants of statehood. In fact, territorial claims are often layered in such a way that the vindication of one nationalist destiny would displace another. As a result, sovereignty is difficult to evade, even if political self-determination is accepted as an authoritative norm. Its application necessarily involves tensions, contradictions, and conflict. Also, states that are inherently incapable of mobilizing resources to meet the needs of their population present serious problems of viability, even if their political structure is accepted as legitimate.

Could one imagine denationalized states as a basis for a more constructive role of sovereignty? Of course, most modern states already claim to be secular entities that confer nationality by legal, not ethnic, criteria and govern on a nondiscriminatory basis.[8] But the secularization of sovereignty has not succeeded in extinguishing the primacy of nationalist identities or their perception of many existing states as repressive vehicles of ascendant forms of nationalism. Hence, unfortunately, at a time of long-range, global-scale challenge it is likely that the political energies of many states and discontented nations will focus on immediate struggles over autonomy, human rights, and contested movements for statehood.

What is the overall prospect for cooperative undertakings in a world menaced as a whole by disintegrative forces associated with the limits of "carrying capacity" and an absence of sufficient capabilities to define and protect global interests? These limits must be tested, stretched, and, one hopes, relocated; the intellectual and political significance of a global integrative process is to identify the limits as they bear upon the challenges and capabilities of political actors in our world, premised on a shared affirmation of the value of sustaining, and even enhancing, the quality of life for the peoples of the world, including those of future generations. With such a normative premise, the collaborative endorsement of an emergent global civilization seeks to expand the *resources* of both citizens and leaders by making public opinion more attuned to the dangers and to possibilities for constructive action, by abolishing destructive polarities between "us" and "them" without losing the special qualities of diversity that give the particularities of human existence their special glow of enchantment.

States do participate cooperatively in wider political communities that fall into three general categories: (1) hegemonic "communities," in which most of the glue is supplied by the dominant state, and the weaker participants have had their autonomy gravely compromised, and their legitimacy as well, to the extent that a governing elite in subordinate countries loses control over vital sectors of policy and acquiesces in such arrangements; (2) alliance "communities," especially during wartime, periods of high international tension, and in reaction to expansionist drives of antidemocratic and imperialist states; (3) cooperative "communities," in which the mutual benefits of economic integration or common regimes for environmental protection and technical relations provide rational incentives for weakening state boundaries. These arrangements are extensions of ordinary diplomacy, fulfilling goals of state actors. Their scope is normally regional, motivated either by domination, fear (of an enemy), or calculations of gain. Such patterns do not as yet respond directly to either the affirmative reality of a global ethos or the more negative dangers associated with the deterioration of the global commons. From the perspective of world order values, such extended political communities can be either regressive or positive, depending on the circumstances. The normative effects can be complex, as is illustrated by debates about the impact of the 1992 plans for further economic integration in Western Europe or the recently concluded free trade treaty between the United States and Canada. Even when the economic effects suggest mutual benefit, a weaker state that participates in such a widening process risks its autonomy and often gives up political space in which to explore alternative lines of policy.[9] Wider frameworks do not necessarily represent a positive adjustment from the perspective of world order values. Quite the contrary, the most prevalent patterns of "suprastatism" often jeopardize some of the most desirable features of national identity that are preserved by states operating on a secure basis of legitimacy: that is, providing their people with human rights, political democracy, a sense of community and tradition, and overall security.

One focus of this effort to adapt political behavior to the global setting is to reinterpret sovereignty, weakening its conflictual preoccupation with threats to territorial space, without depreciating its role in safeguarding to the extent possible the autonomy of particular nations (or, more problematically, of groups of nations joined together as a single state beneath a common flag). Changing the perceptions of the character of the threat—from "the other" as enemy to the current enfeebled arrangements of "the whole" as menacing—can change the choice of instruments for upholding autonomy (that is, the exercise of sovereignty), especially if these instruments of political assertion become denuclearized and demilitarized. Such a process centers, of course, on rethinking "security," shifting the locus from "national security" (part versus part) to "common security" or "comprehensive security" (parts depending on the whole), but it also involves adapting the agenda and priorities of states so that they respond by the most effective means available to challenges directed at their citizenry. The assumptions here are decidedly selfish rather than altruistic, presupposing that a collective response to ozone depletion, for example, is necessary for the sake of national well-being. In this regard, effective sovereignty entails establishing an ambitious regime of prohibition on the basis of negotiation and cooperation among states rather than on the typical basis of a threat posed by an external enemy which can be countered only by counterthreats and capabilities. It may be better to grasp the integrative tendencies of international life as a challenge to a militarized and highly spatial orientation toward sovereignty rather than to sovereignty per se. Part of the analysis being made rests on the diminished ability of territorial boundaries, as defended by military capabilities, to keep a given society free from external penetration. Increasingly, even the most impressively protected boundaries cannot keep out unwanted drugs, persons, ideas, or polluting substances.

Part of the resilience of political life in general derives from the multiplicity and interaction of forms for acting in the world. The role of independent voices is crucial in placing problems on the main political agenda, because vested interests are often mobilized to keep as "invisible" and ineffectual as possible any such challenges to current patterns of "profitable" practices. To initiate action requires an acknowledgment of the gravity of a problem, as well as enough time to overcome destructive patterns of practice. The existence of democratic space is indispensable, as is the protection of those who are the messengers of bad news. Yet individuals who break "the silence" of institutions are vulnerable to severe forms of abuse. Their voices are stilled by the oppressive reflex action of even democratic political traditions under such labels as "treason," "espionage," or "national security." When Mordechai Vanunu disclosed and verified the extent of Israel's nuclear weapons program in 1986, he breached Israel's official silence and was abducted abroad by Israeli secret agents, prosecuted, convicted of treason, and sentenced to eighteen years in jail. With such rigid bureaucratic reflexes the state damages its own resilience by responding severely to challenges, especially those associated with "national security" at the core of its militarist orientation toward sovereignty. Exposing the state to such challenges on grounds of policy and practice, from within and without (transnational democracy), is part of what might enable sovereignty to become potentially more adaptive. Such constitutional conceptions as "checks and balances," "separation of powers," "inalienable rights," and periodic elections to obtain "the consent of the governed" are part of an effort to make government more flexible in the face of changing conditions and values but not so fluid as to be able too easily to transgress limits on the exercise of power. Notions of "civil disobedience" and, more recently, "civil resistance" are ways of underscoring the relevance of conscience to the assessment of official policy. After World War II the notion of moral assessment was given an obligatory character in the course of the Nuremberg trials and the subsequent formulation of a notion of responsibility to uphold international law in the war/peace area, even as against direct commands by the head of state.[10] There are, then, many connections between a revitalized political democracy, positive sovereignty, and a relatively smooth transition to a more integrative, less territorial stage of international relations.

It is these "resources" of sovereignty, often unappreciated and even scorned and suppressed, that I discuss below under the phrase "the evasions of sovereignty." "Evasion" refers here to political action by nonstate actors that addresses the agenda of global concerns. The implicit argument is both functional and normative, raising issues of practicality and desirability. Patterns of evasion are increasing in frequency and scale for several reasons: the growing complexity and interrelatedness of international life; the failure of states to fashion sufficient responses on their own. The motivational basis for many evasions is associated with humanistic convictions that are broader in scope than normal state action. One consequence of the cumulative effect of evasion-oriented action is to form political communities that cannot be encompassed by state boundaries and do not yet appear on maps designating membership and participation in the world political system. What is emerging are transnational and intranational linkages that build up a body of practice and engender new patterns of loyalty, a cumulative process associated in this volume with the dawn of global civil society, a political process generating a civilizational identity that is both diverse and encompassing.

PATTERNS OF EVASION

By a "pattern of evasion" I mean a locus of action distinct from the state but not necessarily in opposition to it. Indeed, many of the most ambitious patterns of evasion have been initiated and managed by concerted state action, including the formation and operation of the United Nations. Those who act within these patterns draw their inspiration, in part at least, from a nonterritorial outlook that embodies to some degree a cosmopolitan outlook. Their intention or influence may be directed toward the state and, to this extent, can be perceived as a resource *additional* or *complementary* to states confronted by the need to cope with global-scale challenges and opportunities. In this reinforcing role, patterns of evasion are an expression of the adjustment capabilities of states and hence manifest the resilience, as well as the shortcomings, of states and the state system. As such, they have a mainly stabilizing relevance, at least in the short run, and they can be regarded as efforts to realize the order-producing and justice-realizing potential of the state system.

But as we shall see, patterns of evasion are often more ambiguous in intention and effect. Transformative implications can arise from those interpretations of a global ethos that reject either fundamental behavioral traits of statism (for instance, domestic jurisdiction, violence, and militarism), its basic organizational features (for instance, subordinating global claims to the assertion of territorial supremacy), or its psychopolitical priorities (for instance, favoring territorial and fragmentary loyalties, putting patriotism ahead of the global ethos). In this regard, there is a natural disposition to perceive the state as opposing these patterns of evasion, as seeking to constrain or even eliminate such fields of action.

Both perceptions of reinforcement and of antagonistic roles are accurate, making an overall evaluation of evasive tendencies confusing and controversial. The proper assessment of a particular "evasion" depends on a convincing interpretation of its actual role in relation to the state and its project for the future, as well as some judgment of its relation to world order values. To extend the argument, I discuss three principal patterns: evasions *across* boundaries (transnational); evasions *within* boundaries (internal); and evasions *beyond* boundaries (supranational).

EVASIONS ACROSS

A concrete instance of evasion is the Great Peace Journey (GPJ), conceived and implemented over several years by a group of Swedish women and culminating its initial stage of activities in the First Global Popular Summit held at the United Nations headquarters in New York City during several days in late September 1988. The GPJ used as a tactical mechanism, five questions posed to governments belonging to the United Nations, questions embodying the ideals of the UN Charter on matters of nuclear weaponry, foreign bases, disarmament, arms sales, development assistance, and governmental accountability under international law.[11] These questions adopted the formulation "Are you willing . . . if all other UN members undertake to do the same?" Multinational delegations visited as many countries as possible to obtain "Yes" or "No" responses from government representatives as prominent as they were able to arrange access to, including several heads of states and senior ministers. In the course of three years, most major countries were visited, more than a hundred in all, with "Yes" responses obtained from some ninety-one. The organizers were aware that these responses were not by themselves real political commitments or even very suggestive of policy; they expressed no more than an endorsement of a common and hypothetical vision of what was required in response to the call for a peaceful, just, and sustainable world. But the main impulse of the project was to reverse two features of modern political participation: the passivity of the citizenry in relation to the attitude of foreign governments on issues of world policy, and the presumed territorial character of relations between state and society. The GPJ intuitively proceeded on the basis of the transnational democratic conviction that governments in an interdependent world are accountable to *all peoples,* not just to their own citizens, other governments, and international institutions. In effect, it converted the entire planet—including those portions governed by principles of sovereign control—into a *global commons* whose well-being was the responsibility of all peoples.

The GPJ was also aware of its dual role: to motivate governments to renew and express their attachment to a vision of a more desirable world order; and to expose any encountered unwillingness even to affirm the imperative of drastic global reform going well beyond what was embodied four decades before in the United Nations Charter (of course, the Charter's mandate has itself never been carried out, given the Cold War, North-South conflict, and a variety of geopolitical maneuvers by many states). More to the point, the GPJ devoted a considerable portion of its limited resources and energies to working with local and regional peace groups and grassroots initiatives, both to build a global network of activists and to establish a foundation for a *transnational* political process that would combine local, regional, and global priorities and be kept coherent by the vision of transforming "No" answers into "Yes" answers and "Yes" answers into a "Yes" world.

The GPJ by itself does not possess the perseverance to transform world order or even to evade sovereignty, but it can act as a catalyst for grassroots activism. Its main "weapon" is to mount verbal, symbolic, and normative challenges to established forms of state power and militarism. At the same time, GPJ is exploring and prefiguring a new sovereignty-evading politics: a community of adherents that is transnational; a commitment to nonviolent practice; an emphasis on feminist insight and leadership; a combining of "gentle anger" with songs of celebration, with flowers, and with art; an image of peace that encompasses social justice and ecological priorities. For such adherents, territoriality is not synonymous with loyalty, nor does an outsider lack standing to challenge governments. The GPJ delegations that circled the globe included regional and extraregional members, making the double point that there persists a special relationship of rights and duties to one's government (citizens should expect greater access and accountability from their own government) but that all people everywhere have a right to insist that every government act for peace, justice, and environmental quality. The field of action is planetary, and its animating ideology is transnational democracy.

Another apparent evasion of sovereignty is related to the use of information as a base of power. Groups such as Amnesty International and the Swedish International Peace Research Institute (SIPRI) gather information on crucial issues of international policy, build a reputation for integrity, and then disseminate materials that speak to policy issues with an authority that is not easily discredited. Whereas the allegations of governments can often be dismissed as propaganda or ideological slander, these transnationally funded and staffed associations disseminate information across boundaries without partisan affiliation or bias. The effectiveness of such information arises partly from the concern of virtually all modern governments with their *normative reputation* at home and abroad. Governments do not want to be perceived as perpetrators of torture or as suppliers of forbidden (say, biological or chemical) weaponry, and therefore exposure by an objective source is itself a sanction and even a deterrent, although its strength in each instance is difficult to gauge. Governments are reluctant to acknowledge the influence of moral or legal censure, especially when it exposes objectionable behavior and induces corrective action.

Often, transnational information is used by activists to put pressure on particular governments to take action against a pariah state. The anti-apartheid campaign is an excellent example. Without transnational networks that had access to information damaging to the South African regime, it would have been impossible to mount an anti-apartheid campaign throughout the world, especially in the United States and Great Britain, where economic and strategic interests are linked to maintaining the status quo. A related initiative concerns efforts by groups seeking to achieve improved standards of corporate accountability, as expressed by transnational campaigns to boycott certain products. The recurrent campaign against Nestlé for its effort to promote infant formula in impoverished regions of Africa is illustrative.

Sovereignty is also evaded by transnational environmental groups that disseminate information and offer symbolic resistance to nuclear testing, whaling, and sealing. Greenpeace is the best known transnational actor in the environment sector. Its effectiveness is difficult to assess or measure, but its obstructive activities often capture the imagination of peoples throughout the world and, beyond this, their gratitude for mounting opposition to what states do or allow beneath the banner of sovereignty. Greenpeace activists have been called "ecological terrorists" by Japanese officials because their boats have obstructed "illegal" Japanese whaling activities. Other undertakings are informational, as in reports on naval activities. Greenpeace sponsored hearings in Stockholm on nuclear weapons in Sweden, a controversial topic because the official policy of the Swedish government is to prohibit nuclear weapons from entering the country, but it does not challenge the U.S. policy ("neither confirm, nor deny") relative to its nuclear-capable ships. The Greenpeace Report, a model of fact-finding and documentation, presents strong evidence that, in fact, many nuclear weapons have been on ships making Swedish port calls over the years.[12] What is striking about the Stockholm hearings held on September 4, 1990, was that they were chaired by a well-known member of the Swedish Foreign Ministry and that the widely known and influential Undersecretary of State for Foreign Affairs Pierre Schori appeared on the program to defend the Swedish approach. Such a close, cooperative relationship between Greenpeace and a government could happen in very few countries and on only selected issues, but that it can happen at all is confirmatory of the growing legitimacy and prominence of transnational groups dedicated to far-reaching global reforms. Such a challenge of state policy, the basis of Greenpeace's report and hearings, is, in effect, an evasion of sovereignty because the format imposed a kind of accountability on the Swedish government that its participation confirmed.

A wide range of transnational undertakings have a more or less specific character. Their programs of action and tactics help shape responses
by states, as well as perceptions as to whether the evasion is tolerable
or not. These perceptions are also closely linked to varying attitudes
toward democratic opposition and to the role of civil society. If the transnational initiative challenges state sovereignty in the national security
sphere, however, responses are likely to be hostile and suppressive. Even
democracies with decent human rights records claim virtually absolute
control in this sphere, including their prerogative to restrict information
via procedures of secrecy, classification, and espionage laws; in setting
nuclear weapons policy, this tendency is maximized with exceedingly
harmful consequences for the quality of constitutional democracy.[13]

To the extent that the traditional prerogatives and legitimacy of a state
are not called into questions, political democracies tend to be generally
tolerant of criticism and opposition. However, to the degree that bitter
controversy exists, the transnational identity of an initiative can be used
to imply a lack of patriotism on the part of citizens who join in the activity. Often "laws" are invoked by governments to constrain transnational
initiatives that challenge state policy. For example, the U.S. government
claims exclusive regulatory authority over immigration policy and refuses
to allow any contradictory claims, such as those of the Sanctuary Movement. The degree of latitude given to such evasions depends on the issue,
the precariousness of the existing political arrangement, public attitudes,
and the political style adopted by leaders, especially their sensitivity to
international and domestic criticism. Long-range abstract issues with less
immediate policy implications tend to be better tolerated, even if their
substance is subversive of state power, than are transnational challenges
to concrete policy that is already in place.

EVASIONS WITHIN

Here the denial of sovereignty can be direct or indirect, but its essence
consists in acts by citizens against the governing process in their own
state. The initiative can have as its goal the change of a given policy or a
much broader revision of official policy, practices, and even institutional
arrangements (for example, a call for constitutional amendment or even
a constitutional convention). My focus is on evasions within territorial
boundaries that respond to the call of a global ethos, and circumvent to
some degree the state's control over civil society.

These evasions can involve the formation of permissible political
vehicles for the promotion of a global ethos, the essential story of the
Green parties in West Germany, the Netherlands, and elsewhere. The
status of this phenomenon is problematic, especially because the par-

ticular Green political formation may be committed to a reforming or a transforming mandate, or to some mixture.[14]

The Vanunu case mentioned earlier is an instance of evasion generating a suppressive backlash by the state in the form of prosecution for treason. Vanunu disclosed sensitive information, previously publiclly disseminated only in its broad contours, on Israel's nuclear weapons program and did so in an atmosphere of persisting tension that justified for many Israeli observers strong procedures to limit dissent and opposition.[15] Most expressions of sympathy and appreciation for Vanunu derived from outside of Israel, especially from transnational sources avowedly dedicated to a stateless global ethos (for example, Vanunu was the recipient of the Right Livelihood Award, a citation by the Danish Peace Foundation, and even received nominations for the Nobel Peace Prize).

The encouragement of whistle-blowers in the modern state seems of great benefit, even if it appears as an "evasion." Society is thus given information about matters that may concern their well-being in fundamental respects. Secrecy is often used by governments to hold back from their own citizenry information that undermines societal confidence in official competence and integrity. The Freedom of Information Act, despite loopholes, acknowledges the right of citizens to gain access to information previously withheld. As the ill effects of interdependence stretch the capacities of most, if not all, states to or beyond their limits, an increasing official impulse to withhold damaging information is likely to ensue, making evasions (and direct challenges) more functionally necessary than ever before—in the first instance, as a safety valve or early warning system; more fundamentally, as an exposure of structural defects in the governing process.

Often the implications are mixed. We now know that in several instances governments have withheld from people in their own society damaging information about nuclear reactor accidents and safety or health problems, often over a long stretch of time.[16] More than this, local officials, for fear that their own competence would be questioned, failed to inform national officials of serious nuclear reactor accidents at the Savannah River Plant, which was producing nuclear weapons.[17] Yet the implications can be read narrowly or broadly, either as showing the need to expose specific harm at particular reactors or to confirm those who oppose reliance on the particular technology.

The underlying observation holds: when legitimacy rests partly on competence, and competence is eroded by new challenges, then the impulse to deny the magnitude of the challenge grows strong, and those that question the denial will be generally treated as "enemies"—even if their intentions and effects are constructive—and must accept personal costs and risks to get the story out. The life of Karen Silkwood—a worker whose job involved handling nuclear materials in a manner dangerous to her health, and who was "accidentally" killed when she attempted to go public—is emblematic of these costs and risks but also of the importance of information to societal well-being.

EVASIONS BEYOND

There are two forms of evasion at issue here: behavioral patterns that are located beyond the reach of a state but have significant impact upon it (such as a nuclear accident in a foreign country, or the overseas production for export of hard drugs); and transfers of authority to international institutions and regimes (such as entrusting certain categories of claims to regional and global dispute-settlement procedures, or establishing international regimes to prohibit commercial whaling and to set quotas on "research").

The first form involves a loss of control by states in the face of many varieties of interdependence, including those that threaten health, agriculture, climate, and financial stability. The rise of these evasive patterns tends to foster perceptions of limits to state power, as well as to erode claims of competence and adequacy. The magnitude of evasiveness encourages the search for alternative, or at least supplemental, forms of order. For instance, Bangladesh is especially vulnerable to the effects of global warming because of its densely settled, low-lying coastal lands, yet its contribution to the greenhouse effect is virtually nil. Thus, its sovereignty is of no help if conceived in territorial terms. Only by entering external arenas to strengthen attempts to reduce reliance on fuels that produce carbon dioxide could Bangladesh relate its sovereign status to limiting the damage done to its society by global warming.

The first form of evasion, then, leads to the second form; that is, states use their discretion to extend their reach by transferring authority to institutions and regimes. Such "exercises" of sovereignty are also "evasions" in the sense that the state gives up discretion and transfers authority in the hope of restoring claims to territorial competence and political legitimacy. Only by institutionalizing adequate nonterritorial regimes of cooperation can territorial well-being be safeguarded.

CONCLUSION

As interdependence grows more salient, the competence and confidence of the state tends to be eroded unless it can facilitate the development of innovative and imaginative formats for problem-solving. In a sense, the state must learn to get out of its own way if over time it is to retain, and regain the full plenum of its legitimacy. But the cumulative consequence of such adaptation is likely to be a far less state-centric global political system. Paradoxically, in order to remain potent the state must give way to a variety of alternative ordering frameworks; the more willingly and forcefully it does so, the better its legitimate sphere of authority can be eventually sustained. The three categories of evasion just considered are producing new allegiances and establishing nascent political communities of local, transnational, regional, and global scope.

The state has demonstrated a remarkable degree of resilience over the several centuries of its existence, but whether it can significantly reorient its sense of sovereign prerogative from space (protecting territory) to time (contributing to a viable and desirable future) is uncertain in the extreme. The realization of such a possibility depends on abandoning the realm of reification. Only if specific persons, acting on behalf of the state, can develop the sort of understanding and backing needed can states be led away from **their** boundary-obsessed territorialism to a more formless contouring of authority that responds to the bewildering array of dangers and opportunities in the world today.

To make this shift at all viable requires an active civil society that gives its citizens "the space" to explore "adjustments," including transnational initiatives, and depends on the secure establishment of human rights and democracy, including on the internal accountability of leaders for violation of international law. As discussed in the preceding chapter, citizens need an enforceable right to a lawful foreign policy if initiatives from below are going to be protected in sensitive times. The natural flow of political life in response to the agenda of global concerns is to encourage evasions as a matter of deliberate tactics. Is the state flexible enough to preside over its own partial dissolution, circumvention, and reconstitution?

CHAPTER X

The Realist School and Its Critics: Interpreting the Postwar World

H OW WE REMEMBER the past shapes the way we understand the present and prepare for the future. A period of forty years is an interval of traditionally deep significance for Western civilization, commencing, of course, with its intense biblical resonance. Was the forty-year period from 1947 to 1987 a time of exodus and liberation, or was it a matter of waiting in the wilderness without even a glimpse or prospect of a promised land? Even without the benefit of any numerological flight of fancy, those decades seem a brilliantly appropriate focus for a connected series of interpretations of the post-World War II world—its beginning, middle, and seeming end, although this implication of an end of the postwar world remains contested and depends on what criterion is adopted.

Even if the Soviet-American rivalry had persisted, it made sense several years ago to talk of the ending of the postwar world, because of at least three factors: the active entry onto the world scene of Japan and Germany, the defeated powers in World War II; an apparent resolution of the most controverted East-West issues in Europe by an acceptance of post-1945 territorial boundaries in the Helsinki Accords; and, finally, the decentering of the world system as a result of the completion of the decolonization process and the loss of U.S. primacy in economic, diplomatic, and cultural domains. That is, even if the Cold War had continued and 1989 had not occurred, it seemed helpful to treat the post-World War II epoch as at an end.

Now what does realism have to do with our understanding of these developments? Is it connected with a debate between realists, and others, as to the political significance of those forty momentous years of international history? Does such a debate help us determine why the Cold War unfolded as it did and analyze such issues as intervention in the South and reliance on a nuclear weapons option? And beyond this, does it enable us to uphold and strengthen our vision of what is desirable and possible on the global level of politics during the years ahead?

REALISM AND ALTERNATIVES

It is first necessary to acknowledge that realists have successfully dominated the political imagination of both policy-makers and their counterparts in the academic world. A realist orthodoxy has emerged in this period that has both sharpened and constrained discussions about foreign policy. Having said this, it is only proper to point out that realists span a fairly wide ideological spectrum that has quite diverse policy consequences, ranging from free-wheeling cowboys seemingly always eager for a good fight in international relations to those who diligently build upon realist premises to bolster their case for moderation. The tension between Zbigniew Brzezinski and Cyrus Vance during the Jimmy Carter presidency illustrates the gap between a tough-minded realist who relishes the prospect of military encounters and the more judicious realist who seeks to pursue national interests through negotiations and diplomacy.

What, then, do the various realist perspectives have in common, and what alternatives to "realism" are worth considering when one sets out to interpret the recent international history of U.S. foreign policy? Realists, no matter how many their divergencies, at least share these several features:

- a focus on sovereign states as the basic units in international relations, and especially on the leading state (or states) as the provider of international order at a given period. Such a focus remains "realist" even if the emphasis is explicitly shifted to the perception of those who act on behalf of the state, or takes into account economic and domestic dimensions of statecraft; the crucial distinguishing mark of realist thought is i'ʲ state-centric character.[1]
- an acceptance of the state system—of interacting states—as the only feasible framework for international order, implying a rejection of alternative forms of world order as utopian or chaotic.
- an acceptance of conflict as the most essential though not exclusive wellspring of political relationships among states whose interests and beliefs are mainly antagonistic and the application of such presuppositions to East-West, Soviet-American relations in the post-1947 period.
- an unspoken ethical assumption (or the suppression of the ethical inquiry to the contrary) that any side in an international conflict can be legitimately expected to threaten unlimited destruction to the extent that doing so effectively discourages attacks and provocative challenges by its enemies; in other words, an essentially amoral acceptance of the security role

of violence, maximized as nuclear deterrence—even in the form of mutual assured destruction. Reliance on deterrence is treated as an acceptable, if unfortunate, basis for stabilizing security in the nuclear age;

■ an acknowledgment that the character of conflict is influenced by international economic policy, by the degree to which war is perceived as a rational instrument of statecraft, and by the domestic political culture and prevailing ideological outlook of principal international rivals.

Existing as partial alternatives to realism have been at least three traditions of thought, each with a following in intellectual circles but none consistently influential in Washington or capable of loosening the main grip by which realism has controlled the academic discussion of United States foreign policy during these years.

■ several varieties of Marxist and post-Marxist interpretations of international relations. These highlight the economic motivation for and class basis of political conflict and tended to consider the Cold War as mainly a pretext for capitalist expansion as facilitated by United States militarism, a pattern claimed to be especially evident in the postcolonial struggle to retain influence and markets in the Third World;

■ various self-serving and deterministic extensions of the belief that conflict is at the center of human experience. One expression of this fatalism, generally associated with religious fundamentalism, views even the prospect of nuclear annihilation as a kind of "blessed assurance" that divine providence is helping history along toward its preordained endpoint.[2] Another, mobilized by the Islamic republic in Iran, provides a rationale for bloody religious warfare and assures each casualty on the side of Allah of immediate ascent to heaven as a reward for a martyr's death in the course of sacred struggle. All fundamentalisms hold in common the conviction that the control of history is shaped not by political or economic forces but by the divine will, and that the decisive actor is the community of true believers as opposed to societies of infidels.

■ continuation of idealism by other normative concepts, especially by reference to the comprehensive reform of the current system of world order. There are almost as many world order approaches as there are variations on the realist theme, but a unifying thread is their shared conviction that the reality of the realist is something to be overcome, to be superseded by safer, more equitable, more durable political arrangements than can be provided over the long haul by the state system. World orderism has sometimes in the past placed its bets on some scheme for world government, or at least on a strengthened United Nations. More recently, world order thinking has emphasized liberation from below by way of grassroots democracy and new social movements that erode the cultural and societal foundations of statism, but it avoids at this stage offering any blueprint of a preferred world order structure. Just as realism is distinguished by its state-centric orientation, world orderism may be identified by its stress on a larger "whole" than the state—most often "the world," but in some variations "the region" or "the civilization." The choice of a unit of analysis other than the state as the foundation of inquiry and the acceptance of normative conviction as social force and political factor are characteristic of all varieties of world order thinking.

Each of these partial alternatives to realism has had some adherents in the United States in the period since 1947, but save for brief exceptions (noted below), none has seriously threatened the realist consensus in either academic or policy circles. The realist triumph over each alternative preceded along distinct lines. Accompanying the rise of the Cold War, especially through the 1950s, was a generalized stigma attached to Marxist orientations, a hostility that swept the society as a tidal wave of intellectual suppression during the late 1940s and early 1950s in the form of McCarthyism, which, even when it receded as an overt attack upon left dissent, cast a dark shadow over radical thinking. And with the severe corrosion of Soviet reputation during the 1950s and 1960s following exposures of internal repression and harsh occupation of Eastern Europe, few academics and no policy-makers in the United States were willing to risk being seen as a subversive because of espousing of a Marxist reading of international relations. Indeed, a shameful process of institutional self-censorship in the supposedly "free world" led to a virtual disappearance of Marxist influence in educational and governmental arenas of influence; despite the power of Marxism elsewhere in the world, it absented itself from the American scene almost completely until the aftermath of the Vietnam War, when some greater tolerance for radical political thought was evident for a short period within university settings—although at no time within policy-making circles.

The realist mainstream has generally met the idealist, world orderist challenge either by showing that statism cannot be tamed through normative approaches, by scornful innuendo, or in some circumstances by co-opting its rhetoric. Arguments contending that the state system is heading for a crash landing or including in the normative potential of international relations the abolition of war as a social institution are derided by hard-core realists either as wallowing in doomsday or as an exercise in utopianism. Especially realists on the liberal, Democratic party side of the scale often validate their realist credentials by world order bashing. Stanley Hoffmann and Joseph Nye are examples of social scientists with moral concerns who locate their thought on the left side of the realist camp by claiming liberal credentials but retain mainstream credibility, in part by combining their sharp criticisms of tough-minded realists with an attack upon their supposedly utopian colleagues who espouse world orderist positions. Mainstream realism fights off the right and the left by seeking to occupy the moderate center, claiming for itself the high ground of reason and the golden mean between the unhealthy and unworkable extremes associated especially with the role of force in international relations.

Oddly enough, it is only the fatalists who have challenged the realists in the counsels of government. They are powerfully represented in the bureaucracy and are especially prevalent among military and business elites, who often have close links with the political and religious right. They have the resources to make their voices heard and, occasionally, even the political clout to threaten realist control over policy-making. For example the Iran-Contra network (Casey, North, Secord) revealed geopolitical fatalists taking charge of government policy. Their basic outlook involved the belief that the Soviet Union and Communism were irremediably evil and that a struggle to the bitter end between the superpowers was both inevitable and uplifting. Fatalists with such views are never far from the centers of power in the United States, even if they do not exert much visible influence in the national media or in academic life, except in the setting of evangelical pedagogy. They can also lay claim, with passion, to the mantle of patriotism and to societal virtue and tradition, exhibiting a purist loyalty to flag, family, and church. Their normative enthusiasm often puts the realist consensus on the defensive in a manner that leftist attacks never do. It was fascinating to watch realists in Congress and the media hastily leave the scene of battle after Oliver North's fundamentalism, with all its intensity, aroused such a powerful response among the American people.

THE EMERGENCE OF THE REALIST CONSENSUS

The triumph of realism is specifically restricted to the period following World War II yet remains impressive more than forty years later. In academic life, virtually all serious search for appointments in higher education and major research proposals to leading foundations can succeed only if they survive realist screening criteria, procedures that are more insidious because largely unacknowledged. Nonrealists and surely anti-realists are rejected if identified or, at most, given a token status at the outer margins of discussion. It is difficult to publish consistently in leading professional journals if one's perspective is regarded as belonging to any of the three nonrealist approaches mentioned above. Additionally, the editorial columns of the most influential newspapers are mainly filled with realist commentary, plus some fatalist presence and an occasional Marxist voice, usually a public official of a Communist country. And in the higher reaches of state power the realist net closes even tighter; more moderate realists such as George Kennan, George Ball, and Cyrus Vance have not fared nearly so well over the years in Washington as have tough-minded realists such as Kissinger, Brzezinski, and Nitze.

Before 1947 the idealists and even the Marxists exerted influence and had some access to power in the United States; only the fatalists were then excluded, as foolish extremists, and were at the time everywhere marginalized by secularist thought control. The image of a Jerry Falwell being sent out by the White House to explain U.S. arms control policy was definitely a 1980s phenomenon, a media event that seems equally inconceivable in either the pre- or post–Reagan era. How then can we explain this extraordinary ascendancy of realism in the four decades since 1947?

Above all, there was a widely shared reading of interwar history (1918–39) as beset by normative illusion and by a refusal to guide thought and action so as to take account of the role of force and counterforce in the adjustment of conflict. The realist approach crystallized around criticisms of the earlier American tendencies to exaggerate the role of law and morality in relations among sovereign states. The writings and personal stature of E. H. Carr, Hans Morgenthau, Reinhold Neibuhr, Walter Lippmann, George Kennan, and Dean Acheson were the core of realist thought and influence in the early postwar period. Much of the criticism of idealist tendencies focused on an appraisal of the diplomatic effort by Woodrow Wilson after 1918 to lift international relations above the messy domain of power politics and alliances, and on the appeasement policies pursued subsequently by the European democracies. The Western democracies were determined after 1945 not to repeat the mistakes of the 1930s. They became convinced that the aggressiveness of Hitler's Germany, Mussolini's Italy, and imperial Japan could have been blunted earlier by superior military force, possibly with the avoidance of World War II. The lessons of Munich and Pearl Harbor were construed to mean that national interests could be defended only by military strength and peacetime preparedness and by commitments to protect victims of aggression even in distant places, which also implied a posture of constant military readiness. Lyndon Johnson summarized this diplomacy in the mid-1960s by saying that it was better for Americans to fight in the jungles of Vietnam than on the beaches of San Francisco. To secure peace required the country to be prepared for war in a manner that would confront any likely adversary with the unmistakable prospect of defeat.

This general disposition was reinforced by a postwar consensus that the Soviet challenge would test immediately the will and capacities of the industrial democracies. The Soviet pressure for hegemony in Eastern Europe, well-organized and large Communist parties in several key war-torn West European countries, and the Soviet bid for an extension of influence to Iran and then to Greece and Turkey clinched the realist claim by 1947 to provide authoritative guidance for policy-makers, including the warning that a repetition of earlier patterns of sterile legalism and isolationist withdrawal from contested geopolitical zones would likely bring on an intolerable third world war within the century.

Further, the realists presented themselves in a nonaggressive idiom as a new variety of peace-maker and, hence, their policy outlook as one that did not overtly threaten the surprisingly redoubtable American image of innocence and virtue. To the realists, even those who favored intervention in the Third World, it was a matter of adopting a posture suitable to a Hobbesian setting in which the most destructive forms of state power will push expansively as far as they can until deterred by credible prospects of resistance and pain. The realists as policy-makers were never adventurers or crazies; they were often as worried about macho warriors as they were by what they conceived to be the naiveté of nuclear pacifists and the outmoded romanticism of isolationists. The realist approach to policy was premised on the assumptions of shared rationalism: confront a potential aggressor with a prospect of pain greater than any anticipated gain; under such circumstances an adversary was rationally receptive and likely to be contained or, in nuclear settings, deterred.[3] Extending this approach to the Soviet challenge required a Western appreciation of the deeper rhythms of revolutionary nationalism, including the realization that aggression could proceed indirectly by way of Moscow-controlled Communist parties situated as Trojan Horses in targeted foreign societies. The move to containment, then, necessarily disposed realists to engage in overseas interventionary diplomacy. Such a marriage of academic sophistication and power politics peaked during the Kennedy-Johnson years when "the best and the brightest" championed the Vietnam War as a watershed of realist wisdom. For the sake of fairness, and improved dialogue, let me note that there were realist defectors, such as George Ball, John Herz, and Hans Morgenthau, who all along as realists in good standing questioned the viability of the Vietnam undertaking and who were generally opposed on prudential grounds to U.S. interventionary diplomacy elsewhere.

This realist mind-set seemed responsive to the complex demands of security in the nuclear age. Considerations of survival put a premium on war-avoidance (as distinct from war-fighting), and the requirements of post-Munich international order made it essential to discourage geopolitical expansion. Thus, containment plus deterrence evolved naturally and coherently as central elements of United States postwar foreign policy.

Realists were also conscious of the importance of centralized international economic management and Keynesian fiscal strategies to avoid recurrence of a worldwide depression. The 1930s fixed the image of a challenge to capitalism as strongly on postwar leadership in the United States as fascism had challenged the stability of political democracy; planning for trade, currency exchange, and capital flows was deemed part of the overall notion of security in the postwar world.

Finally, the realist interpretation opened the way after 1945 to U.S. economic expansion. The collapse of the colonial order and the depletion of the economies of Western Europe and Japan gave the United States an extraordinary opportunity to fill a geoeconomic vacuum. The Marshall Plan, foreign aid programs, and multinational financial institutions were creative instruments of expansion that incidentally served the purposes of containment and were consistent with the geopolitical master plan of meeting the Soviet challenge without the need to fight World War III.

Explaining the ascendancy of realists is distinct from understanding how realists themselves interpreted these four critical decades. Because realists dominated the political landscape, most of the debates given currency were *among* realists, not between realists and their critics. There were two exceptions. One was the period during the Vietnam War from shortly after the Tet offensive in February 1968 to the signing of the Paris Peace Accords in early 1973. The discrediting of the American claims in Vietnam created a temporary opening for wider debate and discussion about militarism and the loss of democracy. This opening scared a portion of the realist establishment—Henry Kissinger remembers the period as one in which the country was on the brink of civil war—and provoked a realist backlash illustrated by Samuel Huntington's contribution to the Trilateral Commission volume *The Crisis of Democracy*.[4] But containment realists recovered control over the policy process, ending the Vietnam War, defeating George McGovern, and bringing a temporary lull in international relations during Richard Nixon's first presidential term by way of normalization of relations with China, detente, and a renewed emphasis on the arms control process. These initiatives were pleasing to liberals yet were long overdue moves on the geopolitical chessboard of international relations.

The second exception to the realist consensus was associated with the early years of the Reagan presidency, when fatalist rhetoric and policy gave realists (and others) several jolts—by careless nuclearist posturing, by appearing to move the goal from deterring nuclear war to prevailing in a nuclear war and from containment to rollback as a basis for Third World diplomacy, by utopian claims for military technology (especially the initial presentation of the Strategic Defense Initiative), and, contrariwise, by endorsing a proposal to abolish nuclear weapons at the 1986 Iceland summit. The Reagan presidency with its mixture of ideological geopolitics and utopianism unwittingly and intermittently challenged the realist domination of debate and policy, both by placing ideologues in positions of influence and by seeming to have some penchant for its own special variant of utopianism: a belief in technocratic panaceas to overcome the hard choices of war and peace.

Having depicted the realist ways of seeing, one can go on to describe briefly how the realists (and their critics) interpreted the last forty years, emphasizing how they construe the past as a foundation for present questioning and reflection, and how they would adjust U.S. foreign policy in the decades ahead to what all sides admit to be a new global situation.

The claims made for the accomplishments of realist control over American foreign policy in the last four decades are substantial:

- the avoidance of World War III despite acute geopolitical tension;
- the containment of Soviet expansion by way of military conquest either directly undertaken or carried out by proxies; responding in 1950 to the North Korean attack on South Korea illustrates the American commitment to containment;
- the reconstruction of a world trading system that helped all sectors of international society to achieve a period of robust and sustained economic growth;
- the stabilization of Europe as a conflict zone, including an apparent "solution" to the German problem;
- acquiescence to the Soviet presence in the world as a legitimate actor if confined to its own sphere of interests.

Realism as an orientation avoided the poles of appeasement and interventionary rollback, but between these poles considerable controversy occurred over appropriate foreign policy. The several strands of realism produced many tactical disagreements, especially on issues of nuclear weapons policy and of intervention in the Third World. Nor have realists fully regained their assured control over foreign policy in the post-Reagan years. The Reagan efforts to support the contras in Central America, to sustain "constructive engagement" in southern Africa, and to push ahead with the militarization of space were policy initiatives difficult to justify within a realist framework.

Realists have been criticized all along by those who take idealist and progressive positions. These criticisms focused on the need to take more dramatic steps to end the nuclear arms race and renounce reliance on nuclear weaponry, as well as to declare an end to all efforts to intervene against revolutionary nationalist movements in the Third World. On more constructive lines, most left antirealists wanted to rely on law and institutions, especially the United Nations, to displace reliance on power politics and calculations of national interests; they anticipated the emergence of an organized global community to replace the dominance over international relations associated with the sovereign state and the state system. Such criticisms assumed prominence in the last years of the Vietnam War (1968–1972) but never threatened realist direction of governmental policy.

These elements of opposition to realism on both the right and left, when taken together with the opportunities afforded by the early period of Gorbachev leadership and the altered setting of relative decline in United States power, have induced realists to begin asking harder questions about the path forward.

There is, first of all, the feeling that the forty years of realist ascendancy are generally a success story whose policy and practice should be only altered gradually, if at all. In the background is an anxiety that the postwar order could unravel dangerously, especially in Europe, and that any rapid dissolution of NATO or withdrawal of U.S. troops could lead to a new version of "the German problem," even to a German drive to acquire nuclear weaponry. Yet realists acknowledge that cumulative pressures make it desirable to make some adjustment, however cautiously, in U.S. foreign policy, with at least two objectives: to cut the financial costs of foreign policy in light of deficits and the falling dollar; and to diminish still further the risk of general warfare, especially as connected with nuclear weaponry. The events of 1989 and subsequent years have accelerated this trend toward readjustment.

Realists also generally agree that the Gorbachev leadership and changes in Eastern Europe offer unprecedented opportunities for improving East-West relations, but they were not prepared to regard the superpower rivalry as over until the early 1990s. The crisis occasioned by Iraq's invasion of Kuwait displayed the widest zone of great power consensus inside and outside the United Nations since the united struggle against the Axis Powers in World War II, although its limits were exposed during the latter stages of the war.

Some realists argue that political economy issues became a far greater challenge to U.S. national interests in the 1980s than the East-West rivalry, and that a redirection of energies is required to meet the challenges of relative economic decline, to avoid further deterioration of the U.S. position, and to manage international indebtedness and the volatility of financial markets in order to guard against an overall breakdown in the world economy. On these matters realists are now in agreement.

Beyond these generalized views there are several more distinct realist variations on these themes which would lead to quite different policy outcomes:

(1) The Cold War has mutated from a corrosive confrontation to a kind of constructive framework for problem-solving and tacit cooperation. Underneath this view, most ably argued by John Lewis Gaddis, is the sense

that nuclear deterrence has provided a bedrock of stability that should not be scrapped too readily.[5] In the background of such thinking lies the belief that bipolar forms of stability tend to work better than multipolar forms. This kind of understanding found the Cold War a source of benefits as well as detriments. In particular, the Soviet-American rivalry as played out in Europe during the Cold War contributed to a solution of the German problem by way of a legitimized division into two countries—which, of course, gave way to the great emancipatory events of 1989 that climaxed in German reunification. In addition, the Cold War facilitated tacit cooperative arrangements between the blocs in Europe that helped reduce the risk of inadvertent nuclear war.

(2) The success of the postwar arrangements was linked to U.S. hegemony and cannot be adapted to increasing multipolar circumstances; therefore, some realists argue, it is necessary to reduce U.S. commitments and shift a greater portion of the burdens of alliance security to Europe and Japan.

(3) Some realists assert that the persistence of Cold War fixations has distracted policy-makers from the need for politically unpopular adjustments at home, especially higher taxes and smaller deficits; similarly, an overemphasis on military research and development has undermined the relative U.S. competitive position, as demonstrated by declining increments in productivity increase for the United States, which result in an unfavorable record relative to its main industrial rivals. Proponents of this thesis contend that the next real war is with Japan.

(4) Some realists contend that the United States consistently misunderstood the Soviet challenge by construing it as primarily military in character; such a misunderstanding generated dynamics that were dangerous, especially with regard to the nuclear arms race. Denuclearization should have been, then, a higher priority than maneuvering for tactical advantage on Cold War issues. This view was put forth vigorously in the 1980s by such influential realists as George Kennan and Robert McNamara, among others, who earlier were in the Cold War mainstream.

(5) And some realists in the late 1980s believed that the Soviet Union remains an implacable foe that has become either more vulnerable or more dangerous—depending on whether the weakness of its economy or the vigor of its new leadership is emphasized—and that now is the time to push against this weakness or at least not to drop the Western guard. Tough-minded realists (and, of course, their fatalist collaborators) who espouse such a view even attacked Ronald Reagan from time to time as succumbing to tender-mindedness. The *Wall Street Journal*, the 1988 Republican nominees for president, Henry Kissinger, Richard Nixon, and Zbigniew Brzezinski have all argued in different ways the wisdom of taking full advantage of Soviet economic weakness, political disunion, and ideological defeat.

The realist sense, then, of the forty years under consideration is currently undergoing a period of creative flux, accounting for the emergence of a wide range of interpretations. Realist thought has recently displayed a capacity for conceptual and policy innovation, yet there are those who remain disturbed by the limits of the realist approach. I leave aside the fatalist viewpoint as a merely more extreme and dogmatic version of the tough-minded-realist belief that the struggle against Communism must be waged unconditionally and inevitably, and that there is no way out other than the victory of one side and the defeat of the other. Of greater relevance are criticisms of realism associated with world orderist perspectives. Although here, too there exist crucial variations of position, world orderist critics generally concur in charging the realist approach with certain weaknesses.

Perhaps the most basic charge is what might be called "the Melian syndrome": that is, the tendency of realists to reduce international relations to tests of force as measured mainly by military capabilities, a view bolstered in realist theorizing by selective readings of key texts and events from Thucydides onward.[6] One doesn't have to be a devotee of Jacques Derrida and deconstructionism to take issue with the extreme selectivity with which realists have read past history and political thought to validate their imagery of the present and future. In effect, the world orderist critique of realism contends that policy-makers have been overly preoccupied with tests of force in their interpretation of conflict and security, thereby missing both opportunities and dangers based on other considerations.

A closely related criticism is an alleged realist tendency to discount both the normative aspirations of society and the normative potential of institutional arrangements that challenge the state system. Especially prominent in realist writing is a tendency to denigrate the United Nations, as well as international law, by misleading claims that international legal approaches have been tried and have failed as foreign policy instruments. Realists are also charged with neglecting the contributions and potential further development of international law and institutions.

A further contention is that realists have a disappointing record when it comes to the new agenda of problems associated with the global commons; matters pertaining to the oceans, space, and the environment are either ignored altogether or treated as technical and managerial details. In their accounts of international relations realists rarely pose or confront the challenge of evolving a long-range, unified approach to this new international environmental agenda or consider how such an agenda can be effectively enforced in a world framework as politically fragmented and anarchic as the state system. The failure of realists to address these issues is a shortcoming of analysis which, if not corrected, will result in serious harm to human health and well-being.

It is also alleged that by excluding the long-term effects of political fragmentation in an interdependent world from their assessment of national interests, realists are able to keep challenges to their interpretations of the world at a safe distance from the main policy-making and opinion-producing arenas. In effect, at a time when the need for new approaches is most critical, the political imagination is kept preoccupied with the traditional agenda of conflict among states, inducing a sense of entrapment within society in relation to such fundamental concerns as nuclearism and interdependence. The realist position makes one believe that the framework is fixed for the indefinite future.

In the end, then, world orderist critics contend that realism is a source of both misleading reassurance and undue caution, fostering the illusion that traditional concerns about power and wealth are all that matter in international relations, as if no conditions of urgency or relevance arise from the normative issues of nuclearism, mass poverty, and environmental decay.[7] This cumulative indictment of realism is, I believe, quite convincing, and engenders a wider cultural atmosphere of complacency or despair. By restricting foreign policy debate to its main postwar points of geopolitical reference, the realist position creates a basic impression that changes of tempo and modality in relations among rival states and groups of states are about all that can be achieved: that is, at best a temporary sense of stability and moderation.

Marxists and world orderists reject this realist assessment. Marxists believe, of course, that the pretext of the Cold War has been the mask behind which militarism, neocolonialism, and interventionary diplomacy could hide and that realism gave the mask credibility in mass public opinion. Beyond this, Marxian objection to the forty year postwar period is partly to unnecessary risks of catastrophe—to what E. P. Thompson has called exterminism—and partly to the eroding of the fabric of political democracy that resulted from making national security the permanent centerpiece of peacetime concerns.[8]

World orderists emphasize the global structural dangers of present trends and the importance of building a capacity both to realize human values and to meet the functional challenges of interdependence and the overwrought global commons.[9] World orderists want to encourage a belief that the world can potentially be unified around a sense of human identity and global interests; they rely on supportive cultural developments and social movements to build a transnational societal basis for developing a foreign policy that is both more hopeful and more responsive to the particular challenges of this era.

In the end, world orderists acknowledge that the realist school performed an important historical function by presiding successfully over the complex dynamics of economic and political reconstruction in the years following World War II, and further, that realism managed to prevent post-1945 tensions from degenerating into open warfare without a repetition of the appeasement diplomacy of the 1930s. In this regard, realism functioned as a viable ideology for the political democracies of the liberal West in the specific setting of one stage of international history.

But now that stage is being superseded by the new complexities of global interdependence and by the decentering of political and economic control, as well as by the removal of the Soviet challenge. In this altered setting of the early 1990s, realism seems far less satisfactory as an account of international relations, although it retains a utility by its focus on relations of power and wealth and by its refusal to be blinded by sentimental considerations in analyzing the play of forces that constitute international relations.

Nothing is more uncertain than the future, but the complexity and fragility of international life make it inconceivable that the next several decades will be as dominated by the narrative of superpower rivalry as have the last few. The Gulf War has been allowed to extend the realist consensus beyond the Cold War, shifting the fulcrum of its interpretation from East-West to North-South and casting Iraq, at least temporarily, in the role of aggressor, thus endangering world stability and prosperity. George Bush's use of the term "new world order" is mainly a rhetorical move *within* the realist framework, seeking to mobilize support for an activist foreign policy in the early stage of a post–Cold War world. As of 1991, such a move seems to signal a geopolitical transition beyond the East-West logic of bipolarity, but little else. The argument of this entire book is that such realist preoccupations operate as a gigantic distraction from the deeper challenges associated with political, economic, and social restructuring in light of the precepts of this new political entity—global civil society!

NOTES AND INDEX

NOTES

CHAPTER I

1. This is the thesis of my book *Revolutionaries and Functionaries* (New York: Dutton, 1988).

2. Martin Buber, *Paths in Utopia*, trans. R.F.C. Hull (Boston: Beacon Press, 1970), p. 7.

3. Lewis Mumford, *The Transformation of Man* (New York: Harper, 1956), p. 95.

4. The two titles are *Citizen Summitry* and *Securing Our Planet*, both edited by Don Carlson and Craig Comstock, and published the same year (Los Angeles: Tarcher, 1956).

5. Raymond Williams, *The Year 2000* (New York: Pantheon Books, 1985), p. 268.

6. Two elaborations on this generalization seem appropriate: the distinction is not meant to pose a choice—safeguarding modernism to defer catastrophe is as necessary as overcoming it is desirable. At the same time, modernism cannot be sustained indefinitely, nor should it be. Whether the modernist mindset, itself caught up in either/or polarities, can embrace the complementary pulls of reformist and transformative energies is itself questionable. There are many cultural hints that it cannot—the anti-utopianism of the mainstream, expressed by the aphorism "the best is the enemy of the good" and the general tendency of those with the longer, transformative vision to neglect current struggles against injustice and dangers. Resolving this connection between the immediacies that summon modernist energies and the postmodern call of the future remains a central challenge, the first step toward forming a response being its acknowledgment.

7. Arthur Schopenhauer, *Essays and Aphorisms* Baltimore, Md.: Penguin Books, 1970), p. 84.

8. See Hebrews 11:13–16.

9. See Chapter III for discussion of the Chinese experience from a different angle.

10. "The Philippines Constitution," *Wall Street Journal*, Jan. 14, 1987, p. 22.

231

11. Quoted David J. Garrow, *Bearing the Cross* (New York: Morrow, 1986), p. 459.

CHAPTER II

1. For general assessment, see, e.g., Andrew Reding, "Seed of a New and Renewed Church: The 'Ecclesiastical Insurrection' in Nicaragua," *Monthly Review*, July–August 1987, pp. 24–55; also Reding, ed., *Christianity and Revolution: Tomas Borge's Theology of Life* (Maryknoll, N.Y.: Orbis Books, 1987). Cf. statement by the National Directorate of the Sandinista government, October 7, 1980, "The Role of Religion in the New Nicaragua," in Tomas Borge et al., *Sandinistas Speak* (New York: Pathfinder Press, 1982).

2. In the 1990 elections administered by the Sandinistas, the anti-Sandinista coalition prevailed. The United States government interpreted the outcome as confirmatory of its decade of support for the contras and as further evidence of the failure of Marxist-Leninist governments to gain popular support. Those more friendly to the Sandinistas attributed their electoral defeat to the years of hardship and suffering caused by the U.S. economic and paramilitary squeeze so relentlessly administered.

3. This focus is developed powerfully in Upendra Baxi, "Taking Suffering Seriously: Social Action Litigation before the Supreme Court of India," *Delaware Law Review* 91 (1979–80): 8–9; cf. Baxi, *Courage, Craft and Contention: The Indian Supreme Court in the Eighties* (Bombay: N. M. Tripath, 1985).

4. See Chapter III for further elaboration.

5. Cf. A. G. Mojtabai, *Blessed Assurance: At Home with the Bomb in Amarillo, Texas* (Boston: Houghton Mifflin, 1986).

6. The Western victory in the Cold War, signaled by the events of 1989, induced a kind of Manichean triumphalism that associated market-oriented constitutionalism with political legitimacy. As such, it encouraged a self-congratulatory mood at the very historical moment when a culturally self-critical posture would have been far more appropriate. See Chapter I for the underpinnings of such an assertion.

7. Sharon D. Welch, *Communities of Resistance and Solidarity: A Feminist Theology of Liberation* (Maryknoll, N.Y.: Orbis Books, 1985).

8. Of course, some religious traditions are notoriously indifferent to earthly suffering, either deferring salvation to the afterlife or giving spiritual striving priority over the torments of earthly existence.

9. Gregory Bateson, *Mind and Nature: A Necessary Unity* (New York: Dutton, 1979).

10. Gary Snyder, "Revolution in the Revolution in the Revolution," in *Regarding Wave* (New York: New Directions, 1970), p. 39.

11. For ethical and legal rationale, see Christopher D. Stone, *Earth and Other Ethics: The Case of Moral Pluralism* (New York: Harper & Row, 1987).

12. See *New York Times*, Oct. 3, 1987, p. 42.

13. Yet not necessarily adherence to unconditional nonviolence; the context

of oppression may make defensive violence the only option, selected as a last resort and within a disciplined framework of respect for civilian innocence.

14. E.g., cf. Petra Kelly, *Fighting for Hope* (Boston: South End Press, 1984), with Rudolph Bahro, *Building the Green Movement* (Philadelphia: New Society, 1986). See also the report of tension among the German Greens, *New York Times*, Oct. 11, 1987, p. 22 (cf. Chapter I).

15. For a convenient summary of the Green perspective, see Charlene Spretnak, *The Spiritual Dimension of Green Politics* (Santa Fe, N.M.: Bear, 1986), pp. 78–82.

16. For excellent information on India, see the regular issues of the *Lokoyan Bulletin* published in Delhi under the editorship of Smitu Kothari and Harsh Sethi.

17. Personal communication, Professor Catherine Keller of the Drew Seminary.

18. See Zsuzsa Hegedus, "The Challenge of the Peace Movement: Civilian Security and Civilian Emancipation," in Saul H. Mendlovitz and R.B.J. Walker, eds., *Toward a Just World Peace* (London: Butterworths, 1987), pp. 191–210.

19. For intriguing speculations with scientific foundations, see J. E. Lovelock, *Gaia: A New Look at Life on Earth* (New York: Oxford University Press, 1979).

CHAPTER III

1. A strong argument along these lines is contained in Stanley Diamond, *In Search of the Primitive* (New Brunswick, N.J.: Transaction Books, 1974).

2. Cf. Arnold J. Toynbee, *A Study of History*, vol. 1 (New York: Oxford University Press, 1934).

3. See Richard Falk, "The Grotian Quest" and "A New Paradigm for International Legal Studies," in Falk, Friedrich Kratochwil, and Saul H. Mendlovitz, eds., *International Law: A Contemporary Perspective* (Boulder, Colo.: Westview Press, 1985), pp. 36–42, 651–702.

4. For background relating to the assertion of Nuremberg claims in domestic courts, see Francis Anthony Boyle, *Defending Civil Resistance under International Law* (Dobbs Ferry, N.Y.: Transaction Books, 1987).

5. Of course, there are many variations of expression on these two "faces" of modernism, but the commitment to a materialist conception of individual and collective fulfillment provides the consistent element of identity.

6. On the specific concerns of nuclearism, the most revealing treatment is probably Joseph Nye, *Nuclear Ethics* (New York: Free Press, 1983); on the broader themes of reassurance about modernism, see the influential book by Herman Kahn and Anthony J. Wiener, *The Year 2000: A Framework for Speculation on the Next Thirty-Three Years* (New York: Macmillan, 1967); cf. also Zbigniew Brzezinski, *Between Two Ages: America's Role in the Technetronic Age* (New York: Viking Press, 1970).

7. These are not the only paths to the future: cultural pluralism, non-Western forms of postmodernism, and relapses into various types of anarchy are also possible.

8. See Donella Meadows et al., *The Limits to Growth* (New York: Universe Books, 1972); Edward T. Goldsmith et al., *Blueprint for Survival* (Boston: Houghton Mifflin, 1972). My own analysis during this period is contained in *This Endangered Planet* (New York: Random House, 1972). See also Robert L. Heilbroner, *An Inquiry into the Human Prospect* (New York: Norton, 1974).

9. For a fictionalized interpretation to this effect, see Günter Grass, *The Rat* (New York: Knopf, 1987).

10. Other leaders in the region who have gained control over their countries in a postcolonial setting include Gamal Abdul Nasser, Muammar Qaddafi, Saddam Hussein. Each has combined an ardent nationalism—often ethnically enlarged to encompass the Arab world—with some sort of invocation of Islam. Because religion in the Middle East provides the basis for political legitimacy, religious identity and cultural authenticity are closely linked in the Islamic world but not necessarily elsewhere. In Asia, for instance, traditional culture and religion have been kept in the background of political life, both internally and regionally. There is no Asian or Latin American equivalent to the idea of a pan-Arab or Islamic nation. Early in the postcolonial period some African leaders such as Kwame Nkrumah attempted to mobilize enthusiasm for pan-African sentiments, but such appeals fell flat. Indeed, African tribal identity has disrupted efforts to promote national identities.

11. See Chapter I for a fuller account of the characteristics of modernism and postmodernism.

CHAPTER IV

1. The period of bipolarity is difficult to delimit with precision; arguably, it did not begin before Winston Churchill's Iron Curtain speech in 1946, or possibly not until the Truman Doctrine was enunciated in 1947, or the Soviet Union exploded its first atomic device in 1949, or, much later, when the Soviet Union achieved some sort of parity with respect to nuclear weaponry. My more expansive dating corresponds with the general opinion of the public and leaders alike that international relations since the end of World War II have been dominated by the rivalry between the United States and the Soviet Union, which in turn produced opposing alliance systems (and blocs) organized on both geopolitical and ideological principles. The ending of bipolarity in 1989 is less controversial, being unilaterally implemented by a Soviet withdrawal from points of geopolitical encounter. This withdrawal was confirmed during the August 1990 Kuwait crisis, in which the Soviet Union joined the anti-Iraq consensus despite the strong overtones of ideological and geopolitical challenge to the United States and to the West generally.

In a different vein, bipolarity can be questioned conceptually. The Soviet Union never managed either to be a formidable presence in the world economy as constituted by the capitalist countries or to constitute a parallel trading bloc of its own that accounted for a significant percentage of global gross national product. Except in relation to its resource base and industrial potential, the Soviet Union never became an economic superpower, nor did the world appear bipolar from the perspective of political economy. There are two responses here. First, during most of the Cold War period, strategic considerations dominated the political imagination, and from this viewpoint the prospect of World War III arose out of a bipolar structure of conflict. Second, even from an economic perspective, Moscow's capacity to catch up to Washington at the strategic level and to threaten U.S. supremacy was related to the perception of the Soviet Union as a formidable economic rival.

2. Petra Kelly, *Fighting for Hope* (Boston: South End Press, 1984), p. 32.

3. Ernest Gellner, *Nations and Nationalism* (Ithaca, N.Y.: Cornell University Press, 1983), pp. 44–45.

4. See, e.g., Lawrence Wittner, *Rebels against War* (Philadelphia: Temple University Press, 1984).

5. See Dean Acheson, *Present at the Creation: My Years in the State Department* (New York: Norton, 1969); and George Kennan, *Memoirs, 1925–50* and *Memoirs, 1950–63* (Boston: Little, Brown, 1967, 1972).

6. The work of the World Order Models Project (WOMP) is especially relevant in this regard. See Saul H. Mendlovitz, *The Struggle for a Just World Order: An Agenda of Inquiry and Praxis for the 1980s*, WOMP Working Paper 20 (New York: Institute for World Order, 1982); and Richard A. Falk and Samuel S. Kim, *An Approach to World Order Studies and the World System*, WOMP Working Paper 22 (New York: Institute for World Order, 1982).

7. A recent study is Harry Eckstein, "Civic Inclusion and Its Discontents," *Daedalus* 113 (Fall 1984): 107–45.

8. One popularization of this view is Marilyn Ferguson, *The Aquarian Conspiracy: Personal and Social Transformation in the 1980s* (Los Angeles: Tarcher, 1981).

9. Paul Wapner, "Making States Biodegradable: Ecological Activism and World Politics" (Ph.D. diss., Princeton University, 1990), is an important exception, completed too late to be taken into account in this book.

10. For elaboration of D-5 orientation see Chapter VI.

11. See Richard A. Falk, *Normative Initiatives and Demilitarization: A Third System Approach*, WOMP Working Paper 13 (New York: Institute for World Order, 1982).

12. For parallel discussion, see Chapter VI.

13. On Greenham Common, see Caroline Blackwood, *On The Perimeter* (Baltimore, Md.: Penguin Books, 1983).

14. For Ground Zero's world view and political vision, see James Douglass, *Lightning East to West* (Portland, Ore.: N.p., 1980), and the group's excellent newsletter during the 1980s titled *Ground Zero*.

15. Independent Commission on Disarmament and Security Issues, *Common Security: A Blueprint for Survival* (New York: Simon & Schuster, 1982), p. 178.

16. Ibid., pp. 178–81. In all, there were twenty short-term and sixteen medium-term proposals plus a few for strengthening the UN Security Council and regional security mechanisms.

17. See Lester Brown, et al., *State of the World 1985: A Worldwatch Institute*

Report on Progress toward a Sustainable Society (New York: Norton, 1985).

18. This distinction is elaborated in Chapter VI.

19. *New York Times*, Feb. 18, 1985, p. A3.

20. See *The Bomb and the Law: London Nuclear Warfare Tribunal 1985—A Summary Report* (Stockholm: Myrdal Foundation, 1989).

21. Ursula Le Guin, *The Dispossessed: An Ambiguous Utopia* (New York: Avon Books, 1975).

22. See Chapter II for fuller discussion.

CHAPTER V

1. See Theodore Roszak, *Unfinished Animal* (New York: Harper & Row, 1975); Stanley Diamond, *In Search of the Primitive* (New Brunswick, N.J.: Transaction Books, 1974); Sharon Olds's poem "The Paths," in Jim Schley, ed., *Writing in a Nuclear Age* (Hanover, N.H.: University Press of New England, 1984).

2. Dorothee Sölle, *The Arms Race Kills Even without War* (Philadelphia: Fortress Press, 1983), p. 111.

3. This perspective is elaborated in Chapter III.

4. Marguerite Yourcenar, *The Memoirs of Hadrian, and Reflections on the Composition of Memoirs of Hadrian*, trans. Grace Frick and Marguerite Yourcenar (New York: Modern Library, 1984), p. 333.

5. Dhirubhai Sheth, "Grassroots Stirrings and the Future of Politics," *Alternatives* 9:1 (1983): 1–24, at 8–9.

6. See the report of Harvard Nuclear Study Group, written by Scott Sagan et al., *Living with Nuclear Weapons* (New York: Bantam Books, 1983).

7. Schley, preface to *Writing in a Nuclear Age*, [p. iv].

8. For an important overall examination, see Eric Nordlinger, *On The Autonomy of the Democratic State* (Cambridge, Mass.: Harvard University Press, 1981).

9. Elizabeth McAlister, "For Love of Children," in *The Hammer Has to Fall* (privately distributed, 1983), p. 32.

10. Ibid., p. 32.

11. Ibid., p. 34.

12. "The Challenge of Peace: God's Promise and Our Response," Pastoral Letter on War, Armaments, and Peace, *Origins* 13, no. 1 (May 19, 1983).

13. For general implications, see Chadwick Alger, "Bridging the Micro and the Macro," *Alternatives* 10 (1984–85): 319–44, at 333–36.

14. For excellent introduction and analytic assessment of the main split within Green politics, see Andrew Dobson, *Green Political Thought: An Introduction* (London: Unwin Hyman, 1990); see also Fritjof Capra and Charlene Spretnak, *Green Politics* (London: Hutchinson, 1984).

15. Despite slight differences in terminology, such a positive image of the future is similar to what Elise Boulding envisages in *Building a Global Civic Culture* (New York: Teachers College Press, 1988).

16. For an early systematic attempt to specify this proposed normative re-

orientation of politics at the state and global level, see Robert Johansen, *The National Interest and the Human Interest* (Princeton, N.J.: Princeton University Press, 1980).

CHAPTER VI

1. A helpful assessment of social movements from a variety of angles is to be found in "Social Movements, *Social Research* (symposium issue, ed. Jean L. Cohen) 52 (1985): 664–890. What qualifies as a "social movement" is the subject of debate, especially among sociologists. I use the term loosely in this text to describe any societal initiative that is sustained in time and space and that includes a normative element and a commitment to change.

2. There is here an apparently semantic choice that relates in a basic way to substance: do we encompass the new social movements within an expanded conception of politics, or do we regard this activity (following Antonio Gramsci's lead) as a struggle for the cultural terrain that conditions politics (conceived mainly as governance structures of a formal institutional character)? In this chapter I adopt an intermediate posture; for related discussion see Chapter II.

3. For confirmation, see Harry Eckstein, "Civic Inclusion and Its Discontents," *Daedalus* 113 (Fall 1984): 107–45.

4. A perceptive discussion of assessment of influence may be found in Paul Wapner, "Making States Biodegradable: Ecological Activism and World Politics" (Ph.D. diss. Princeton University, 1990), chap. 1.

5. This framework has benefited from collaborative work with Mary Kaldor under the auspices of the United Nations University. See, e.g., our joint introduction in Kaldor and Falk, eds., *Dealignment: A New Foreign Policy Perspective* (Oxford: Basil Blackwell, 1987), pp. 1–27. See also the related discussion in Chapter X.

6. This point is made dramatically by Robert Jungk, *The Nuclear State* (London: John Calder, 1979), p. vi: "There is no fundamental difference between atoms for peace and atoms for war." It is made historically by the similarities between Hiroshima and Chernobyl.

7. See Brundtland Commission, *Our Common Future: The World Commission on Environment and Development* (New York: Norton, 1987).

8. Cf. the first section of this chapter on the evidence for normative hazards arising from certain *democratic* sentiments.

9. For the text of these proceedings, see John Duffet, ed., *Against the Crimes of Silence* (Flanders, N.J.: O'Hare, 1968).

10. See *Israel in Lebanon: The Report of the International Commission*, (London: Ithaca Press, 1983).

11. For accounts, see *Rainbow Warrior*, Insight series of the *Sunday Times* (London: Arrow Books, 1986); David Robie, *Eyes of Fire: The Last Voyage of the Rainbow Warrior* (Philadelphia: New Society, 1986).

12. Complementary to reassurance are counterterrorist campaigns to sus-

tain the security functions of government against actual and imaginary disruptive threats.

13. See Chapter II for more extensive discussion but in the different context of postmodernism.

14. Quoted in Conor Cruise O'Brien, "God and Man in Nicaragua," *Atlantic*, August 1986, pp. 50–72, at 63; this section draws on O'Brien's perceptive account.

15. There is now a rich feminist literature on religious renewal. Among the most perceptive works is Catherine Keller, *The Broken Web* (Boston: Beacon Press, 1987).

16. Both quotations from "Focus on Women," *Breakthrough*, Summer 1986, p. 14; this special issue includes illuminating accounts of the Nairobi conference.

17. For broader cultural, political, and economic reflections, see Stanley Diamond, *In Search of the Primitive* (New Brunswick, N.J.: Transaction Books, 1974).

18. Christian Bay, "Toward a World of Natural Political Communities," *Alternatives* 6 (1981): 525–60. Also cf. Chapters I–III.

19. These metaphors are creatively explored in another kind of inquiry by Russell Banks in his fine novel *Continental Drift* (New York: Harper & Row, 1985).

20. Raymond Williams, *The Year 2000* (New York: Pantheon Books, 1985), pp. 243–48.

CHAPTER VII

1. See generally Richard Falk, *A Global Approach to National Policy* (Cambridge, Mass.: Harvard University Press, 1975), pp. 146–66.

2. For a perceptive assessment in the context of the Vietnam War, see John Hart Ely, "The American War in Indochina, Part I: The (Troubled) Constitutionality of the War They Told Us About," *Stanford Law Review* 42 (1990): 877–926.

3. See the persuasive analysis in John Hart Ely, "The American War in Indochina, Part II: The Unconstitutionality of the War They Didn't Tell Us About," *Stanford Law Review* 42 (1990): 1093–1148. Ely ends his article with this quotation from Congressman William Hungate: "It's kind of hard to live with yourself when you impeach a guy for tapping phones and not for making war without authorization."

4. For an early characterization of these elements, see Jonathan Marshall, Peter Dale Scott, and Jane Hunter, *Iran-Contra Connection: Secret Teams and Covert Operations in the Reagan Era* (Boston: South End Press, 1975).

5. This is a principal thesis of Louis Henkin, *Constitutionalism, Democracy, and Foreign Affairs* (New York: Columbia University Press, 1990).

6. *Youngstown Sheet and Tube Co. v. Sawyer*, 342 U.S. 579 (1952).

7. *Flast v. Cohen*, 392 U.S. 83 (1968).

8. Many of these cases are discussed in Francis Anthony Boyle, *Defending Civil Resistance under International Law* (Dobbs Ferry, N.Y., Transaction Books, 1987).

9. The leading decisions are in Leon Friedmann, ed., *The Law of War: A Docu-*

mentary History, 2 vols. (New York: Random House, 1972), esp. vol. 2.

10. See Richard Falk, "The Spirit of Thoreau in the Age of Trident," *Agni Review* 23 (1987): 31–48.

11. It remains to be seen whether the end of the Cold War reverses this trend, and if so, by what degree. The new moderateness in East-West relations gives added weight to fiscal argument for reduced budgetary expenditures on defense, but the Persian Gulf crisis of 1990 gave rise to one of the most extensive military operations since World War II, despite U.S.-Soviet cooperation and consensus.

12. Such a view is given indirect encouragement by a new current of *political* realism that has recently entered international legal scholarship in the United States. See, e.g., Thomas M. Franck, *Judging the World Court* (New York: Priority Press, 1986).

13. Powerfully depicted in Mary Kaldor, "The Imaginary War," in Dan Smith and E. P. Thompson, eds., *Prospectus for a Habitable Planet* (Middlesex, Eng.: Penguin Books, 1987), pp. 72–99.

14. I have discussed these issues more fully in "Nuclear Weapons and the End of Democracy," in Richard Falk, *The Promise of World Order* (Philadelphia: Temple University Press, 1987), pp. 77–92.

15. See generally Louis Henkin, *Foreign Affairs and the Constitution* (New York: Norton, 1972); on these matters I find Henkin's Cooly Lectures, delivered at the University of Michigan Law School in 1988 and published in *Constitutionalism, Democracy, and Foreign Affairs*, far more congenial to my own views.

16. "The courts, despite sometimes misguided efforts to compel them to do so (as on Vietnam), are not likely to step into intense confrontations between President and the Congress, or inhibit either when the other does not object" (Henkin, *Foreign Affairs*, pp. 274–75).

17. Ibid., p. 278.

18. *United States v. Curtiss-Wright Export Corp.,* 299 U.S. 304 (1936).

19. E.g., see Thomas M. Franck and Michael J. Glennon, eds., *Foreign Relations and National Security Law* (St. Paul, Minn.: West, 1987), pp. 38–43.

20. See Chapter I.

21. E.g., *Ground Zero* (Bangor, Wash.); *Year One* (Jonah House, Baltimore, Md.); *Nuclear Resister* (Arizona).

22. For informed discussion of "first-strike" weapons systems and doctrines, see Robert Aldridge, *First-Strike! The Pentagon's Strategy for Nuclear War* (Boston: South End Press, 1982).

23. Cf Falk, *Global Approach*, pp. 146–66.

24. Examples are well discussed in Boyle, *Defending Civil Resistance*.

25. Such a legal acknowledgment would reinforce the declining utility of military force as a source of political leverage. This development registers partly the impact of the nuclear stalemate on international politics and partly the rising capabilities for defense against intervention associated with the sort of political mobilization that can be generated by nationalism in the Third World. Resistance is also facilitated by prior militarization of Third World countries by way of military assistance and arms sales.

CHAPTER VIII

1. Carolyn Merchant, *The Death of Nature: Women, Ecology, and the Scientific Revolution* (San Francisco: Harper & Row, 1980); Langdon Winner, *Autonomous Technology: Technics-out-of-Control as a Theme in Political Thought* (Cambridge, Mass.: MIT Press, 1977).

2. See Daniel Berrigan, "A Famous Book, Its Infamous Misuse," September 1987 (mimeographed).

3. Carl H. Builder and Morlie H. Graubard, *The International Law of Armed Conflict: Implications for the Concept of Assured Destruction*, R-2804-FF (Santa Monica, Calif.: RAND, 1982).

4. See Rajni Kothari, "Peace in an Age of Transformation," and Ashis Nandy, "Oppression and Human Liberation: Toward a Third World Utopia," both in R.B.J. Walker, ed., *Culture, Ideology, and World Order* (Boulder, Colo.: Westview Press, 1984).

5. Robert Jay Lifton, and Richard Falk, *Indefensible Weapons: The Political and Psychological Case against Nuclearism* (New York: Basic Books, 1982).

6. United Nations General Assembly Resolution 1653 (XVI), 1961.

7. Arthur Selwyn Miller and Martin Feinrider, eds., *Nuclear Weapons and International Law* (Westport, Conn.: Greenwood Press, 1984).

8. Richard Falk, "Methods and Means of Warfare," in Peter Troboff, ed., *Law and Responsibility in Warfare* (Chapel Hill: University of North Carolina Press, 1975), pp. 37–53.

9. As collected in Miller and Feinrider, *Nuclear Weapons.*

10. Robert S. McNamara, *Blundering into Disaster* (New York: Pantheon Books, 1986).

11. See Albert Carnesale, et al., *Living with Nuclear Weapons* (New York: Bantam, 1983); Michael Mandlebaum, *The Nuclear Future* (Ithaca, N.Y.: Cornell University Press, 1983); Joseph S. Nye, Jr., *Nuclear Ethics* (New York: Free Press, 1986).

12. See Robert Jay Lifton, *The Broken Connection: On Death and the Continuity of Life* (New York: Touchstone Books, 1979).

13. "The Challenge of Peace: God's Promise and Our Response," Pastoral Letter on War, Armaments, and Peace, *Origins* 13, no. 1 (May 19, 1983).

14. See, e.g., Pam McAllister, ed., *Reweaving the Web of Life: Feminism and Nonviolence* (Philadelphia: New Society Publishers, 1982).

15. See Alice Cook and Gwyn Kirk, *Greenham Women Everywhere* (Boston: South End Press, 1983).

16. See Christopher D. Stone, *Earth and Other Ethics: The Case of Moral Pluralism* (New York: Harper & Row, 1987).

17. Bill Devall and George Sessions, *Deep Ecology* (Salt Lake City, Utah: Peregrine Smith, 1985).

18. See Chapter I.

19. See McGeorge Bundy, et al., "Nuclear Weapons and Atlantic Alliance," *Foreign Affairs* 60 (Spring 1982): 753–68.

20. See Robert C. Aldridge, *First Strike! The Pentagon's Strategy for Nuclear War* (Boston: South End Press, 1983).

21. George F. Kennan, *The Nuclear Delusion* (New York: Pantheon Books, 1982), pp. xxviii–xxix.

CHAPTER IX

1. Lewis Lapham, "Leviathan in Trouble," *Harper's Magazine*, Sept. 1988, pp. 8–11, at 10.

2. The quality of political independence has become quite confusing. Third World countries are recipients of modern arms and have an increased political and military capability to resist overt forms of intervention; at the same time, the interdependent character of international life makes weaker states especially vulnerable to various forms of unwanted penetration.

3. See Richard Ashley, "The Poverty of Neorealism," in Robert O. Keohane, ed., *Neorealism and Its Critics* (New York: Columbia University Press, 1986), pp. 255–300.

4. For a more extended argument, see Robert Jay Lifton and Richard Falk, *Indefensible Weapons: The Political and Psychological Case against Nuclearism* (New York: Basic Books, 1982); see also, of course, Jonathan Schell, *The Fate of the Earth* (New York: Knopf, 1982).

5. *New York Times*, Sept. 27, 1988, p. A20; see also Cynthia Pollock Shea, *Protecting Life on Earth: Steps to Save the Ozone Layer*, Worldwatch Paper 91, (Washington, D.C.: World Watch Institute, 1988).

6. In theory, there are no impediments to agreements by states to establish supranational institutions with funding and police authority, or to strip themselves of capabilities and prerogatives. In practice, states have been reluctant to diminish their discretionary space, despite the weight of functional considerations. The main obstacles to such structural adjustment seem situated in the domain of psychopolitics.

7. The international law of human rights is an explicit intrusion on the domestic territorial authority of states in the sensitive issue area of governmental treatment of citizens and other persons subject to jurisdiction. The intrusion is mainly symbolic, although it can have consequences if foreign governments withhold benefits or impose sanctions. The United States has for years denied the Soviet Union most-favored-nation treatment in trading relations because of an alleged Soviet failure to allow Jewish emigration freely.

8. Religion, class, and race also provide a governing elite with the basis for coercive and exploitative rule that discriminates against excluded minorities.

9. Among alternative policy paths are neutrality and nonalignment; "soft" energy; smaller economic units with forms of social accounting other than reliance on GNP.

10. For a fuller discussion of the Nuremberg tradition, see Richard Falk,

Robert Jay Lifton, and Gabriel Kolko, eds., *Crimes of War* (New York: Random House, 1971), pp. 73–176.

11. The text of the GPJ questions appears as follows in *Report from the YES Conference. The Great Peace Journey, Ronneby, Sweden, May 5–7, 1986*, ed. Nina Widstrand (Lund, Sweden, 1986), p. 116.

(1) Are you willing to initiate national legislation which guarantees that your country's defense forces, including "military advisers," do not leave your territory for military purposes (other than in United Nations peace-keeping forces)
—if all other Members of the United Nations undertake to do the same?

(2) Are you willing to take steps to ensure that the development, possession, storage and employment of mass-destruction weapons, including nuclear weapons, which threaten to destroy the very conditions necessary for life on this earth, are forbidden in your country
—if all other Members of the United Nations undertake to do the same?

(3) Are you willing to take steps to prevent your country from allowing the supply of military equipment and weapons technology to other countries
—if all other Members of the United Nations undertake to do the same?

(4) Are you willing to work for a distribution of the earth's resources so that the fundamental necessities of human life, such as clean water, food, elementary health care and schooling, are available to all people throughout the world?

(5) Are you willing to work to ensure that any conflicts, in which your country may be involved in the future, will be settled by peaceful means of the kind specified in Article 33 of the United Nations Charter, and not by the use of threat of force?

12. Hans M. Kristensen, William M. Arkin, and Joshua Handler, *U.S. Naval Weapons in Sweden*, (Washington, D.C.: Neptune Press No. 6, Greenpeace, 1990), pp. 1–99.

13. See Richard Falk, *The Promise of World Order* (Philadelphia: Temple University Press, 1987), pp. 77–116.

14. For a wider assessment of the progressive potential of environmentally based political coalitions, see Robert C. Paehlke, *Environmentalism and the Future of Progressive Politics* (New Haven, Conn.: Yale University Press, 1989).

15. For a descriptive account, see *Israel's Bomb the First Victim: The Case of Mordechai Vanunu* (Nottingham, Eng.: Spokesman, 1988).

16. For news accounts, see *New York Times*, Oct. 1, 1988, p. A1, and also reports carried on Oct. 2 and 3, 1988.

17. Cf *New York Times*, Oct. 5, 1988, pp. A1, A26.

CHAPTER X

1. In this respect, I take a more inclusive view of realism than that which forms the conceptual basis of Joseph S. Nye, Jr., "Neorealism and Neoliberalism," *World Politics* 40 (1988): 235–51. Whereas Nye treats Robert Gilpin's *War and Change in World Politics* (New York: Cambridge University Press, 1981) as an instance of updated realism and Richard Rosecrance's *The Rise of the Trading State* (New York: Basic Books, 1986) as an expression of liberalism, I regard both as within the realist tradition. Both are state-centric, influenced by the shifting structure of international relations and by the impact of technology on the viability of the military instrument. Both authors offer adjustment strategies based on their interpretation of the current phase of geopolitics.

2. A. G. Mojtabai, *Blessed Assurance: At Home with the Bomb in Amarillo, Texas* (Boston: Houghton Mifflin, 1986).

3. See T. C. Schelling, *Arms and Influence* (Cambridge, Mass.: Harvard University Press, 1966).

4. Samuel P. Huntington, "The United States," in Michel Crozier, Samuel P. Huntington, and Joji Watanuki, *The Crisis of Democracy: Report on the Governability of Democracies to the Trilateral Commission* (New York: New York University Press, 1975), pp. 59–118.

5. John Lewis Gaddis, *The Long Peace: Inquiries into the History of the Cold War* (New York: Oxford University Press, 1987).

6. The destruction of Melos by Athens after the Melian leaders refused to give in to Athenian demands illustrates "power politics" and the disaster that can befall those who neglect it.

7. For elaboration, see Richard Falk, *The Promise of World Order* (Philadelphia: Temple University Press, 1987).

8. E. P. Thompson, "Notes on Exterminism, the Last State of Civilisation," *New Left Review* 121 (May–June 1980): 3–31.

9. For a range of thinking, see Saul H. Mendlovitz, ed., *On the Creation of a Just World Order* (New York: Free Press, 1975); and Mendlovitz and R.B.J. Walker, eds., *Towards a Just World Peace* (London: Butterworths, 1987).

INDEX